AMERICAN PARADOX

YOUNG BLACK MEN

Renford Reese

CAROLINA ACADEMIC PRESS
Durham, North Carolina

Copyright © 2004
Renford Reese
All Rights Reserved.

Library of Congress Cataloging-in-Publication Data

Reese, Renford, 1967 -
  American paradox : young black men / by Renford Reese.
     p. cm.
  Includes bibliographical references.
  ISBN 0-89089-568-6
  1. African American young men--Social conditions. 2. African American
  young men--Psychology. 3. Masculinity--United States. 4. African Americans in popular culture. 5. Men in popular culture--United States.
  6. African Americans--Race identity. 7. United States--Race relations.
  8. United States--Social conditions--1980- 9. Popular culture--United
  States. I. Title.

  E185.86.R385 2003
  305.242'1'08996073--dc22

                                                        2003060282

CAROLINA ACADEMIC PRESS

700 Kent Street
Durham, North Carolina 27701
Telephone (919) 489-7486
Fax (919)493-5668
www.cap-press.com

Printed in the United States of America

AMERICAN PARADOX

To: Earnest & Artelia Reese

ACKNOWLEDGEMENTS
Gina & Al
CAP Editor: Bob Conrow
Copy Editor: Cheryll Greenwood Kinsley

Nu Rho
CW, MW, KH, LS, MJ, RL, YT, CO, KF, MK, LL, SB, DL, JM

Contents

Introduction

> I am an invisible man. No, I am not a spook like those who haunted Edgar Allan Poe; nor am I one of your Hollywood-movie ectoplasms. I am a man of substance, of flesh and bone, fiber and liquids—and I might even be said to possess a mind. I am invisible, understand, simply because people refuse to see me. (Ellison 1947, Prologue)

More than a half-century after Ralph Ellison wrote the classic book Invisible Man, black men in America are still trying to become visible. An intense quest to become seen, heard, and felt has manifested itself in rebellious and counterproductive behaviors. Whether it is the baggy pants, the bandana, the braids in the hair, the earring, or the tattoo, black men have desperately striven for visibility. Perpetual gang warfare and an overemphasis on living a glamorous lifestyle have had detrimental consequences on an entire generation of young black men.

Young African American males have unwittingly accepted one model of black masculinity. The acceptance of the "gangsta-thug" model-that of the "tough guy"—has derailed many young black men from achieving success in the United States. Black-on-black violence is one consequence of this hypermasculinist behavior.

This book attempts to shine a light on the most pressing problem facing young African American males, the acceptance of the gangsta-thug image and the enthusiastic embrace of society's stereotypes. It also probes the unkindness of "the system." One would be naïve to dismiss the historical impact of discriminatory policies and the systemic perpetuation of stereotypes in U.S. society. Hence, this book examines the internal and external influences on the current black male identity.

A number of books address the complex issue of black masculinity. However, this one departs from the others because it is based not only on my interpretations, perceptions, and contextual analysis, but also on data in support of my thesis. In 2002, I conducted a survey of 756 African American males between the ages of 13 and 19 in Los Angeles and Atlanta. This survey gauges the attitudes, perceptions, and basic knowledge of young African American men regarding black public figures. One component of this survey is a Realness Scale that I constructed to examine the perceptions of young black men regarding the "authenticity" or "realness" of black icons. Along with data collected from the survey, I interviewed a number of young black males to find out why they, or many of their peers, have embraced the gangsta-thug persona. The results of the survey and the interviews are fascinating—and revealing. For example, the bad-boy NBA player Allen Iverson is rated overwhelmingly as being more of an "authentic" black man than David Robinson, the clean-cut graduate of the Naval Academy. As a political science professor and the director of the Colorful Flags program at California State Polytechnic University, Pomona, I was interested in why this might be so.

This book grows from my desire to build healthy race relations in the U.S. I and many others were galvanized in March of 1991 when an African American teenager named Latasha Harlins walked into a South Central Los Angeles convenience store and got into a tense argument over a bottle of orange juice with the Korean American merchant. The clerk shot Harlins fatally in the back. This tragic incident, which partially involved miscommunication, increased ethnic tension in Los Angeles. In 1993, as a second-year doctoral student and Presidential Fellow at the University of Southern California's School of Public Administration, I responded to the Harlins incident and the 1992 Los Angeles riots by creating the Colorful Flags Human Relations Module in August 1993 as an experiment in multicultural education.

Colorful Flags teaches individuals five human relations statements in the five languages most commonly spoken in their communities. The human relations statements are: 1) Hello. How are you doing? 2) What is your name? 3) Thank you. You're welcome. 4) Please. Excuse me. 5) Good-bye. Have a nice day. These are universally important statements.

The Colorful Flags program uses language as a passionate and intimate instrument to reduce mistrust and stimulate cultural curiosity. The program suggests that language is a powerful instrument to show people we respect them and their culture. What matters is not perfect grammar or syntax; instead, it is the genuine effort to learn something about other cultures and the sincere attempt to use what we have learned. This program is a proactive- interactive approach to bridging cultural differences in schools. It is a human relations module that involves multilingual workshops geared to children, teenagers, and adults. The program has been shown to make a significant difference in reducing ethnic mistrust and increasing cultural curiosity.

Colorful Flags has served approximately 130,000 K-12 students in 17 school districts in Southern California. This program has also been implemented in police departments, hospitals, and various other organizations. In 1996 the Los Angeles Human Relations Commission endorsed the Colorful Flags approach as one of its seven recommendations to stem racism and anti-immigrant sentiment in Los Angeles.

Although this book does not discuss the Colorful Flags program, it does suggest that in order to be successful in life, young black men must move beyond the gangsta-thug model to embrace a diverse pool of knowledge and various perspectives and world-views.

Chapter One examines the controversial issue of academic underachievement among African American students and suggests that the African American community has embraced a culture of underachievement. It is this acceptance of low standards that is the most detrimental threat to the academic success of a generation of young blacks. Chapter Two examines the legacy of racism in the U.S. on the black male identity. The harshest forms of punishment and control in U.S. history have been directed towards the black man. Perhaps his rebelliousness today is a consequence of decades of systematic persecution.

Chapter Three treats my ostracism by Jim Brown—the famous NFL player, actor, and activist—for not being a "real" black man. As a graduate student, I attempted to join his nonprofit gang-violence prevention program "Amer-I-can" but was shunned (in my view) because I was too clean-cut.

Chapter Four examines the various symbols of defiance that the young black man has embraced. Earrings, tattoos, anti-intellectualism, and hypermasculinist behavior are all symbols of black male defiance. Popular culture has wrapped itself around the defiant symbols of black masculinity, but so has the criminal justice system. Whereas these symbols may be tolerated and condoned by the entertainment and sports industries, this imagery is having a tragic effect on young black men caught up in the criminal justice system.

Chapter Five analyzes the current black athlete in the context of black sport icons of the past. Today's black athletes have rebelled against the "Ideal Negro" image of Jesse Owens, Joe Louis, and Jackie Robinson and fully aligned themselves with the "Bad Nigger" image of the great heavyweight boxing champion Jack Johnson. I have integrated my personal experiences as a college player in NCAA Division I football into my discussion of this topic.

Chapter Six explores how young black men have squandered opportunities to address publicly the most pressing problems facing their population: lack of equal opportunity, for example, along with appalling police brutality, an unjust criminal justice system, AIDS, and inadequate health care. Whether in sports or music, high profile blacks have not taken full advantage of their currency to influence the system.

Chapter Seven looks at the influence of young black men on popular culture. Society has created various stereotypes of black men. Today's young black men have enthusiastically but unwittingly embraced these negative images as fundamental components of their black male identity. The issues of "white privilege" and the commodification of the gangsta-thug are also explored in this chapter.

Chapter Eight examines the impact of discriminatory policies in the criminal justice system. I use my personal knowledge of issues regarding police brutality and racial profiling to enhance the discussion. For example, I counseled Rodney King between 1997 and 2000. I incorporate my thoughts about Rodney and his infamous beating into my narrative.

Chapter Nine treats the ongoing problem of black-on-black violence. As a four-year resident of South Central Los Angeles during the height of gang warfare in the early 1990s and as a board member of the Charles Drew Child Development Corporation in Watts, California, I acquired a substantial understanding of the causes and consequences of black violence in the inner city.

Chapter Ten consists of brief biographies of black icons and their rankings on my Realness Scale. This chapter also includes interview comments from youth, explaining why they ranked certain individuals in the ways that they did. Their comments are insightful and intriguing.

In the Chapter Eleven, I conclude by discussing the challenges of redefining authenticity among young black men. This chapter explores the issues of embracing new icons and new values. It summarizes the American Paradox.

It is my intention to give the reader of this book a better grasp of the various dynamics influencing the identity of young black males in the United States during these first years of the twenty-first century. It is my hope that the reader will be inspired to do something to counter the negative internal and external influences shaping the lives of a generation of young black men.

Reference

Ellison, Ralph. 1947. Invisible Man. New York: Vintage Books.

Chapter 1

Excuses

Young Black Male Survey **Question 1**

Have you read a book (outside of classwork) in the past year?

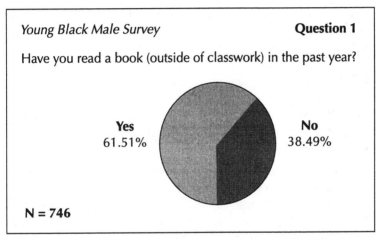

Yes
61.51%

No
38.49%

N = 746

Many black kids do not read books because it is not a *cool* thing to do.

Underachievement

Scott Phelps was the high school science teacher who started a firestorm of controversy with his letter about black students in 2002. Phelps, who is white, wrote in a letter to fellow teachers at John Muir High School in Pasadena, California, that black students were unruly and responsible for the school's low standardized test scores. Phelps contended that the school's miserably low test scores had nothing to do with the teachers or the curriculum. He stated, "standards of behavior, or lack thereof, are to blame." There was outrage among blacks in the Pasadena community and elsewhere about Phelps's criticisms.

Phelps stated,

> Overwhelmingly, the students whose behavior makes the hallways deafening, who yell out for the teacher and demand immediate attention in class, who cannot seem to stop chatting and are fascinated by each other but not with academics, in short, whose behavior saps the strength and energy of us on the front lines, are African American. (Banks 2002, B1)

Is Phelps a racist for stating his observations? Was he being unsympathetic and insensitive to the black students? Phelps was known by his fellow teachers to be dedicated and committed to student achievement. He quit a job at a research lab at the California Institute of Technology to teach high school science. He tutored kids in physics for free, invited students to his house for dinners, and visited their homes to host study sessions. Given his commitment to the students, he was perhaps the best person to make the harsh criticisms of the black youth at his school.

His controversial letter should be taken as the starting point for discussing the behavior of black youth and their academic achievement. Phelps had the courage to say what many teachers and administrators feel. He spoke only from his experiences. Today, political correctness has chilled speech that is valuable to public discourse. Phelps gathered empirical data and was still labeled a racist.

Phelps's criticisms outraged many blacks because he is white. *I can criticize my brother and my sister but you cannot because you are not a part of my family.* It is this rationale that makes blacks uncomfortable with being criticized by individuals outside of their race. It happened in the 1960s when Daniel Patrick Moynihan released his report stating that the family structure among blacks was the fundamental factor in their high poverty rates.

When Richard J. Herrnstein and Charles Murray authored *The Bell Curve* in 1994, it was bound to be controversial. Any discussions of ethnic differences in cognitive ability ignite uniquely heated debates in the U.S. Those who fiercely protest this discussion are wary of the racially biased conclusions of Charles Darwin. In Chapter 13 of their polemical book, the authors state that East Asians (e.g., Chinese, Japanese), whether in America or Asia, typically score higher than white Americans on standardized achievement tests. According to the authors, Asians tend to have higher nonverbal intelligence than whites while being equal, or slightly lower, in verbal intelligence.

In their comparison of African Americans and whites, the authors found that the average white person tests higher than about 84 percent of the population of blacks and that the average black person tests higher than about 16 percent of the population of whites. At every socioeconomic level, there is a variance in IQ between blacks and whites. The variance is greater among those whites and blacks at higher levels of socioeconomic status. In other words, poverty and the various social challenges facing blacks do not fully explain their underachievement (Herrnstein and Murray 1994, 269). No one, to my knowledge, has explained this perplexing phenomenon. Nevertheless, there is a simple explanation. *Blacks have embraced a culture of underachievement.* Parents have embraced this culture and consequently, their children have also.

It is easier to blame the racist system for lack of academic achievement among blacks than it is to say, "We have failed our children by embracing a culture of underachievement." In various therapies for addictive behavior, therapists encourage patients first to admit that they have a problem. They say the acknowledgement of this problem is the first step towards recovery. Indeed, this is an apt metaphor for the black community in the context of academic achievement.

With all of the criticism and the discussions concerning the imposition of stereotypes on the black male, it is my contention that blacks have enthusiastically embraced these stereotypes. Have the stereotypes of black men over the years been so seductive that a significant number of black men have opted to embrace them? I agree that stereotypes of black males have historically permeated our society. I am aware that various institutions such as the criminal justice system and the media have been the primary culprits in shaping the black male identity. The fundamental question is, why have black men capitulated and accepted this construction? Ellis Cose in his book *The Envy of the World* (2002) gives us one explanation:

> Many of us...feel compelled to live the thug life. Why? Like so much about life as a black male in America, the answer is something of a paradox: Self destructive as the macho street attitude can be in the long term, in the short term it can be life

preserving, which is to say that the very attitude that sends so many of us to the morgue sometimes can seem like our only hope for survival. (P. 56)

The traditional response to the black male acceptance of stereotypes is that black men have been forced to accept them. I do not agree. Many blacks continue to criticize the system instead of looking inward. For instance, no one has explained how the children of newly arrived immigrants can score higher than blacks on standardized tests such as the Scholastic Aptitude Test (SAT). I have heard the perennial argument that the exams are culturally biased. Maybe so; but should this cultural bias not also act to the disadvantage of newly arrived immigrants? Asian students consistently score significantly higher than blacks on the verbal as well as the mathematics components of the SAT. The higher test scores in the verbal component are the most puzzling to me. English, for some of the newly arrived Asian students, is their second or third language. One cannot continue to harp on the same excuse if it has been proven to be untenable.

The fact is, the parents of these Asian students do a remarkable job of socializing their children not to make excuses. Instead, they passionately encourage their children to achieve. Many have come from oppressive political environments. Many have experienced poverty at some point in their lives. Nevertheless, they do not complain nor do they encourage their children to complain. They focus all their energies on academic achievement.

It is bewildering to me how most of the Asian students in my Introduction to American Government course outperform my African American students. For example, one quarter I had a student in my class from Beijing, China. Prior to signing up for my class, she had been in the United States for six weeks. She struggled mightily with her English and always carried an English-Mandarin Chinese dictionary. She came to my office during the first week of class and discussed how fearful she was of speaking English and taking my class. One of the African American students was waiting outside my office while I comforted the Chinese student. He came into my office as she was leaving. He wore baggy pants, an extra-large shirt that was not tucked in, and he had an uncombed Afro hairstyle. He wanted to add the class that the Chinese student was taking. I told him that my class was full. He promised that if I let him in, he would be an excellent student and would not let me down. I signed the form for him to add the class. The first exam in the class included 50 questions. The Chinese student scored 82 percent. The African American student scored 56 percent.

Blacks can discuss the ills of the hegemonic, paternalistic, racist system all they want, but at some point they have to stop making excuses for subpar performance. If the example above were an aberration, I would say so. That is not the case. At this point, I have been a university professor for seven years. It is disturbing to see more than a few of my African American students underachieve. This underachievement is not inherited, but learned. Through tolerance and the acceptance of excuses, many blacks have stunted the intellectual growth of their own children.

Achievement

I can make a strong case that the underachievement of African American students is not inherited because, in seven years, five of my ten most talented students have been African American. In one of my upper division courses, the twenty-eight students included four blacks, three males and one female. At the end of the quarter I gave seven A's. All four of the African American students received A's for the course. What made these students the exception?

As I beamed inside with pride while I marked their final grades on my official grade sheet, I paused to ask myself what separated these students from some of my underachieving African American students. Here are my observations.

Sean is the son of a military man. He lived in various places around the world and received a military education. He was in the Air Force ROTC. He was an analytical thinker and an excellent public speaker.

Ronald is the son of Afro-Cubans. He worked at a bank. He had visited the homeland of his parents on several occasions and had taken account of the poverty and despair he saw there. His parents reminded him frequently about how grateful he should feel. He was taught to feel fortunate to be studying in the U.S., and he did not take his education for granted.

Nichola is the daughter of Jamaican parents. Her mother raised her in New York City. Like Ronald, she was frequently reminded by her mother and her grandparents about how fortunate she was. According to her, her mother never discussed what profession she should choose, only that she needed to get a good education. Her final presentation in class was the best I have ever had. She started the Pre-Law Club on campus.

Justin is the son of politically conservative parents, both of whom have master's degrees. Justin was raised in the suburbs of Los Angeles. His parents stressed education and raised him as a God-fearing person. He was a Christian Conservative. He was very quiet unless someone challenged the merits of traditional Christian values. He defied every stereotype imaginable of a young black man.

The parents of each of these students embraced a culture of achievement. They exposed their children to a broader perspective and always held them accountable as individuals for their behavior. These parents did not blame an unfair system. In the cases of Nichola and Ronald, their parents did not blame the U.S. system because they had experienced highly oppressive systems in their homelands. In Sean's case, his father did not blame the system because he had used it as a military man to launch a successful career.

Not one of these students embraced the various stereotypes put forth by society. The males never came across as trying to be "hard." The female did not project herself as a "don't-mess-with-me-I-got-attitude" sister. There was no "I'm trying to keep it real" in their attitudes or demeanors. They actually kept it "real" by articulating their thoughts in their writing and their speaking. They kept it real by making A's on all of their assignments. I realize that this observation is not based on a rigorous social science experiment; but for the sake of this brief discussion, it will suffice.

Let us deconstruct the profiles of my four star students. Two of the four were born to parents from other countries; their parents put into context for them the opportunities they were afforded because they lived in the United States. One of the students was the son of a no-nonsense military man whose different assignments exposed his son to different cultures. Another was the son of no-nonsense Christian parents. They instilled in him principles, values, and a sense of pride.

In speaking to these students, I wanted to know how their parents raised them. I found that all of their parents stressed the importance of education. None of the parents blamed the system for their problems. They taught their children that they could excel in any field of human endeavor. Each of the students was strongly encouraged to ignore stereotypes. These are a few of the success stories of blacks who refuse to embrace society's stereotypes. There are others.

One of the most intriguing stories I have read is that of James McBride and his siblings. In his book *The Color of Water*, McBride brilliantly documents how his Jewish mother and black father taught him that education tempered with religion was the best way to climb out of poverty. McBride was taught that money without knowledge is worthless. After his father died, his mother, a poor woman, was responsible for preparing him and his eleven siblings for college. All twelve of them graduated. Ruth McBride raised her children in the housing projects of New York. She never commented on how cruel the system was to her or to them. She was too busy encouraging them to broaden their horizons and to achieve.

> The question of race was like the power of the moon in my house.... Mommy kept us on a frantic living pace that left no time for the problem. We thrived on thought, books, music, and art, which she fed to us instead of food. At every opportunity she loaded five or six of us onto the subway...parading us to every free event New York City offered: festivals, zoos, parades, block parties, libraries, concerts.... We did not consider ourselves poor or deprived, or depressed. (McBride 1996, 94–95)

After I read this book, I tried to think of what other argument could be made for how Ruth McBride nurtured twelve children through college. Her children, although of mixed race, were black. She raised them in the housing projects. They were poor.

We should learn from the remarkable McBride story that it takes an unwavering commitment to academic excellence to escape the grip of poverty. It also takes zero tolerance for the embrace of negative stereotypes. As McBride states, "Excuses for not doing your homework were not accepted and would draw a beating."

A World Perspective

I have visited thirty-five countries. During my travels, I have become accustomed to meeting people who are fascinated with the black urban experience in the United States. On my trip to South Africa, I remember being in Crossroads, a shantytown of the Western Cape Province. As the black South African tour guide escorted a group of us around, he wanted to know what it was like to be a black man in America. He wanted to know if black men were really persecuted daily by the police. He wanted to know if the racism of America was comparable to the racism of South Africa. He wanted to know if the poverty among blacks in America was as oppressive as the poverty among black South Africans. As I walked through the community, I silently questioned the need to answer the South African tour guide's inquiry. The thousands of tin-roofed shanties had no running water, no electricity, and no bathrooms. One of every four adults was infected with HIV/AIDS. Obviously, the guide wanted to point out that we all had our crosses to bear. The issue is the weight and size of our respective crosses. The problems that African American men face in the U.S. pale in comparison to the problems confronted by the black population in South Africa.

Later in my journey, I was taken to the Tshebedisanong School in Soweto. This school included grades K–6. They had approximately two hundred students and five classrooms. The assistant principal of the school gave me a tour of their library, which contained only thirty-one books. This school, and other schools like it in Soweto, desperately lacked resources. While I was there, I met children who asked me for books to read. The strong desire of these students to get an education stuck with me. This was one of the poorest schools in and around Johannesburg. I decided to make a donation. My experience prompted me to collaborate with the Trust for Educational Advancement in South Africa (TEASA) to start a Soweto Schools Book Drive in the United States.

During a trip to Ghana, I had the opportunity to speak to a local elementary school assembly, a group of 2,000 students. Their school, like many others, desperately lacked basic resources. As I toured the schoolyard, I saw both ambition and frustration in the eyes of the students. My words to these students were *Ebe Ya Ya*. In the native Twi language this means, "It will be all right." Their response was, *Ebe Ya Ya*.

I once had a Cambodian student in my class who could not understand the self-destructive nature of black maleness. I remember a black student in the class trying to discuss the implications of racism in America. The Cambodian student remained confused. At the end of the quarter, this student walked me to my office and divulged that he had lived through one of the worst tragedies in human history. He survived the vicious assaults of the Khmer Rouge regime. From 1975 to 1979, the Khmer Rouge killed at least 1.7 million of their countrymen—21 percent of the entire population of Cambodia.

This student told me that his entire family was placed in the Khmer Rouge work camps. Confined to the women's camp, his mother worked in the rice fields from four in the morning to nine at night, with only one outfit and one pair of shoes. The workers got one bowl of rice or porridge to eat each day. People in the rice fields could not talk while they were working. The consequence of talking was death.

He told me that he was in the work camp for children. He was once caught scrambling for a chicken bone under a table and was beaten into unconsciousness. He told me he saw children who had disobeyed orders thrown into the air and punctured with knives like stuffed animals. He saw people forced to dig their own graves and then stand in them while the officers filled the grave with dirt so only the head would show. Then the officers would pound the head with sticks, pipes, or rifles until the person died. My student's mother dodged officers and periodically risked her life by walking five miles to check on him.

In 1980 he and his mother escaped. As war raged, they navigated on a boat, with others, through a sea of thousands of dead bodies on their way to Thailand. Perhaps it is his experience that fuels his confusion over how blacks continually blame the system for their woes. His father—and his hero—was a prisoner of war and is now one of the richest men in Asia.

My conversation with this student was so powerful that after speaking to him I was on the verge of tears. I went back to my office to ponder what I had just heard. I reflected on the plight of African Americans in this country. I became angry that in the name of victimization we have allowed ourselves to become marginalized. We have allowed ourselves to embrace a culture of underachievement.

The paradox of racism is perhaps America's most complex phenomenon. The fact is, there is no place in the world in which blacks can prosper like they can in the U.S. Europeans like to brag about how open they are to minorities. When I was in Amsterdam, I asked a person of African decent from Suriname if he experienced much racism. He said, "very little." I asked an African gentleman in Gothenburg if he experienced racism living in Sweden. He said, "very little." Finally, I asked an African living in Copenhagen if he experienced any racism. He said, "not at all." In each case I asked what blacks did for a living. The most common answers were domestic work, janitorial work, or security work. I asked in each instance, did their country have any black politicians, prominent black lawyers, police, police chiefs, or black judges? The answer in each case was, "few or none." What does it mean if you tolerate a black male sitting next to a white female at a bus stop? What about the bigger picture?

The Illusion of Racism

The knee-jerk response of many blacks who have failed, underachieved, or been unsuccessful in an endeavor is to say it was because of racism. In fact, "because of racism" is the universal response to black underachievement. The race game in the U.S. is an American paradox. Racism exists but it does not. It is real but it is not. It's overt but covert. Some people know it when they see it but cannot quite put their finger on it otherwise. For black conservatives, racism is an optical illusion. However, for black liberals it hovers around like a cloud in the sky. On any given day it can bear down and transform its environment.

The history of blacks in America is one of humiliation and degradation. Blacks have had to endure blatant discriminatory policies and overcome consistent acts of racial intolerance. These experiences have obfuscated the judgment of some blacks when it comes to racial bias. Even the generations that have not endured the harshest forms of racial intolerance are enveloped by its legacy.

A friend who worked at a prominent university in Southern California was fired from his job during his third month of work. I asked him why he was fired. He said, "Man, you know how racist that school is." I candidly asked, "Are you sure you weren't fired because you were always late and took long lunch breaks?" His response was, "Well, that's what they were trying to say." I asked, "Were you consistently late to work and did you take longer than allotted lunch breaks?" He said, "A few times, but it wasn't all of that."

A couple of years ago I was having a discussion with one of my African American friends about racism in America. He reflected on a racist incident he experienced while in a restaurant with his African American wife. He and his wife ordered a meal. Some fifteen minutes after they placed their order, a white couple sat down next to them and ordered their meal. The white couple received their food before my friend and his wife. According to my friend, this was blatant racism. I asked the question, "How do you know it was an act of racism?" He responded by saying it was obvious. I then asked him if he saw what the white couple ordered. His response was no. I asked, "So how do you know the waitress (who was white) was being racist? Maybe the white couple ordered soup and salad while you ordered filet mignon and lobster." He did not get it. Most of us do not.

In 1990, Marion Barry, the mayor of Washington, D.C., said that he was a victim of racism when he was caught smoking crack cocaine. Over the years, other black public figures who have run afoul of the law have used the because-of-racism defense in explaining their dilemmas. I learned the story of the "little boy who cried wolf" when I was in elementary school. The lesson of this childhood story is timeless. Racism does exist in American society. However, some minorities justify the negative results of their actions by automatically alleging racism. Unjustified calls of racism undermine the significance of truly racist acts. We must start to take the extra step in analysis before we automatically assume an incident is racist.

When I visited an ATM in Los Angeles one night recently, an Asian male in his fifties and an Asian female in her thirties were using the only two machines available. The Asian male completed his transaction before the Asian female was finished. As he walked to his car, I approached the open ATM. I noticed that he waited in his car until the woman was finished and had made her way to her own car.

My first thought was that he waited because I was an African American male. Was the Asian male a racist because he watched until the woman was finished and in her car? I do not know. Perhaps he was being a perfect gentleman. I asked myself, would he have waited for an African American female to get to her car safely? What if I were a thirty-year-old white male or a thirty-year-old Asian male—would he have done the same thing? Only by knowing the answers to these questions would I know if his act was truly racist.

I remember going out with a few of my African American friends while I was in the doctoral program at the University of Southern California. While we were driving to a restaurant to dine and dance, one person in the car said, "America is racist." Another person responded, "Everything that affects us is based on race." My response was, "That's crazy." There were five of us in the van. Four were in their "blacker than thou" mode. I said that most of the things you do daily have nothing to do with race. "When was the last time you were harassed or beaten by a cop?" I asked. "When was the last time someone denied you entrance into the library or restaurant because of your race?"

"If everything that affects us is based on race, how did all of you get into the graduate programs at this university? How can you explain Tom Bradley being the mayor of Los Angeles, a city that lacks a black majority, for over a decade? How can you explain Norm Rice—then the mayor in Seattle—leading a city that is less than 10 percent African American? How can you explain the more than 300 cities that have had African American mayors since the 1970s? How can you explain the visibility of blacks on commercials and throughout popular culture? No other minority of the majority population anywhere in the world has the clout and visibility that African Americans have in this country." After I made my points, there was no response. The crew immediately began to discuss the upcoming season of the Los Angeles Lakers.

The American Dilemma

After reading the previous section, one might conclude that racism does not exist in America and indeed is an illusion, a figment of one's imagination. I am not naïve enough to think that injustice does not exist in the United States. My father is from Mississippi. My mother is from Alabama. I was born and raised in Georgia. I know racism when I see it—I think. Seeing racism when it is not there is counterproductive, like "crying wolf." Not seeing it when it is there is equally counterproductive.

Who is to blame for the systematic neglect of America's inner-city schools? According to the California State Department of Education, the California High School Exit Examination (CAHSEE) aims to "significantly improve pupil achievement in public high schools and to ensure that pupils who graduate from public high schools can demonstrate grade level competency in reading, writing, and mathematics." At Crenshaw High School, a predominantly black school in Los Angeles, only 20 percent of the class of 2004 (the test is first administered to 10th graders) initially passed the math portion of the test and 47 percent passed the language arts portion. By contrast, at Beverly Hills High School, 95 percent of the class of 2004 passed the mathematics section and 100 percent passed in English/language arts. This might be due to the cognitive intelligence argument posited by Hernnstein and Murray, or it might be due to the lack of resources at Crenshaw. Many students did not yet have textbooks one month after classes started in the fall of 2002. More than one-third of the teachers at Crenshaw lack full credentials. In fact, across the state of California, minority students are five times more likely than other students to have underqualified teachers.

Contrast the scenario at Crenshaw to that at Beverly Hills High School, where all students are taught by fully credentialed teachers. The students are given high-quality textbooks. To optimize the learning experience, their classrooms and learning facilities are equipped with the most cutting-edge instructional technologies.

The CAHSEE is another hurdle that many black students are asked to jump while wearing ankle weights. Some 72 percent of African Americans who took this exam in the spring of 2002 failed to pass it. The fundamental question is, how can they be expected to succeed with inferior resources? A recent Louis Harris Poll found that 42 percent of teachers in schools with the largest concentrations of low-income children do not have enough books for their students to take home, and 21 percent use books that do not cover the state standards (Oakes and Rogers 2002). Given the nature and extent of resource disparities, CAHSEE can be considered to have results that are racially biased. Historically, the lack of resources appropriated to black schools has been one cause of black underachievement.

The poignant fact is that America was built on a racially biased ideology. Even when strides were made to do the right thing, politicians, policymakers, the courts, and those in power shirked their responsibilities to make this society equal. Agents of the government have established a strong and reliable tradition of giving blacks rights and then taking them back.

Self-Help

Sampson Davis, George Jenkins, and Rameck Hunt (with Liza Frazier Page) wrote the powerful book *The Pact*, which tells how these three young black men overcame the odds of growing up in tough neighborhoods in Newark, New Jersey—plagued by crime, drugs, and violence—to become doctors. They write, "Where we lived, hustlers reigned, and it was easy to follow their example. Two of us landed in juvenile detention centers before our eighteenth birthdays." Nevertheless, today Davis and Hunt are medical doctors and Jenkins is a dentist.

There were no doctors or lawyers walking the streets of our communities. But one of us in childhood latched on to a dream of becoming a dentist, steered clear of trouble, and in his senior year of high school persuaded his two best friends to apply to a college program for minority students interested in becoming doctors. We studied together. We worked summer jobs together. We partied together. And we learned to solve our problems together. We are doctors today because of the positive influence our friendship had on us. (Davis et al. 2002, back cover)

The Pact is a must-read for young black men. This story shows that discipline, strategy, commitment, and dedication substantially improve one's probability for success. It proves that when young black men are given opportunities through special programs that guide them into certain career paths, some will succeed. These gentlemen are special because they started a process, persevered, and met their goals. I am certain that many young black men have the equivalent intellect of these individuals. However, peer pressure and the cultural standards of the streets have stunted their intellectual growth and sabotaged their career options. In explaining why they wrote *The Pact*, the authors state, "We did this because we hope our story will inspire others, so that even those young people who feel trapped by their circumstances, or pulled by peer pressure in the wrong direction, might look for a way out, not through drugs, alcohol, crime, or dares but through the power of friendship."

As blacks we should strive harder to help ourselves. This in-house effort, however, should be coupled with certain sensibilities of the government. The government must jettison its mean-spirited, "zero-sum game" philosophy and reacknowledge its role in assisting its truly needy populations. Policymakers should send the message that the Bill of Rights of the U.S. Constitution protects the civil liberties of *all* citizens, not just a select population. They should also send the message to police officers that all individuals in our society are protected from haphazard victimization by the Equal Protection clause of the Fourteenth Amendment.

I am a cultural critic, neither a "liberal" Afro-centrist nor a "captured" conservative. I continue to state and believe that racism is not the source of all or even most of the problems that African Americans endure. African Americans should take responsibility for a portion of the cyclical social ills that challenge their community. With strong community institutions, this population should not have to wait on the government to solve most of its problems. The expanding black middle class shows us, even with the prevalence of racism, that it *can* be done.

Perhaps my travels have caused me to have scant tolerance for the hackneyed excuses for the multiple problems facing blacks in the United States. Maybe it was my exposure to the dire poverty of South Africa and Ghana or to the horrifying stories of the Khmer Rouge that prompted my intolerance for the same old excuses. I am sure that my perspective is derived from a culmination of various cultural learning experiences.

I refuse to rationalize, overconceptualize, or explain away certain social phenomena that have victimized the African American community: black-on-black crime, for example, and the disintegration of the black family, as well as academic underachievement, the proliferation of drug abuse, and increase in teenage pregnancies. The black community must acknowledge and banish behavior that is detrimental to its well-being. It is the responsibility of the black community to hold those accountable for *any* activity that is destructive and counterproductive to its population.

Is racism today more virulent and oppressive than it was sixty years ago? Are the barriers higher and more fortified? Are the options more restricted? I ask that question because while I was working on this section of the book, Benjamin O. Davis, Jr., a hero to many blacks of my father's generation, died at the age of 89. Davis was a pioneering military officer who led the fabled Tuskegee Airmen during World War II and was the first African American to become a general in the U.S. Air Force. When Davis graduated from the U.S. Military Academy at West Point, New York, in 1936, he was only the fourth African American ever to do so. At the academy, Davis was shunned. Other cadets refused to speak to him throughout his four years at West Point, yet he persevered.

I wish I could have interviewed Davis to find out what he thought about the frequent claims of "racism keeping us down," and about young black men embracing the "gangsta-thug" image. I wish I could ask Davis, who flew sixty missions in P-39s, P-40s, P-47s, and P-51s, what his impressions were of today's young black street soldiers. Indeed, it would have been insightful to get responses to the same questions from black men such as Benjamin Banneker, Frederick Douglass, Paul Robeson, Jackie Robinson, Benjamin Mays, Malcolm X, Martin Luther King, Jr., and Arthur Ashe.

Given the fact that these black men risked their lives to pave the way for future generations, what does it say that a substantial number of black men do not want to take advantage of their efforts? How did we go from these pioneers being our role models to thugs serving the same purpose? How did we shift from trying to contradict stereotypes with all of our might, to embracing them?

Solutions

In order to deal constructively with the culture of underachievement among black children, there are several issues that stakeholders must address. These suggestions are couched in reality, not in political ideology.

- Blacks must acknowledge that they have embraced a culture of underachievement.
- Blacks must work vigorously to embrace a culture of achievement.
- Black policymakers and civil rights organizations should increase pressure on the government to invest in schools in low-income areas.
- Young black men must be encouraged to read more.
- They must be taught that there is nothing soft, weak, or unmanly about being educated.
- They must be taught not to make excuses for things that they can control, e.g., reading and studying.
- They must be taught that there are people around the world who are much worse off than they are.

- They must learn not to be handicapped by the illusions of racism.

- They must learn to identify true acts of racism and devise effective strategies to counter these acts—e.g., involvement in protests, writing letters to local and national political representatives; voting.

- They must learn their history and never take for granted the strides that great black leaders have made on their behalf.

References

Banks, Sandy. 2002. Debate on black students rages. *Los Angeles Times,* 1 December.

Cose, Ellis. 2002. *The Envy of the World.* New York: Washington Square Press.

Davis, Sampson, George Jenkins, and Rameck Hunt (with Liza Frazier Page). 2002. *The Pact.* New York: Riverhead Books.

Hernnstein, Richard J., and Charles Murray. 1994. *The Bell Curve: Intelligence and Class Structure in American Life.* New York: The Free Press.

McBride, James. 1996. *The Color of Water.* New York: Riverhead Books.

Oakes, Jeannie, and John Rogers. 2002. Diploma penalty misplaces blame. *Los Angeles Times,* 6 October.

Chapter 2

Race Matters

Blacklash

In order to understand the psyche of the contemporary black man, it is paramount to understand the historical context of his existence in America and the legacy of racial discrimination on the black male identity. The struggle for civil rights in America is the backdrop for the black man's struggle to create a positive male identity. Indeed, the harshest forms of punishment and control in U.S. history have been directed towards the black man. Perhaps his rebelliousness today is a consequence of decades of systematic persecution.

In *An American Dilemma: The Negro Problem and Modern Democracy*, Gunnar Myrdal captures America's struggle with its "Negro problem."

There is a "Negro problem" in the United States and most Americans are aware of it, although it assumes varying forms and intensity in different regions of the country and among diverse groups of the American people. Americans have to react to it, politically as citizens and, where there are Negroes present in the community, privately as neighbors.... The Negro problem has distinctly negative connotations. It suggests something difficult to settle and equally difficult to leave alone. It is embarrassing. It makes for moral uneasiness. (Myrdal 1944, xlv)

According to E. Franklin Frazier, the development of sociological theory at the turn of the twentieth century made the idea of segrega-

19

tion in society palatable. Sociologists suggested that "the Negro was primarily a social problem and would remain a social problem because he could not be assimilated.... He has a 'racial' temperament and his 'shiftlessness and sensuality' are partly due to heredity and that he is inferior in his adaptiveness to a complex civilization" (Frazier 1968, 34).

During the early 1900s Social Darwinism was gaining acceptance among members of a guilt-ridden society eager to rationalize their racist and prejudiced feelings. Myrdal reports that according to Darwin's theories, "the Negro race is said to be several hundreds or thousands of years behind the white man in development. Culture is then assumed to be an accumulated mass of memories in the race, transmitted through genes. A definite biological ceiling is usually provided: the mind of the Negro race cannot be improved beyond a given level" (Myrdal 1944, 99).

Immediately following the Civil War, the U.S. attempted to put its egalitarian principles of democracy into practice. During the period of Radical Reconstruction in the South from 1866 to 1877, blacks had an unprecedented degree of political access. Indeed, blacks sat in political offices at the national, state, and local levels (Trefousse 1971, 58). The first Civil Rights Act was passed in 1866, guaranteeing all persons—including nonwhites and noncitizens—the same legal rights as white citizens.

Efforts to democratize American society continued with the passage of the Fourteenth Amendment to the U.S. Constitution in 1868. This amendment contains the Equal Protection clause that prohibits states from depriving any person of life, liberty, or property without due process of law, or denying any person equal protection under the law. Furthermore, with the Civil Rights Act of 1875, Congress attempted to uphold America's creed of democracy and equality by legislating equal treatment in public facilities—e.g., public transportation, theaters, hotels, and restaurants. However, in 1883 the courts ironically declared this Civil Rights Act to be unconstitutional (Dye 1995, 47).

Most of the progress made towards civil rights between 1866 and 1876 quickly evaporated with the 1876 presidential election of Rutherford B. Hayes. Southerners pledged their support for Hayes only after they were guaranteed the termination of Radical Reconstruction, which was a form of martial law imposed on the Southern states by the North (Blumberg 1984, 6). Although Samuel J. Tilden won more popular votes than Hayes, Hayes prevailed in this controversial election. The North had officially reneged on its promise to rearrange Southern society so that it would be representative of America's egalitarian creed (Myrdal 1944, 88; Dye 1995, 47).

Although the election of Hayes and the advent of terrorist organizations such as the Ku Klux Klan solidified segregation in the South, the 1896 Supreme Court ruling in the landmark case Plessy v. Ferguson legalized strict segregation in the South. Jim Crow laws separating blacks from whites further perpetuated segregation in the South (Blumberg 1984, 6). The Supreme Court inverted the interpretation of the Fourteenth Amendment by stating that the amendment's Equal Protection clause did not prevent state-enforced separation of races (Dye 1995, 47). In short, the Supreme Court's interpretation of the Equal Protection clause of the Fourteenth Amendment in Plessy v. Ferguson stated:

> The object of the [Fourteenth] Amendment was undoubtedly to enforce the absolute equality of the two races before the law, but in the nature of things it could not have been intended to abolish distinctions based upon color, or to enforce social, as distinguished from political equality, or a commingling of the two races upon terms unsatisfactory to either. Laws permitting, and even requiring, their separation in places where they are liable to be brought into contact do not necessarily imply inferiority of either race to the other....
> (Dye 1995, 47)

It took American society and the Supreme Court fifty-eight years to realize the "separate but equal" clause was unjust, unconstitutional, and undemocratic. In the historic 1954 case Brown v. Board of Education of Topeka, the Supreme Court ruled public-school segregation unconstitutional (Dye 1995, 48). This decision—along with the Rosa Parks experience—was the impetus for the civil rights movement. The Montgomery bus boycotts, sit-ins, and various other protests effectively precipitated social change (Kelman 1996, 256).

Segregation laws were put in place because of the fear of miscegenation. However, in the U.S. it was not the fear of all forms of miscegenation but the fear of the black man interacting with the white woman. No other issue is responsible for so much hate and volatility in America. The fear of the black man interacting with the white woman impacted the Plessy v. Ferguson decision and the subsequent Jim Crow laws in the South.

In 1911 U.S. Representative Seaborn Roddenberry of Georgia introduced a constitutional amendment to ban interracial marriages. In his appeal to Congress, Roddenberry stated:

> Intermarriage between whites and blacks is repulsive and averse to every sentiment of pure American spirit. It is abhorrent and repugnant. It is subversive to social peace. It is destructive of moral supremacy, and ultimately this slavery to black beasts will bring this nation to a fatal conflict. (Gilmore 1975, 108)

Influenced by Roddenberry and others, miscegenation bills were introduced in 1913 in half of the twenty states where this law did not exist.

The Sexualization of Racism

There were three black football players recruited in my freshman class at Vanderbilt University. At that time, the school was about 95 percent white. It was impossible not to interact and study with whites. I had a black roommate, and the white guys on the team would stop by from time to time to pal around with us. When we were studying, the guys knew our room was off-limits. If one of us was studying with a white female, however, the whites ignored study etiquette and remained in the room or stopped by frequently to act as monitors. If they perceived something was going on besides studying, they would become visibly irritated. If the white guy could prove to his white comrades beyond a reasonable doubt that the white student had been intimate with one of us, she was labeled as "undesirable" for the rest of her college career. The majority of the white girls were in sororities and this label would be humiliating to them. Few of the girls risked getting this label. This type of extortion was an effective way of regulating interracial dating.

On one occasion, one of the black guys on the team had a white girl in his room. No one on the floor thought what they were doing was studying. One of the white guys was so disturbed that he began knocking on the door. When there was no answer, he began bouncing a basketball on the door until their intimacy was interrupted. It was puzzling to me how we were teammates and brothers on the football field, but as soon as we got on campus our teammates imposed restrictions on our dating options.

On another occasion, one of my best friends was a white guy, a non-athlete. He was very nerdy but cool. We liked hanging out together. One of my other close friends was a Norwegian political science major, a female. One night we were studying late, and she fell asleep at my place. My male friend knew we were studying. He knocked on my door and when there was no response, he knocked louder. Suspecting we were being intimate, he attempted to put his key in the door to see if he could open it. By this time I was awake and realized what he was doing. I jumped up, opened the door, grabbed him by the collar, and told him never to disrespect me like that again. He apologized profusely and stated that he did not know what had gotten into him. Best friend or not, he could not accept my being intimate with this beautiful Norwegian student. He had no explanation for his actions. Their root causes were deep and complex.

As a child growing up in Georgia, I knew that interracial dating was the greatest of taboos in the South. I knew that intimacy with a white female, even in the 1970s, could cost a black man his life. Our high school basketball coach blatantly let us know that interracial dating would not be tolerated. Our team was all black and all of our cheerleaders were white. There was to be no mixing, even in seating arrangements on bus trips.

It was not until I arrived at Vanderbilt that I was in constant contact with white men. It was there that I began to understand the depth of their resistance to interracial dating. The issue went to the core of my white male cohorts' self-concept, their masculinity.

In 1995, as a third-year doctoral student at the University of Southern California (USC), I toured Japan with a group of twenty other USC Presidential Fellows. The purpose of the tour was for us to examine Japanese culture and leadership styles. During our first lecture, an American expatriate painted a comprehensive portrait of Japanese culture. One of the African American women in our group asked the lecturer what the Japanese thought of African American men. His response was that the Japanese admired African American men for their athletic and sexual prowess but not for their intellectual capacity. If what the lecturer stated was accurate, the Japanese had accepted a widely popular concept of black masculinity that America created. According to Cornel West in *Race Matters*:

> White fear of black sexuality is a basic ingredient of white racism. And for whites to admit this deep fear, even as they try to instill and sustain fear in blacks, is to acknowledge weakness—a weakness that goes down to the bone. Social scientists have long acknowledged that interracial sex and marriage are the most [widely] perceived sources of white fear of black people—just as repeated castrations of lynched black men cry out for serious psychocultural explanations. (West 1993, 55)

Teenager Emmett Till was murdered in Mississippi in 1955 because he disrespected the sanctity of white womanhood. Till took a dare from friends and went into a store and said, "Hey baby" to a white woman. Ignoring tradition cost Till his life.

Historically, the black man's interaction with the white woman has been prohibited. Miscegenation was illegal in all of the Southern states until the 1967 Supreme Court decision in the case of Lovings v. Virginia that declared antimiscegenation laws to be unconstitutional.

Calvin C. Hernton, in his seminal book *Sex and Racism in America*, poignantly describes the sexualization of racism in the United States. Hernton writes that "the white man, especially the Southerner, is overtly obsessed by the Negro desiring sexual relations with whites" (Hernton 1969, 4). He continues:

> White men, especially Southerners, are afraid of the so-called superior, savage sexuality of the Negro male and they are

dead set against any measures that will lift the Negro's status, because they are certain that such measures will bring the Negro one step nearer to the white woman's bedroom. (Hernton, 1969, 6)

Hernton is correct in asserting that black masculinity is a cause of tension in dealing with matters of race relations. How else can one explain the castration celebrations that consistently took place during lynching festivals in the South? If a black man was found guilty of a crime that was punishable by capital punishment, then lynching should have been the gross punctuation of that punishment. However, castration became an "exciting" element of the lynching ritual in the South. This cultural exercise revealed a uniquely intense perversion and obsession with the sexual nature of the black male body.

Since racism is centered in and revolves around sex, the Negro cannot help but see himself as at once sexually affirmed and negated. While the Negro is portrayed as a great walking phallus with satyr-like potency, he is denied the execution of that potency.... (Hernton 1969, 7)

In reality, the black woman never posed a threat to the social order in American society. For most of U.S. history, she has been economically oppressed and politically disenfranchised. Working as a domestic, she was the one who raised and parented the white politicians who made public policies in our country. Segregation laws were not put in place because of her; she was already intimately involved in the most sacred ritual in society, child-rearing. The black woman, through sexual interaction, also helped to affirm white masculinity. White masculinity is defined by a callous paternalistic and hegemonic dominance over people and things.

Historically, the black man, like the black woman, has been economically oppressed and politically disenfranchised. However, because of the perceived potency of the black male body, black men have posed a consistent and unremitting threat to white masculinity and to the white power structure. According to the authors of *The Color Complex*, "The black man's dark skin became the sign of a dangerous and potent sexuality, and the darker the skin, the greater the threat to white manhood" (Russell, Wilson, and Hall 1992, 23). Indeed, the muscular, athletic black male body type is synonymous with sexual perversion and sexual liberation. It was the threat of the potency of the black male body that was at the root of many segregationist policies in the United States.

The Roots of Rebellion

Langston Hughes asked in his famous poem "What happens to a dream deferred?" Does it sag like a heavy load or explode? In 2001 Cornel West-then a professor at Harvard, now at Princeton—released *Sketches of My Culture*, a ten-track, spoken-word album that infuses poetry with rap, jazz, and rhythm and blues to capture the history of African Americans. On the track "Stolen King," West rhythmically speaks:

> No other people in the modern world have had such unprecedented levels of unregulated violence against them. Psychic violence taught us to hate ourselves and told us we have the wrong hips and lips and noses and hair texture and skin pigmentation. Physical violence, slavery, Jim Crow, lynching, police brutality...but we engage in a sweet and sad indictment of such misery with the strength of our souls and with the vision of our struggle. Through great sadness and sorrow we forge a grand faith and hope in the future.

Black rebellion has always been a part of American society. Nothing is more symbolic of this rebelliousness than Alex Haley's descendant Kunta Kinte, of whom Haley wrote in his landmark book, Roots. Kunta Kinte's staunch refusal to change his name to Toby is the root and the legacy of black male rebellion in America.

In 1829, David Walker authored the first African American book to advocate the overthrow of the system of slavery. In *Appeal to the Colored Citizens of the World*, Walker urged his people to resist schemes of colonization. He declared: "Let no man of us budge one step.... America is more our country than it is whites'.... The greatest riches in all America have risen from our blood and tears... " (Brown in Robeson 1971, xxxvi). Walker's appeal laid the foundation for black rebelliousness in the United States.

Early leaders of slave revolts—Nat Turner, Denmark Vesey, and Gabriel Prosser-were the progenitors of H. Rap Brown, Bobby Seale, Huey P. Newton, and Eldridge Cleaver. These activists of the 1960s are in turn the predecessors of today's black rebels. The rebels of the past had cause, plan, and purpose. The rebels of today share the same cause-oppression—but they lack plan and purpose. Rebellion has defined the black man's existence in America. In language, dress, style, attitude, and behavior, the black man has resisted the pressures to conform to the ways of the status quo.

Ironically, the black man has resisted conforming to the status quo because historically he has not been allowed to integrate or assimilate into the mainstream. He has not been accepted. When people are not accepted and embraced, they rebel. When factions within interest groups do not feel appreciated, they rebel and form splinter groups. When kids do not get the approval and acceptance of their parents, they rebel and go wayward. When populations within nation-states feel unappreciated and isolated, they rebel and attempt to secede. It is the same type of isolation and nonacceptance that has defined the black man's rebellious tenure in America.

Accommodationist vs. Non-Accommodationist

As I settled into my airplane seat for a flight to Los Angeles from Atlanta, an older white gentleman sat down next to me. I turned to acknowledge and speak to him. He turned away and didn't so much as mumble a word. I turned away from him. On the inside, I rebelled, cussing him out, and then tried to sleep. I was tired—tired of trying to make people like him feel comfortable with me, tired of trying to get their approval. Throughout American history, many blacks have unsuccessfully striven to gain acceptance from whites. As I sat on that plane, I thought about the great black educators Booker T. Washington and W.E.B. DuBois.

In one of the great speeches in U.S. history, Booker T. Washington made an eloquent and energetic plea for white acceptance. In the 1895

Atlanta Exposition Address, Washington told a mostly white audience that if they invest in the Negro race, "you can be sure in the future, as in the past, that you and your families will be surrounded by the most patient, faithful, law-abiding, and unresentful people that the world has ever seen" (Washington 1995, 128). Factions of blacks have always been opposed to Washington's "we will do whatever it takes to make you like us" ideology. Many opposed what they perceived to be Washington's acceptance of black inferiority. Washington's most intense plea for white acceptance came in the middle of his Exposition speech:

> As we have proved our loyalty to you in the past, in nursing your children, watching by the sick-bed of your mothers and fathers, and often following them with tear-dimmed eyes to their graves, so in the future, in our humble way, we shall stand by you with devotion that no foreigner can approach, ready to lay down our lives, if need be, in defence of yours....
> (Washington 1995, 129)

W.E.B. DuBois responded to Washington's accommodationist appeal in *The Souls of Black Folk,* first published in 1903. DuBois represented the rebellious strain of blacks who grew tired of trying to accommodate whites. He states, "Mr. Washington distinctly asks that black people give up, at least for the present, three things—first, political power, second, insistence on civil rights, third, higher education of Negro youth" (DuBois 1968, 51). DuBois goes on to state that blacks had acquiesced to Washington's philosophy for ten years with no positive consequences: "As a result of this tender of the palm-branch, what has been the return?" (P. 51). DuBois provides the answer to his own question: "1) The disenfranchisement of the Negro 2) The legal creation of a distinct status of civil inferiority for the Negro 3) The steady withdrawal of aid from institutions for the higher training of the Negro" (P. 51).

In *The Souls of Black Folk,* DuBois articulates why blacks should not be passive and accommodating towards whites. Indeed, it was his voice and that of Paul Robeson that laid the foundation for the rebellious spirit of future generations of blacks. DuBois and Robeson shared a similar ideology and world-view. DuBois said of Robeson:

He is without doubt today, as a person, the best known American on earth, to the largest number of human beings. His voice is known in Europe, Asia and Africa, in the West Indies and South America and in the islands of the seas. Children on the streets of Peking and Moscow, Calcutta and Jakarta greet him and send him their love. Only in his native land is he without honor and rights. (Brown in Robeson 1971, xxvi)

Paul Robeson was perhaps the most internationally revered black rebel. Although he was lionized internationally, he was feared and ostracized in the United States. Robeson was valedictorian of his graduating class at Rutgers College and a two-time All-American football player. He was a lawyer, concert singer, renowned stage and movie actor, and a staunch activist for the liberation of oppressed people around the world. It was his activism that prompted the U.S. government to coordinate efforts to undermine his message and credibility. During the peak of his career, the U.S. government took away Robeson's passport. They labeled him a dangerous communist and a threat to national security.

In protest against Robeson in 1949, Peekskill, New York, witnessed one of the ugliest riots of the twentieth century. This came after Robeson stated that colored people of Afro-Asia did not want a war with the Soviet Union. Robeson stated it was "unthinkable that American Negroes would go to war on behalf of those who have oppressed them for generations against the Soviet Union which in one generation has raised our people to full human dignity" (Brown in Robeson 1971, xvii). Immediately after these comments were made, Robeson became the object of intense hate by the establishment in America. Even blacks began to view him with suspicion. His annual income dropped from $100,000 to $6,000 and remained at this level for ten years (Brown in Robeson 1971, xvii).

Robeson paid a heavy price for his unwavering commitment to social justice and human rights. When he was summoned before the House Un-American Activities Committee in 1956, one of the congressional inquisitors asked if he liked Russia so much, why did he not stay over there? Robeson's swift and unabashed response was, "Because my father was a slave, and my people died to build this country, and I'm going to stay right here and have a part of it, just like you. And no fascist-minded people like you will drive me from it. Is that clear?" (Brown in Robeson 1971, xxxv). Robeson was a rebel with cause, purpose, and conviction.

Blacks have often rioted in America because they have felt discriminated against, ostracized, and neglected. Indeed, the race riots of the 1960s were a consequence of this neglect. They followed the same general pattern. Usually there was some incident (sometimes alleged) in which the police victimized a black. News of the confrontation quickly spread to an already frustrated and angry black population. This population acted out its anger by looting, burning, and destroying property. In nearly all the incidents that have sparked race riots in the United States, systematic discrimination, injustice, and neglect have been the underlying problems.

The Los Angeles Watts Riots of August 11-16, 1965, started when a highway patrolman stopped a black man on the suspicion that he was driving under the influence of alcohol. A crowd gathered to protest the police behavior. They became angry and unruly and riots began. The July 12-17 riots of Newark, New Jersey—in 1967—began after a black taxicab driver was arrested. The handcuffed driver resisted officers outside the police station. Witnesses falsely reported that the cab driver had been killed. A crowd threw rocks at the police station, prompting more widespread rioting. In another incident, a police raid on an after-hours club led to rumors of police brutality, enough to spark riots in Detroit that lasted from July 23 to 30 in 1967 (Gilje 1996, 158; Boskin 1976).

The *National Commission on the Causes and Prevention of Violence* identified 239 separate urban riots between June 1963 and May 1968, involving approximately 200,000 participants. These riots resulted in 8,000 injuries and 190 deaths. These numbers include the riots that took place immediately after the assassination of Martin Luther King, Jr. After Dr. King was assassinated, riots took place in 28 states and in 125 cities nationwide. These riots claimed 46 lives (Gilje 1996, 158).

The report of the *National Advisory Commission on Civil Disorders-the Kerner Commission*—stated that the cause of the urban disorder was the unequal treatments of blacks and whites, which created two separate societies: one suburban and white, and the other urban and black. This report examined issues of job opportunities, education, and housing. It concluded that the solution to preventing riots was not to add more police to departments, but rather to confront the underlying cause of the riots: racial injustice. In fact, all of the high-powered commissions that have been assembled after urban riots have reached the same conclusions.

Forms of Control

Perhaps the establishment has always feared the Bigger Thomas-like characters within American society. Bigger is the fictional character in Richard Wright's *Native Son*. Bigger accidentally kills a white woman after coming very close to raping her. He embodies the violence and uncontrollable rage that U.S. society has long feared and accepted as a characteristic of black maleness. The U.S. has seemingly been obsessed with controlling the behavior of black men. How else can we explain the countless lynchings and cases of police brutality? How else can we explain the disproportionate number of black men who have been subjected to capital punishment?

The freedom and liberation that blacks felt immediately after slavery and during the period of Radical Reconstruction was met with the most vicious form of "blacklash" in U.S. history: lynchings. In *Without Sanctuary: Lynching Photography in America*, the authors trace the history of lynching in the United States. According to the authors, lynching was a response to the emancipation of the slaves and rose from fear of black progress, from "folk pornography," and even from boredom (Allen et al. 2000, 13).

From 1877 until the mid 1940s, each event that blacks could take pride in was met with this form of blacklash. Whether it was blacks celebrating the title victory of flamboyant black heavyweight boxing champion Jack Johnson over white opponent Jim Jeffries in 1910 or the defeat by mild-mannered Joe Louis of the German Max Schmeling in 1938, black exhilaration, euphoria, and pride were consistently met with vicious forms of terrorism (Reese 1999, 4).

Lynching was not only accomplished by hanging, but also by burning, shooting, stabbing, and whatever other means, as long as the suffering was maximized.

> To kill a victim was not enough; the execution became public theater, a participatory ritual of torture and death, a voyeuristic spectacle prolonged as long as possible (once for seven hours) for the benefit of the crowd. Newspapers on a number of occasions announced in advance the time and place of a lynching, special "excursion" trains transported spectators to the scene, employers sometimes released their workers to attend, parents sent notes to school asking teachers to excuse their children for the event, and entire families attended, the children hoisted on their parents' shoulders to miss none of the action and accompanying festivities. (Allen et al. 2000, 13)

In the 1890s lynchings claimed an average of 139 lives each year, 75 percent of them black. The number of lynching victims declined in subsequent decades but the percentage of blacks lynched increased to 90 percent. Between 1882 and 1968, an estimated 4,742 blacks were victims of lynchings (Allen et al. 2000, 2).

Many states passed anti-lynching laws in the 1940s and 1950s. As lynchings subsided, other forms of capital punishment replaced this gruesome act. The electric chair and other new forms of capital punishment have had a similarly disproportionate effect on black males.

The Eighth Amendment in our Bill of Rights prohibits "cruel and unusual punishment" and the United Nations' Universal Declaration of Human Rights forbids "torture...cruel, inhumane, or degrading punishment." The UN Commission on Human Rights has called for a moratorium on the death penalty. The death penalty has been abolished by a record number of 105 nations, including all of Western Europe.

In 1972, the United States followed the path of the international community by banning capital punishment. As a result of the 1972 Supreme Court decision in Furman v. Georgia, executions were halted in the U.S. for four years. This 5-4 decision held that the death penalty was not, in principle, cruel and unusual punishment and not, therefore, unconstitutional; but its implementation through existing state laws was unconstitutional. According to the Furman decision, many of these state laws violated the Eighth and Fourteenth Amendments. Because black men were disproportionately the victims of capital punishment, this move appeared to be a noble gesture. It spared this population from the vagrant injustices that were embedded in the system. The reinstitution of the death penalty in 1976 had a similarly disproportionate impact on black men.

The following data from *Death Row USA*, a quarterly report by the Criminal Justice Project of the NAACP Legal Defense and Education Fund, suggest that blacks are significantly more likely than whites to get the death penalty. They also suggest that the death penalty is more likely to be imposed if the victim is white.

Between the reinstatement of capital punishment in 1976 and April 1, 2003, there were 842 executions carried out in the United States.

Capital Punishment in the U.S.
Top number = year, Bottom number = executions

77	78	79	80	81	82	83
1	0	2	0	1	2	5

84	85	86	87	88	89	90
21	18	18	25	11	16	23

91	92	93	94	95	96	97
14	31	38	31	56	45	74

98	99	00	01	02	03
68	98	85	66	71	22

Gender of Defendants Executed
(842 total executions)

Female	10	1.19%
Male	832	98.81%

Gender of Victims
(1271 total victims)

Female	623	49.02%
Male	648	50.20%

Race of Defendants Executed
(842 total executions)

White	447	56.65%
Black	290	34.44%
Latino/a	56	6.65%
Native American	13	1.54%
Asian	6	0.71%

Race of Victims
(1271 total victims)

White	1022	80.41%
Black	174	13.69%
Latino/a	50	3.93%
Native American	3	0.24%
Asian	22	1.73%

Defendant-Victim Racial Combinations

	White Victim	Black Victim	Latino/a Victim	Asian Victim	Native American Victim	
White Defendant	448 (52.02%)	12 (1.43%)	6 (0.71%)	3 (36%)	0	(0%)
Black Defendant	182 (21.62%)	87 (10.33%)	10 (1.19%)	7 (0.83%)	0	(0%)
Latino/a Defendant	28 (3.33%)	2 (0.24%)	22 (2.61%)	1 (.12%)	0	(0%)
Asian Defendant	2 (0.24%)	0 (0%)	0 (0%)	4 (0.48%)	0	(0%)
Native Defendant	12 (1.43%)	0 (0%)	0 (0%)	0 (0%)	1	(0.12%)
Total	672 (79.81%)	101 (12.00%)	38 (4.51%)	15 (1.78%)	1	(0.12%)

Note: In addition, there were 15 defendants (1.78%) executed for the murders of multiple victims of different races. Of those, 8 defendants were white, 4 were black, and 3 were Latino.

Source: NAACP Legal Defense and Educational Fund, Death Row USA, 1 April 2003.

Cases of Police Brutality

As Human Rights Watch pointed out in 1998:

The excessive use of force by police officers, including unjustified shootings, severe beatings, fatal chokings, and rough treatment, persists because overwhelming barriers to accountability make it possible for officers who commit human rights violations to escape due punishment and often to repeat their offenses. Police or public officials greet each new report of brutality with denials or explain that the act was an aberration, while the administrative and criminal systems that should deter these abuses by holding officers accountable instead virtually guarantee them impunity. (Human Rights Watch 1998, 25)

On March 3, 1991, motorist Rodney King was brutally beaten by four Los Angeles Police Department (LAPD) officers. On April 26, 1992, those officers were tried in the white enclave of Simi Valley, California, and found not guilty of criminal acts. This decision sparked the infamous 1992 Los Angeles riots. The King case and the subsequent civil unrest were a cathartic experience for Americans. Because King's beating was captured on video, it forced Americans to confront once again the issue of racism. In the context of police brutality, police reform, and dialogue on race relations, the King case has become the reference point. Since this case, America has been consistently reminded of the horrors of police brutality. There have been other high-profile cases of police brutality during the past decade.

• In July 2002, a home video was released of an Inglewood, California, police officer hoisting a handcuffed 16-year-old to his feet and then slamming his head on the trunk of the police car. Seconds later, the same white officer punched the teenager, Donovan Jackson, in the face. The police report revealed that another police officer had punched Jackson in the face twice before he was handcuffed (Howlett 2002, 3A).

• Also in July 2000, Thomas Jones was chased by Philadelphia police officers for allegedly hijacking a car and possibly wounding a police officer. A videocamera showed officers beating and kicking Jones after he had been shot by a police officer. Black officers and white officers perpetrated this act of brutality. Although the video clearly showed Jones being brutally beaten after he was held captive, the police commissioner refused to state that his officers were culpable (Scherer 2000, 3). Many who viewed this act of police brutality compared the incident to the Rodney King beating. In fact, today there is hardly an act of police brutality that is not compared to the King incident.

• On November 5, 1992, Malice Green, an unemployed steelworker and father of five, was stopped in his car by two white plainclothes Detroit Police Department officers. They pulled their unmarked car in front of his car outside a suspected crack house in Detroit. Green was dropping off a friend. According to witnesses and court testimony, the officers walked over and leaned into Green's car. Green reached into his glove compartment and pulled out a clenched fist that officers suspected held drugs. When Green refused to open his fist for inspection, the two officers, known to the people in the community as "Starsky" and "Hutch," began beating Green with their heavy steel flashlights. Green suffered fourteen blows to the head and part of his scalp was torn off. He died about thirty minutes after the beating. One of the officers was sentenced to twelve-to-twenty-five years in prison and the other to eight-to-eighteen years for second-degree murder (Walsh 1992, A3; Terry 1993, 2, 4).

• In August 1997, three New York City police officers assaulted Abner Louima, a thirty-year-old Haitian immigrant in the restroom of Brooklyn's 70th Precinct station house. One of the officers mistakenly thought Louima had punched him from behind during a fight outside a Brooklyn nightclub. Among other forcible tactics, officers sodomized Louima with a broomstick. He was hospitalized with severe injuries that included a ruptured bladder and colon. Officers threatened to kill him and his family if he screamed or told what happened. Two of the officers involved in the assault were indicted, found guilty, and sentenced to serve up to thirty years in prison. At the 70th precinct, a total of eighteen officers were disciplined (Fried 1999, 2, 4).

• In the same spirit, at 12:40 a.m. on February 4, 1999, four New York City police officers killed an unarmed West African immigrant named Amadou Diallo. Diallo was a devout Muslim with no criminal record. The officers mistook him for a rapist as they approached him in the vestibule of his apartment. They commanded Diallo to put up his hands. Diallo nervously reached in his back pocket for his wallet and one of the officers shouted "Gun!" The officers used forty-one shots to hit Diallo nineteen times. According to court testimony, Diallo was shot even while he was lying down. In a two-month trial that ended in March 2000, an Albany, New York, jury found the police officers "not guilty" on a range of charges, the least of which was official negligence (O'Shaughnessy 2000, 8).

The July 24, 1999, murder of the former professional football player and Notre Dame All-American linebacker, Demetrius DuBose, shocked many people. The San Diego district attorney found that two white officers were justified in shooting DuBose.

On the last day of his life, DuBose had been playing in a volleyball tournament at Ocean Beach in San Diego. According to court testimony, DuBose—who at autopsy was found to have alcohol and cocaine in his system—climbed over the balcony of his apartment into a neighbor's apartment and fell asleep. The neighbor came home and suspected DuBose of burglary and called the police. DuBose was sitting on the steps of the apartment when the police showed up.

He refused to be handcuffed by the police officers and stated that he had done nothing wrong. Witnesses say that DuBose ran from the officers and then fought with them and disarmed them of their nunchaku martial arts weapons. Police sources say that DuBose turned towards the officers and looked as though he would pursue them. The officers, fearing aggression, shot DuBose multiple times. These facts make this case difficult to determine the rightness of the police behavior (Thornton 1999, A-1).

The fact that DuBose was shot nine times, including five times in the back, suggests foul play. The two officers who shot DuBose stood over him while he was dying and waited ten minutes without making any attempt to help him. This scenario suggests unethical and indeed sinister police behavior (Gross 1999, B-2).

Irvin Landrum, an 18-year-old African American, died January 17, 1999, six days after he was shot three times by police officers in Claremont, California. A Claremont police officer pulled Landrum over at 1:00 a.m. for speeding. As the officer questioned Landrum, a backup officer arrived and stood nearby. According to the police accounts, when the first officer told Landrum he would have to be searched for weapons, Landrum stepped back, reached under his sweater, and pulled a revolver from his waistband. The officers stated the suspect said, "No. No. I'm gonna kill you. I'm gonna kill you." An investigation of the incident showed that the gun Landrum allegedly used was never fired and did not bear his fingerprints. Many accused the police of planting the gun. To make matters worse, the Claremont city manager gave the two officers who shot Landrum $1,000 rewards as "Employees of the Year." The Los Angeles County district attorney concluded that the police officers involved in the controversial shooting were not criminally culpable, and therefore they were not prosecuted (Mozingo 1999, B-1).

The race-driven tragedies of the past several years support the conclusion that Cornel West comes to in *Race Matters*. Race still matters.

• In South Carolina in 1994, Susan Smith claimed that a black man had kidnapped her two white toddlers. There was an immediate and enormous outcry. Black men were detained in six states while Smith's small children sat seat-belted in a car at the bottom of a pond where she had left them.

• In 1995, a wrong turn in Los Angeles brought three-year-old Stephanie Kuhen and her white family to a dead-end street where gang members peppered their car with bullets, killing the toddler. This tragedy prompted a regional and national outcry. On the same day, two black youths were killed in Los Angeles. However, there was no mention of these tragedies on the local news.

As it is with any social phenomenon, the rebellious behavior of the black man is complex. Historical dynamics have converged to create today's black deviant. Those who simply dismiss the wanton behavior of today's young black man as silly and ignorant fail to examine how American society has meticulously sculpted this behavior.

The objective of this book is to examine the sociopolitical and cultural complexities that have created today's young black man.

References

Allen, James, ed., Hilton Als, Jon Lewis, and Leon Litwack. 2000. Without Sanctuary: Lynching Photography in America. Sante Fe, New Mexico: Twin Palms.

Blumberg, Rhoda Lois. 1984. Civil Rights: The 1960s Freedom Struggle. Boston: Twayne Publishers.

Boskin, Joseph. 1976. Urban Racial Violence. 2d ed. Boston: Glencoe Press.

DuBois, W.E.B. [1903] 1968. The Souls of Black Folk. New York: Johnson Reprint Corporation.

Dye, Thomas. [1972] 1995. Understanding Public Policy. 8th ed. Englewood Cliffs, New Jersey: Prentice-Hall.

Foreman, Thomas E. 1957. Discrimination against the Negro in American athletics. Master's thesis, Fresno State College and Rand Research Associates.

Frazier, E. Franklin. 1968. E. Franklin Frazier on Race Relations. Edited and with Introduction by G. Franklin Edwards. Chicago: University of Chicago Press.

Fried, Joseph. 1999. Sentencing in Louima case. New York Times, 19 December.

Gilje, Paul A. 1996. Rioting in America. Bloomington: Indiana University Press.

Gilmore, Al-Tony. 1975. Bad Nigger! The National Impact of Jack Johnson. Port Washington, New York: Kennikat Press.

Gross, Gregory Alan. 1999. Chief faces some hard questions on officers' use of deadly force. San Diego Union-Tribune, 13 August.

Haley, Alex. 1976. Roots. Garden City, New York: Doubleday.

Hernton, Calvin. 1969. Sex and Race in America. London: Andre Deutsch.

Howlett, Debbie. 2002. Lawyer: officer on tape acted correctly. USA Today, 15 July.

Hughes, Langston. 1949. Selected Poems. New York: Alfred Knopf.

Human Rights Watch. 1998. Shielded from Justice: Police Brutality and Accountability in the United States. New York: Human Rights Watch.

Kelman, Steven. 1996. American Democracy and the Public Good. New York: Harcourt Brace College Publishers.

Kerner Commission. 1968. Supplemental Studies for the National Advisory Commission on Civil Disorders. New York: Praeger.

Mozingo, Joe. 1999. FBI probes Claremont police in man's death. Los Angeles Times, 10 July.

Myrdal, Gunnar. 1944. An American Dilemma: The Negro Problem and Modern Democracy. New York: Harper and Brothers.

NAACP Legal Defense and Educational Fund. 2003. Death Row USA. Washington, D.C.: National Association for the Advancement of Colored People.

O'Shaughnessy, Patrice. 2000. Making sense of tragedy: jury decision closes a case but not the wounds. New York Daily News, 26 February.

Reese, Renford. 1999. The socio-political context of the integration of sport in America. Journal of African American Men 4 (3).

Robeson, Paul. [1958] 1971. Here I Stand. Reprint, with introduction by Lloyd Brown. Boston: Beacon Press.

Russell, Kathy, Midge Wilson, and Ronald Hall. 1992. The Color Complex. New York: Anchor Books.

Scherer, Ron. 2000. The videotaped beating comes as Philadelphia police try to move past a reputation for brutality. Christian Science Monitor, 17 July.

Terry, Don. 1993. Detroit police beating: two murder convictions, and a city heaves a big sigh. New York Times, 29 August.

Thornton, Kelly. 1999. DuBose killing justified, DA finds; athlete over-powered 2 policemen, Pfingst says. San Diego Union-Tribune, 2 November.

Trefousse, Hans L. 1971. Reconstruction: America's First Effort At Racial Democracy. New York: Litton Educational Publishing.

Walsh, Edward. 1992. Three Detroit officers to stand trial, but charge against fourth dismissed. Washington Post, 24 December.

Washington, Booker T. [1901] 1995. Up From Slavery. Oxford: Oxford University Press.

West, Cornel. 1993. Race Matters. Boston: Beacon Press.

West, Cornel. 2001. Sketches of My Culture. Spoken word CD produced by Derek Allen: Artemis Records.

Chapter 3

Authenticity

After all, since the dominant view holds prideful self-respect as the very essence of healthy African-American identity, it also considers such identity to be fundamentally weakened wherever masculinity appears to be compromised. While this fact is rarely articulated, its influence is nonetheless real and pervasive. Its primary effect is that all debates over and claims to "authentic" African-American identity are largely animated by a profound anxiety about the status specifically of African-American masculinity. (Harper 1996, Preface)

Being Hard

In the spring of 1994 my father was honored in Atlanta by the *100 Percent Wrong Club* as "Sportswriter of the Year." At the awards banquet, my father sat at a table next to NFL great Jim Brown. Brown was being honored with the organization's "Hall of Fame" award. My father told Brown that he had a son who was in graduate school at the University of Southern California. Brown gave my father his telephone number and told him to make sure I called him when he returned home to Los Angeles. I called Brown on a Saturday, a couple of days after the banquet. He invited me to a party that he was having at his home in the Hollywood Hills later that night.

I drove to his house not knowing what to expect. I knew the guests at his party would consist of celebrities such as Richard Pryor and Eddie Murphy or of Crips and Bloods. Brown was the founder and director of a nonprofit organization called Amer-I-Can. In this role, he brokered a truce between the Crips and Bloods, and his organization provided unique opportunities for gang members to make positive changes in their lives. As I walked through the entrance into his house, I was immediately paralyzed by the emotional testimonials of the gang members in the living room. The first person stated his name and said that he had done a five-year bid in Folsom Prison. Others in the room responded to this statement with prideful congratulatory gestures, "yeah, yeah, yeah," as if he said that he graduated Phi Beta Kappa from USC. The next person who got up spoke of his time in the "joint," also to subtle applause. He discussed how much Jim Brown had meant to him. Finally, a person got up and said, "I'm an OG. I started this muthafuckin shit." "OG" stands for "original gangsta." He discussed how he had stolen, assaulted, and murdered and how he had changed his ways since he met Jim. He said he never had a father and Jim was his father figure. "I want to say 'thank you' and 'happy birthday.'" He began to cry as he walked over to give Jim a hug.

That night I saw something that only a few people in the world have witnessed. I saw Jim Brown weep. In his statement to the packed room, Jim said that he never had a father, and he wanted to be the father to them that he never had himself. His commitment to these young men was evident and inspirational. After his comments, he told everybody to kick back, relax, party, and have fun.

As I walked around the room, I saw bodies that had never been cuddled, nurtured, or loved. I saw eyes that lacked hope. I saw fingers that were responsible for taking the lives of countless sons and brothers. Although we were all young black men, I realized that I had little in common with these young men. In many ways I felt like a fish out of water.

I went up and introduced myself to Jim. He warmly welcomed me. He told me to just hang out and have fun. All evening I felt he was monitoring me. I felt that he was checking to see if I was "real." I danced and mingled and had a good time. Later in the night Jim invited me back to his house the next evening for an Amer-I-Can advisory board meeting. I enthusiastically agreed to come over. While I was driving over the next evening I was excited and a bit nervous about what I was about to get involved in. I knew that by agreeing to work with rival gang members, I would be facing potentially life-threatening risks. Nevertheless, I was game.

I parked in Jim's driveway and walked right into his kitchen. Jim was at the table, meeting with one of his facilitators who was his right-hand man and one of the advisory board members. I got a nonchalant reception from Jim as he told me to have a seat. I sat down and heard him discuss business with the facilitator, who was quite articulate and astute. During their conversation, I felt like I was persona non grata. In the vernacular of the street, I "got no love" during their conversation. Not once did either of them look in my direction or bring me into the conversation.

As others trickled into the meeting, I introduced myself. At the time of the meeting, we were all gathered in Jim's living room. Everybody was scared to talk unless Jim talked. He had the persona of "Scarface." We went around the room and introduced ourselves. All of the guys were ex-gangbangers. All of them had served time in prison.

The first person to state his name added, "First giving honor to Allah. I would like to say it is up to us to liberate ourselves from the oppressive hands of the oppressor. We must appreciate and not degradate...." Jim interrupted, "What are you talking about? Shut up. You don't know nothing because you haven't read anything nor have you been anywhere. Next." I wanted to laugh-hard. The next person introduced himself and talked about how he gave up the life of gangbanging and thanks to Jim he was getting his life in order. I was about the fifth person to introduce myself. "Hi, my name is Renford Reese. I'm a second-year graduate student at USC." It would have been impossible for the room to fall any more silent. I felt like I had just said, "Hi. My name is Renford Reese and I work for the Boy Scouts of America."

But after the insightful board meeting I was ready to get involved. I walked up to Jim in the kitchen and told him how excited I was to be getting involved with his organization. I told him he could use me in any capacity.

He nonchalantly said to me, "That's good. Go over and let one of the facilitators get your information." I went over and exchanged numbers with one of the facilitators. He promised to give me a "shout." I waited one day for him to call before I decided to call him. He did not return my call, so I called him again and this time we spoke. We set a date to meet, but he canceled out. He did not return my calls afterward. It took me a few weeks to recover from Jim's nonchalant response to my enthusiasm and the facilitator's nonresponsive behavior towards me. I was dejected. I was willing to immerse myself in the gang truce between the Crips and Bloods, and I was unappreciated.

I let these series of incidents simmer and percolate before I made an effort to deconstruct them. After a couple of days of analyzing what took place, I came to the conclusion that the group did not want me involved in its activities because they felt I could not relate to their plight. They felt that I was "powder-puff" and not "real." I asked myself how I would have responded if I were in their shoes. Would I have excluded someone because they were never affiliated with a gang and never served time?

This brings us to the complicated concept of black masculinity. What is it? Authors such as Robert Staples, Phillip Brian Harper, Karen Ross, Clarence Lusane, Robert Entman, Andrew Rojecki, Darnell Hunt, Michael Eric Dyson, Lawrence Carter, J. Carroll George, Earl Hutchinson, Haki Madhubuti, and Todd Boyd have all tackled the issue of black masculinity in their insightful research. The overarching theme in this body of literature is that black masculinity is a concept that has been socially constructed by the dominant population and imposed on black men. The literature is replete with descriptions of how the white power structure has created stereotypes of the black man as a tough, physically imposing, crime-oriented, hyper-sexed, hedonistic, promiscuous, irresponsible, and barbaric species. Although these descriptions have been exaggerated and socially engineered, many black men have internalized and embraced all of these representations.

I have always considered myself masculine and athletic. However, during the Amer-I-Can advisory board meeting, I might as well have been Opie Taylor. Jim Brown epitomizes our conception of black masculinity. He was the toughest running back in the history of the NFL. Throughout his brief movie career he was seen as a sex symbol. His encounters off the field have given him the persona of what Al-

Tony Gilmore (1975) would call a "Bad Nigger." While reading his 1989 autobiography, *Out of Bounds*, I tried to establish at what point Jim became deprived, underprivileged, and gangsta-oriented. He grew up fatherless on St. Simons Island—according to Brown, St. Simons was a "quiet dreamy islet just off the southern coast of Georgia." When he was eight years old, he moved with his mother to Manhasset, New York. He attended Manhasset High School, a school that he describes as "one of the country's finest schools.... I was one of the school's few blacks, and I was voted Chief Justice of the Supreme Court. I felt loved at Manhasset, on and off the playing field" (Brown 1989, 57). After high school he became a superstar athlete at Syracuse University and then went on to become one of the most celebrated athletes in American history. After retiring from the NFL, he enjoyed a career as a successful actor.

This guy's life was twice as privileged as mine—so what made him a "real" black man and me, a choirboy? In short, he embraced society's representations of black masculinity. I did not. It was his subtle disdain for what he perceived to be my lack of toughness that excluded me from working with his organization.

Keeping It "Real"

Bobby McFerrin became the "whipping boy" of blacks in entertainment after his song "Don't Worry, Be Happy" became widely popular. Black comedians loaded up on jokes branding McFerrin an Uncle Tom. Perhaps if McFerrin had hit with a song titled "Pimpin Ain't Easy" like 8 Ball and MJG, he would have been embraced as an "authentic" black man.

I remember visiting home and going to a *Black College Football Classic* at the Georgia Dome with my sister and two teenage boys from our church that she was mentoring. As we rode home after the game, one of the boys asked us to turn the radio on. Lil Bow Wow was on the radio. This was before he dopped the Lil and embraced a more streetwise image. The thirteen-year-old said, "Oh, you can change the station, I don't like him." I turned to him and asked,

"Why don't you like Lil Bow Wow? He's gifted." The boy responded, "He's too happy." He went on to state that in order to rap you have to be mad and angry or else you are not "real." I looked at his fifteen-year-old brother and he nodded his head in agreement as he said, "That's true." I was shocked and appalled that these young men could not appreciate the talents of Lil Bow Wow because he was not "angry" enough.

The pastor of my home church assigned my sister to mentor these young men because their parents had complained about them underachieving in school. When I came home to visit, my sister wanted me to meet the boys so I could try to inspire them. I remember arriving at their house in an upper-middle-class neighborhood. I met their parents and asked what the problem was with the boys. The mother said, "All they want to do is play video games, watch music videos, and listen to rap music." The tragedy was poignantly ironic. These middle-class parents had worked all their lives to provide unlimited opportunities for their children, but they were virtually powerless to motivate them. It did not matter that the father had had a successful career in the military. The lure and seduction of "being cool" and "keeping it real" had undermined the influence of him and his wife.

I am sure that middle-class parents who read these pages can identify with this tragedy. The story is tragic because the urge for young black men to "keep it real" has permeated all socioeconomic sectors of the black community. In my 2002 survey of young black males, the socioeconomic environment of the schools did not matter. Young black men responded in the same patterns to the Realness Scale that was a part of that survey.

The code of the streets suggests that success should be secondary to street credibility. For instance, it is still a mystery to me why the entertainer MC Hammer was "blackemasculated." He employed 200 workers, mostly black, from his community. He hired more black workers and did more for his community than most, if not all, other black entertainers in his genre. Nevertheless, Hammer was seen as being less of a black man because his music was clean and appealed to a cross section of the population. His mainstream appeal landed him commercials and even a cartoon series. By 1991, he had made over $49 million. Still, Hammer was saddled with the label of not being "hard enough."

After tremendous success, Hammer responded to the criticism of "selling out" with his 1994 album, *Pumps And A Bump*. In the accompanying comeback video he attempted to establish his "thug" credentials. His extreme representations of sexuality and street life got his video banned from MTV and other outlets. Hammer attempted to be someone he was not. He felt the enormous pressure of "keeping it real."

When Cornell Haynes, Jr., nicknamed Nelly, released his first album, *Country Grammar* in 2000, it sold more than 10 million copies. His second album, *Nellyville*, immediately went to No. 1 on the charts. Hip-hop critics did not wait long before they criticized Nelly for "crossing over." Nelly's persona is a cross between Tupac Shakur and Will Smith.

In a home video produced about the life of the late rapper and actor Tupac Shakur, his closest friends offer a counter-narrative to his "Thug Life" image. In the riveting documentary, *Tupac Resurrected* (2003), Tupac analyzes the contradictions in his behavior and persona. This film shows Tupac as a brilliant, articulate, introspective, enlightening and self-constructed thug. According to his biographer, Michael Eric Dyson, Tupac was well read in political philosophy and feminist literature. He was very intelligent and gifted. As a high school student he danced, acted, and enjoyed writing poetry. At some point, however, he realized that being intelligent and gifted was not enough to get him where he ultimately wanted to be-so he created his "Thug Life" image. He got multiple tattoos all over his body. The words "Thug Life" were boldly tattooed in calligraphy on his chest. He must have realized that not even this was enough to be considered a "real" black man. At the height of his rapping and acting career, he began to engage in gangsta behavior.

Until this point, his life had been free of jail and imprisonment. In an extraordinary effort to become accepted as an "authentic" black man, Tupac initiated a series of crimes and embraced a way of life that was foreign to him. This lifestyle ultimately led to his murder in 1996. Tupac went overboard in trying to prove his black manhood.

Like Tupac, other blacks have been vigilant about their black male image. Even Will Smith temporarily attempted to meet the rigid standard of black masculinity. By the early 1990s, Smith's rap songs were widely popular and appealed to a cross section of the population. In 1992, Smith responded to criticisms that he was a "popcorn," "bubble gum," and "light weight" rapper by making a song titled "You Hit My Bumper Bitch." I was shocked to hear his lyrics describe the old woman who hit his bumper as a wrinkled-up, Shar-pei dog. Undoubtedly it was Smith's quest to become a "real" black man that led to this production. He quickly came to his senses and became a superstar without compromise, for a while—until he made the profanity laced film *Bad Boys II* in 2003, co-starring Martin Lawrence. Smith's character goes out of his way to prove his realness.

It seems that black men always have something to prove. Many people—blacks and nonblacks—are puzzled to see black superstars consistently in trouble with the law. What does a thirty-year-old black man who is a multimillionaire need to prove to anyone? He has to prove his hardness, his toughness, and his black maleness perpetually. The more passionately he embraces society's stereotypes of him, the more "authentic" he becomes.

The 50 Cent Phenomenon

The widely popular rapper 50 Cent came on the hip-hop scene with instant credibility. His debut album, *Get Rich or Die Tryin*, broke the record for the most sales for any debut artist in U.S. history. The album sold 827,000 units in its first four days and 2.1 million copies in its first three weeks. The CD cover is designed to look like a target that has been penetrated by multiple gunshots. 50 Cent's album and singles remained at No. 1 on the rap and pop charts for multiple weeks in 2003. His album even reached the top of the pop charts in London. Only two months after releasing his CD, 50 Cent was on the cover of Rolling Stone. The cover featured him with the grimacing look of a hardened criminal, and the profile was entitled "50 Cent: Mastering The Art of Violence."

What is it about this artist that makes him so intriguing to people? Outside of being produced by two of the most powerful men in hip-hop, Eminem and Dr. Dre, 50 Cent is a bona fide "gangsta-thug." He is the real McCoy. Eminem said he recruited the former boxer because of his life experiences. Touré, a contributing editor to Rolling Stone, states: "We love the gangsta, the real gangsta, in hip hop. The guys who really lived it.... Jay-Z really lived it, Biggie really lived it, we love those guys. He [50] really lived it! He's wearing a bulletproof vest for real. He's talking about, I been to jail, a bunch of times. Yeah, I been shot, a bunch of times" (Empire 2003, 5). The ubiquitous motto of hip-hop culture is, keep it real. Indeed, the music world's fascination with 50 Cent is because he is what Eminem calls "the realest, the illest, the killest."

50 Cent was born Curtis Jackson. His father was largely absent during his childhood and his mom, a crack dealer, was killed when he was eight. A convicted crack dealer himself, 50 Cent began selling drugs and hustling when he was 12, inheriting his mom's business that brought in $5,000 a day. He was shot nine times when he was twenty-three years old. One of the 9 mm bullets dislodged one of his teeth. There is also the scar tissue on his thighs from gunshots and a stab wound. He brags about overcoming gunshot wounds in the song "In Da Club," when he raps that he was shot many times but does not walk with a limp. In his hit song "Wanksta," 50 Cent boasts of doing a three-to-nine bid in prison and being on parole since 1994. It is this type of street credibility that an overwhelming number of young black men crave. But the popularity of 50 Cent on the pop charts is an incredible phenomenon. The pop charts have traditionally been reserved for white artists and nonthreatening black artists like Will Smith. The success of 50 Cent on the pop scene is testimony that the gangsta-thug is an enticing phenomenon in the world of popular culture.

My brother-in-law, who is an accountant in Atlanta, went to lunch one weekday with a couple of co-workers. His fifty-year-old, happily married, white female colleague offered to drive to the diner. As they settled into her Jaguar, she began to play what she said was her favorite CD: *50 Cent's Get Rich or Die Tryin*. My brother-in-law was shocked.

This phenomenon illustrates how tremendously difficult it is to preach the dangers and the nonsense of being a gangsta-thug when the world of popular culture is so enamored with this image. It is natural for people to want to be respected and revered; historically, lacking the respect of mainstream society, this is doubly important for black men. When popular culture enthusiastically embraces and romanticizes the gangsta-thug, this acts as a powerful incentive for young black men to want to be "the realest, the illest, the killest." In the 1950s, 1960s, and 1970s, the music world embraced entertainers such as Nat King Cole, Sam Cooke, Johnny Mathis, Smokey Robinson, James Brown, Curtis Mayfield, Marvin Gaye, and Michael Jackson because of their superb music, their seductive charisma, and their humaneness. Tragically, those days are gone—perhaps they will return. For now, however, popular culture is engaged in a trend of worshiping the most dangerous and threatening images found among black men.

Irony

As a board member of the Charles Drew Child Development Corporation in Watts, California, I often sit in meetings with fellow board member Carl Douglas. Douglas is the famed attorney who assisted Johnnie Cochran in freeing O.J. Simpson. As I gazed at Douglas in one meeting, I began to think about the O.J. Simpson trial and the many ironies it produced. While I sat in the meeting, I jotted down one glaring irony of the trial.

Former Los Angeles District Attorney Christopher Darden's "authentic black" card was taken away when he attempted to prosecute O.J. Simpson, but it was buried when he cried on television in the company of whites. To many black men, this was a cardinal sin. He showed weakness and he showed it in the presence of the so-called nemesis. The irony in this example is, although "The Juice" mingled and associated in the social circles of affluent whites and shunned the Afro-centric lifestyle, he became an icon of black masculinity. Why? Because it appeared that he beat the system and remained defiant to the end. Irrespective of his guilt or innocence in the murders of his former wife and her friend, he had a track record of domestic violence. Perhaps it was Simpson's encounters with the criminal justice system that made him "real." This seems to be one widely accepted criterion of black masculinity.

Former Washington D.C., mayor Marion Barry was caught on tape smoking crack, and yet his constituency re-elected him. Barry became an icon of black masculinity. At the same time, many labeled former Los Angeles mayor Tom Bradley a sell-out while he was one of the most successful mayors in U.S. history. Why? Perhaps it is the need of blacks to see a black man challenge the system or be—allegedly—victimized by the system, which makes his black maleness "genuine." For example, what made James Evans of the 1970s sitcom *Good Times* more of an "authentic" black man than Cliff Huxtable of the *Cosby Show*? Evans was a blue-collar worker with a quick temper and a no-nonsense parenting philosophy. Huxtable, on the other hand, was a white-collar professional, a medical doctor, with a lovable sense of humor and a warmly didactic parenting philosophy. Both gentlemen worked hard to provide for their families. Nevertheless, Evans was embraced as an icon of black masculinity because it appeared that the system was always against him. We only saw Huxtable's success; and many refused to accept this as a model of black maleness.

How is Bryant Gumbel less of a black man than Jim Brown? Is it because he contradicts many of the stereotypes that have been constructed about black men? Gumbel is an iconoclast. He speaks the King's English. He has become a success because of his skillful gamesmanship. Who's applauding? What black man holds Gumbel in esteem? Why not? He is the quintessential black male success story. In three decades of being a high profile television anchor, Gumbel has won numerous awards for his work. He worked on NBC's *Today Show* for twenty-five years and was the Today Show co-host for an unprecedented fifteen years. He anchored that network's coverage of the 1992 presidential elections and hosted the primetime coverage of the 1988 Seoul Olympics. Covering the most important stories of the day and interviewing some of the most influential figures in history, Gumbel succeeded in the most highly visible arena of media and journalism.

Much like MC Hammer, Gumbel does not reflect the narrow representation of black masculinity. Instead of applauding the fact that these two gentlemen have been highly successful, black men add a caveat-"Yeah, but they did it by selling out." How did optimizing one's talents become synonymous with selling out?

We should not judge a man's authenticity based on his appearance or his demeanor. If someone came to me and said "Bryant Gumbel never did anything for the black community" and showed me evidence of this claim, perhaps this would warrant a negative label. Unless people know the track record of a person, they should not make harsh judgments.

Randall Robinson discusses Gumbel's commitment to black causes in his book, *Defending the Spirit*, written in 1998. In the early 1990s, Gumbel urged his colleagues at NBC to shoot the *Today Show* in Africa. In 1992, the *Today Show* was broadcast live from Harare, Zimbabwe. This was the first American broadcast of its kind in Africa. As a result, people were enlightened about African culture.

Perhaps the person who has challenged the rigid concept of black masculinity the most is Michael Jordan. His physical appearance and athletic prowess are synonymous with black masculinity. However, he lacks many of the negative characteristics that many have embraced as essential to black maleness. Jordan is not a gangsta; he never represented himself as one. Instead, he personifies the image of class and professionalism. Jordan has had the type of overwhelming cross-sectional success that has immediately undermined the credibility of some black men. Like Hammer, Jordan appeared in commercials and was featured in an animation. How did Jordan escape the detrimental label placed on Hammer?

Ice Cube and Ice-T, two pioneer hard-core rappers who were critical of Hammer's style of music because it was too mainstream, later became successful movie and television actors. This ironically pushed them further into the cultural mainstream. There was nothing hard-core about *Three Kings* or *Anaconda*, two of Ice Cube's films.

I have a good friend who is a young African American professor at a major university in California. He sought my advice on whether he should get a tattoo to go with his two hoop earrings. I asked him what his motive was in getting the tattoo. He said that he had wanted one for a while. I knew the reason he wanted to get the tattoo was so he could be more intimately connected to the student athletes who took his class. The earrings and the tattoo would make him appear to be a "baller"—e.g., a more "authentic" black man. This example shows us that even black professionals have a need to conform to the standard of black masculinity. Ellis Cose affirms this reality in *The Envy of the World*.

Training Day

I have discussed and debated with several people, mostly black, about whether Denzel Washington should have played the rogue cop, Alonzo Harris, in the film *Training Day*. Before I discuss my criticisms, I would like to say that Denzel did a sensational job of acting in the film and he remains an outstanding role model for all black men.

I had mixed emotions as I left the movie theater at the end of this film. On one hand, I felt I had gotten my nine dollars' worth; but I was disappointed because Denzel played this character. Alonzo Harris wields his power without restrictions or boundaries. He lies, cheats, steals, and kills. He drinks alcohol and womanizes on the job. He embraces nearly every stereotype of a black man that society has created. He makes O-Dog in *Menace II Society* look like Renford Reese (who looks like Opie Taylor).

One African American female friend in her early thirties did not see the slightest problem with Denzel playing this role. She said that if white actors have the latitude to choose their roles, why shouldn't black actors?

My response to her was that black actors should, in theory, have the same latitude to choose whatever roles they like. But I think these actors should be selective because they have a social responsibility that white actors do not have. We cannot revert to the misspoken words of Charles Barkeley: "I'm Not a Role Model." I went on to state that white actors do not have to deal with 300 years of negative image construction. Every chance a black person gets to contradict a stereotype, he should. Every chance he gets to enthusiastically embrace a stereotype he should avoid it like the plague, if he has a choice.

In the beginning of their careers, most actors struggle and find themselves in compromising situations as a matter of survival. I am sensitive to this dilemma. This was not the case with Denzel in *Training Day*. He took this role at the pinnacle of his career, when he had the discretion to choose his roles.

My friend and I are usually in agreement in our sentiments about movies, politics, and sports. She was surprised by my response to this film. She stated, "Denzel is a professional. He is an actor; that is his profession. Actors act." I asked about the consequences this role would have on impressionable people watching it. Her response was that people know it's just a movie.

Does an impressionable teenager watching this film know "it's just a movie"? Can we say for certain that Denzel's role in this movie will have no consequences on people who are watching it? For example, can we say that the multiple utterances of the words "my nigger"—in reference to the officer who is his partner—will not cause someone out there to think it is perfectly okay to use the so called "N" word? "Mom, why can't I use it? Denzel used it and he's your favorite actor!"

I concluded my debate with my friend by saying Sidney Poitier would not have played the role of Alonzo Harris—and Denzel is our modern-day Poitier. My final question to her was, how would she feel if Denzel played the role of a straight-up pimp? She said that would not sit well with her. I asked, "Why not? If that's the role he wants to play, he should be able to play it." She said, "Not a pimp." I said, "Why not? Shouldn't he have that choice?" I added sarcastically, "Denzel is a professional. He is an actor; that is his profession. Actors act." She said, "I get your point."

My mother loves Denzel Washington, but she said that she would not go see him in that role. There are many others who share my mom's feeling. My sister said that she cringed throughout the movie, asking herself why Denzel would take such a role. So, the fundamental question is: why did he take this role? And, why would I put this discussion under my chapter titled, Authenticity?

Denzel said he took the role because his oldest son told him he needed to play a bad guy for once. He also stated that the only way he would play the role was if his character got killed in the end so there would be a moral to the story. I think Denzel took this role because of the tremendous challenge it offered. I also think he took it because even he-Denzel Washington—felt a strong desire to affirm his black maleness. He had the urge to show people that he could be "real."

Many of my black friends, fraternity brothers, and colleagues have this strong urge to show The Man they are not like him. Just like Denzel, they have a desire to be down, in a rebellious way. They have an urge to revisit the days when street credibility was paramount, the days most black men discuss in their autobiographies.

Selling Out vs. Fitting In

While I was a graduate student at USC, I was walking to my apartment one day when a black man in his mid-twenties confronted me. He was working security at the Shrine Auditorium. He said, "Hey black man. What's up, my brother?" He asked me if I attended USC, and then he asked me if I had to sell out to fit in. My first instinct was to get mad at him for insinuating I was a sell-out. I told him that a black man does not have to sell out to fit in. As I continued to walk home, I realized that I had not been totally truthful. The fact is, in American society we have to be flexible with our identity to succeed. If some people construe this flexibility to mean "selling out," then they must not understand that it is a necessary component of success in this country.

The fact is that blacks represent only 12.8 percent of the U.S. population. They may have influence, but they do not make the laws in this country. Economically, blacks have influence but do not set the agenda for economic and corporate policies. Hence, the reality is that blacks must play by rules that have been outlined by others. My sister, who graduated from Tennessee State University, came home once with a T-shirt that carried the message: The Blacker the College, The Sweeter the Knowledge. Another one read, It's a Black Thing. You Wouldn't Understand. I understood then and I understand now. The odds were then that she would be working for a white-owned company after she graduated—and she was. The odds were that several years later, she would still be working for a white-owned company— and she is.

Black men should continue to fight for justice. They should not sell their souls and identity for the sake of vertical mobility. However, there is a rigid but flexible system of rules that must be followed by black men if they are to succeed in this society. Traditionally, for black men in the United States, playing by these rules has been a complex endeavor. In the 'hood a black man has to keep it real and prove to his community that he has not sold out. He must personify toughness. In the workplace, however, he must be the complete antithesis of what he is in his community.

When considering the question of what plight is the true plight of the black man in the U.S., it is my contention that black men who enthusiastically embrace the narrowly constructed stereotypes of black masculinity will continue to be degraded, victimized, and oppressed. Those who work diligently to contradict these stereotypes will be more likely to succeed in American society.

To contend that American society is so oppressive that no black man has a fair chance is being dishonest. If this is true, how is it possible to explain the black mayors in our major cities, the many black chiefs of police, judges, lawyers, doctors, dentists, principals, school superintendents, and entrepreneurs?

One of my best friends—a black professor at a major university— and I have gotten into many heated debates over the plight of black men in America. His point is that no matter what black men do, they are always going to be a threat to the hegemonic U.S. system. He says that you cannot compare the lot of blacks in America to any other group.

In the end, says my friend, blacks collectively will never be allowed to achieve their full potential because the system will not tolerate such positive behavior. He makes some good points. However, my response to his argument is that just because the system is harsher on blacks does not mean that blacks should not have a game plan to combat its ills. If there is a conspiracy to hold black men back, there should be an equally potent conspiracy to help black men achieve. I maintain it is ignorance on the part of black men to engage in self-destructive behaviors. My friend holds the system largely accountable for these behaviors. I tell him to look at the Morehouse model. Morehouse College brings young black men to its campus from all over the nation and world and educates and refines them. The institution teaches them to be conscious of their heritage. It teaches them that regardless of the odds, with discipline and perseverance they can be successful in any field of human endeavor. At Morehouse, they do not embrace the defeatist attitude that no matter how hard they study and no matter how much discipline they have, the system is going to keep them down.

I tell my friend to read Joe Marshall's book *Street Soldier* in order to get a grasp of someone who is not blaming the system but trying to change the lives of black men from within. I agree with Marshall in many other ways. For too long, the focus and attention of blacks has been outward-looking instead of inward-looking. Marshall acknowledges that our system is not fair. However, he encourages young black men to have the discipline and vision to avoid America's trap. I usually conclude my argument with my friend by saying that I acknowledge the system is unfair. Black politicians and community leaders must rigorously lobby to change it. I always remind my buddy that it is incumbent upon people like us to inspire change—internally and externally.

References

Brown, Jim, and Steve Delsohn. 1989. Out of Bounds. New York: Zebra Books, Kensington Publishing.

Cose, Ellis. 2002. The Envy of the World. New York: Washington Square Press.

Dyson, Michael Eric. 2001. Holler if You Hear Me: Searching for Tupac Shakur. New York: Basic Civitas.

Empire, Kitty. 2003. He's cool. Dead cool: Eminem sings his praises and Mike Tyson says he's scary. The Observer, 23 February.

Gilmore, Al-Tony (1975). Bad Nigger! The National Impact of Jack Johnson. Port Washington, New York: Kennikat Press.

Harper, Phillip Brian. 1996. Are We Not Men? Masculine Anxiety and the Problem of African-American Identity. New York: Oxford University Press.

Marshall, Joseph, Jr., and Lonnie Wheeler. 1996. Street Robinson, Randall. 1998. Defending the Spirit: A Black Life in America. New York: Plume.

Touré. 2003. 50 Cent: Mastering the art of violence. Rolling Stone, 3 April.

Chapter 4

Symbols of Defiance

The cross is a symbol of redemption and the most sacred symbol of the Christian faith. Once upon a time crosses were worn only by priests, ministers, and the very religious. Today, many young black men wear crosses. They wear them because they have embraced the cross as a symbol of defiance. Many would consider it blasphemy to use profanity while wearing a cross. However, it is the shock effect of wearing a cross while simultaneously being a gangsta-thug that is appealing to many young black men. For example, when reading an article in USA Today titled "50 Cent Rules Year in Radio," I noticed that the accompanying photo of the artist featured him wearing a long gold necklace connected to a miniature book that had "Holy Bible" engraved on it (Barnes 2003, 14D). I immediately wondered how an artist whose album boasts of violence, sex, and drugs with song titles such as "P.I.M.P." and "High All the Time"—as in, "I get high all the time"—could sport a necklace with the Holy Bible on it. Religious symbols such as this have strangely become symbols of defiance. Many young black men who have embraced the gangsta-thug persona wear the cross because they are not supposed to. Indeed, these individuals have embraced other symbols of defiance.

In *Cool Pose: The Dilemmas of Black Manhood in America*, Richard Majors and Janet Mancini Billson state that being "cool" is the black man's way of dealing with racism and discrimination without losing his sanity.

> Being cool invigorates a life that would otherwise be degrading and empty. It helps the black male make sense out of his life and get what he wants from others. Cool pose brings a dynamic vitality into the black male's everyday en-

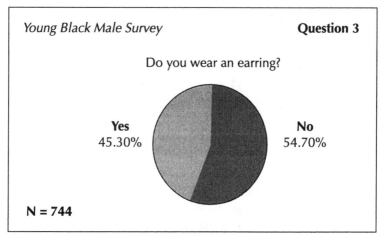

Young Black Male Survey   **Question 3**

Do you wear an earring?

Yes   **No**
45.30%   54.70%

N = 744

Over the past decade, the earring has become increasingly popular among young black men. Why?

counters, transforming the mundane into the sublime and making the routine spectacular. (Majors and Billson 1992, 2)

I agree with Majors and Billson. However, I would add that coolness is also a symbol of defiance for the African American male.

Earrings And Tattoos

There is so much pressure put on black men to conform to one model of black masculinity. Some 45 percent of 744 respondents to the survey of young black males I conducted in 2002 stated that they wore earrings. These respondents were from thirteen to nineteen years of age.

When I entered college in 1985, I was shocked to see that my African American roommate wore an earring. He was unique because at that time earrings had not become accepted. Now it is difficult to find a young black man who does not have one or two earrings. What do these earrings symbolize? I once heard an African American athlete comment that wearing earrings was an African tradition. I have been to Africa three times and the only men I saw wearing earrings were the ones who were trying to emulate African Americans. Young black men began wearing earrings as a symbol of defiance against the conservative white system.

At one point in our recent history, earrings were worn only by women, some homosexual men, and a few hippies. So how did this mostly feminine ornament become transformed into a widely embraced symbol of black masculinity? Donning an earring met one of the fundamental criteria for black masculinity: challenging the system. Earrings remain a taboo in conservative white America. In golf, for instance—a sport that represents the power structure—you will rarely see a player wearing an earring.

I contend that the earring as a symbol of defiance tells the white power structure, "You can't control me." When black men wear their hats backwards or to the side, they are making the statement, "I'm not like you and you can't control me." As various symbols of defiance have become tolerated, young black men have constantly pushed the envelope. For example, as the stud earring became tolerated by the power structure, the symbol of defiance became more visible. Black men moved from the stud to the hoop earring and from the hoops to two earrings. Michael Jordan's sporting of the "Genie Hoop" earring is his subtle symbol of defiance and one affirmation of his black maleness. It would be hard to fathom Joe Montana, John Elway, or Wayne Gretsky adorning themselves with such symbols of defiance.

What statement did the reporter Ed Bradley of *60 Minutes* make when he started wearing an earring in the mid 1980s? At the time, his wearing an earring on the air was a radical and controversial statement. The earring was Bradley's way of telling the conservative operation at *60 Minutes*: "I may work for you but you can't control me."

My mom once asked me, "What are these middle-aged and old black men doing wearing earrings? I saw Morgan Freeman with two hoop earrings. What are they doing?"

Although 11.23% of those surveyed stated that they have tattoos, this is substantial since tattoos are outlawed for those under the age of 18 in California. Tattoos have replaced the earring as a symbol of defiance and authenticity for young black men.

As the earring has become surprisingly tolerated by the power structure, young black men have moved to tattoos. A significant majority of NBA players have tattoos. Even clean-cut Kobe Bryant recently got two tattoos. Tattoos were once seen as a representation of defiance only sported by whites in motorcycle clubs, veterans, and backwoods residents. While growing up in McDonough, Georgia, I cannot recall ever seeing a black person with a tattoo. So why have so many young black men appropriated a cultural phenomenon that was foreign to them just a decade ago?

The fact is that young black men need new symbols of defiance to affirm their black maleness. When one tattoo is not enough of a symbol, then young black men will move to multiple tattoos. Some already have. Allen Iverson of the NBA is a representation of this defiance.

What is Iverson attempting to prove with his multiple tattoos? Because he has so many tattoos, his statement must be that he is the ultimate "Bad Nigger" who cannot be controlled by the system. Perhaps these symbols of defiance are today's versions of the black-gloved fists of Tommie Smith and John Carlos at the 1968 Olympics. Nevertheless, these visual representations of black masculinity can be counterproductive. Although Iverson can get away with wearing multiple tattoos because he is a multimillionaire, the average young black man limits his vertical mobility when he embraces such symbols of defiance. In order for him to get a job and begin a career as a teacher, police officer, salesperson, marketing representative, accountant, or stockbroker, he will invariably have to prove to his employer that he is the anti-thug. In other words, he has to prove that he is the polar opposite of the gangsta-thug. Whether it is the baggy pants, the bandanna, the braids in the hair, the earring, or the tattoo, black men must realize that in certain arenas, there are negative consequences to embracing defiant symbols of black masculinity.

Anti-Intellectualism

More than 38 percent of those included in my survey of young black males responded that they had not read one book outside of classwork in the past year. This is disturbing. Many blacks blame the system for failing our kids. However, public libraries are free. Any student who wants access to a book can get it. Many black kids do not read books because it is not a "cool" thing to do.

Not long ago, I watched the teen competition on the game show *Jeopardy*. There were three contestants, a white male, a white female, and a young black male: Evan, Lindsay, and Bernard, respectively. I was enthralled by the competition. Bernard took an early lead but Evan came back to tie and then pass Bernard in the first round. Lindsay was a distant third. In the second round, using the category "African American Firsts," Bernard mounted a serious comeback. The parents of the two other competitors were probably displeased that Bernard was taking advantage of the African American category—not thinking that all of the other categories were based on the achievements of whites. At the end of the second round, Bernard led Evan by a small margin and Lindsay had closed the gap to be within striking distance. In the final round, the contestants responded to the statement: "A DNA-containing linear body of the cell nuclei of plants and animals." Bernard and Lindsay responded, correctly, "What are chromosomes?" Bernard had wagered enough to hold Lindsay off and win the game. I celebrated like my favorite sports team had won a big game. Bernard Holloway of Mitchellville, Maryland, had just scored the winning touchdown or sunk the final three-point shot—with time running out—to win the game and become the Most Valuable Player. Bernard was a superstar, not a sell-out or a deviant.

When I was growing up in McDonough, the basketball court was the center of our cultural universe. If a person left the court to go the store to get something, you might hear the following exchange:

Ceddy Boo: Hey Fat Rat where you going?

Fat Rat: To the sto'

Ceddy Boo: Straight up? You is?

No one would dare say, "You are?" as a question. Speaking grammatically correct English in my area of town-the part known as Blacksville—automatically got you labeled and your "ghetto card" revoked. Consequently, nearly everyone spoke Black English Vernacular (BEV). If Ceddy Boo had responded to Fat Rat by saying, "You are?" it would have meant that he had accepted the legitimacy of the English language and the system, which meant that he had sold out.

In language, dress, and behavior, it seems that black maleness has been defined by the nonacceptance of norms established by whites. The most troubling aspect of this anti-norm behavior is deliberate underachievement in school.

In the film *Finding Forrester*, actor Sean Connery plays the role of an eccentric mentor to actor Rob Brown. Brown is a standout basketball player from the inner city who is offered a basketball scholarship by an elite private school. He takes the entrance exam for the school and does remarkably well. The private school administrators are puzzled because his public school grades do not match his scores. The movie reveals that Brown's character is brilliant but does not try in school. He frequently writes in a tablet but is careful not to let his homeboys see him do so. The well-read basketball star downplays his intelligence so that he is not labeled a square, called a nerd, or accused of acting white. It is bewildering to see this young man hiding his intelligence in order to conform to the code of the streets.

In the film *8 Mile*, the rapper Eminem battles in a freestyle rap competition against a member of a rival group. He wins the rap competition partially because he exposes the background of his opponent. He raps that his competitor has two parents at home and that he attended an elite private high school. When Eminem's competitor takes the microphone, the all-black crowd begins to boo him for being a fake. Knowing that he has been exposed, the embarrassed rapper gives up and Eminem wins. Imagine being embarrassed for having two parents at home and graduating from an elite high school!

> It's no wonder that the madness is spreading. By its sheer pervasiveness, the gangsta-rap culture imposes a tremendous amount of peer pressure, even on young blacks who try to play it straight. In their songs and in their gangsta personae, some rappers promote the notion that you're lame if you go to school; you're weak if you weren't raised slinging dope; you're nobody if you didn't come up hard. (McCall 1997, 53)

When I was recruited to play football at Vanderbilt, I was among a group of twenty-four scholarship athletes. There were only three blacks in this class. This addition brought the total number of blacks on the team to twenty, of one hundred. The students from neighboring Tennessee State University and Fisk University, historically black universities, thought we were upper-crust blacks of privilege and therefore not "real." A few of my teammates went to extraordinary lengths to prove that they were real. One spent more time hanging out in the Nashville housing projects than he did on campus. It would have been admirable if he had been doing positive work in this community; but his preference instead was to date women from the projects and engage in the activities of the street. My question was, why come to this elite white university if you are going to spend your time in the projects? We had five wannabe thugs on the team. All of them eventually flunked out of school. I guess their rationale was that they did not want to play by the white man's rules. So they "kept it real" and rebelled in the worst way: they underachieved.

The fifteen of us who did not embrace society's stereotypes graduated with degrees in engineering, economics, political science, and human resource management. All of us have successful careers now. We have the power to contribute and influence the black community in a variety of ways. Indeed, our contributions now are more significant than those of the black man who is on the corner talking about how he used to be at the white man's university on full athletic scholarship but dropped out because he did not want to get exploited and brainwashed.

The anti-intellectual subculture of black men is not a recent phenomenon. Young black men have historically shunned intelligence in the context of school achievement. "Street smarts" have been embraced as a more acceptable attribute. In his autobiography, *Vernon Can Read*, Vernon Jordan discusses the challenges of being young, black, and intelligent. He reflects on his teenage years when he states, "There was something of a stigma attached to being too intelligent." He writes of being in the eighth grade when one of the girls in his class wrote on the board "Girls in Our Class" and "Boys in Our Class." She listed his name at the end of the girl's column.

Indeed, young black men who have embraced their intelligence have been called sissies, among other names. The legacy of the anti-intellectual movement has endured and become more calcified today.

Jonathan Miller, the smartest person in my town—black or white—did not reach his full potential because he was labeled a nerd, a square, and a white boy. In trying to meet people's standard of black masculinity, he sabotaged his grades in school and maintained a nonchalant attitude towards academics. The pressures to conform to a rigid standard of black maleness were unforgiving in my town. I escaped these pressures and affirmed my black masculinity by being an outstanding athlete.

If blacks had constructed and enthusiastically embraced a model of black masculinity that celebrated academic success, Jonathan would have undoubtedly excelled and easily become the valedictorian of our class and chosen from a number of prestigious scholarship offers. Instead, he graduated in the middle of a class from which about 15 percent went on to college. Rather than enjoying an illustrious career in engineering, law, or medicine, he is currently working for a department of family and child services, distributing food stamps.

The illogic of the anti-intellectual symbol of defiance is the most disturbing. Many talented young black men sabotage their academic careers to fit in and keep it real. For example, in the brilliantly insightful film *Save the Last Dance*, Derek Reynolds, the main character played by Sean Patrick Thomas, finds himself torn between his desire to help his homie Malakai get revenge on a gang and concentrating on his preparations to enter Georgetown University as a pre-med major. His dilemma is probably perplexing to many who have watched this film. It seems as if the easiest decision in the world would be for Derek to drop the dangerous Malakai as a friend and pursue his own academic career. However, the overwhelming pressure imposed on Derek to keep it real does not allow for such a simple determination.

At the point in the film when Derek is faced with making the complex decision that will determine his fate for the rest of his life, he rebuffs Malakai's invitation to trouble. Malakai is eventually arrested for his drive-by shooting activities. If Derek had made the split-second choice to keep it real, he would have inevitably found himself in prison for murder—his academic career sabotaged and his dreams poisoned.

Countless young black men have undoubtedly been faced with the same choice as Derek. However, many have yielded to the intense pressures of subcultural norms. Imagine the numbers of pre-med and pre-law majors that have been incarcerated trying to conform to an irrational standard of black maleness.

Nathan McCall writes in *What's Going On* that young blacks whose experiences do not mirror those of the streets are looked at as being "illegit." I have witnessed, just as McCall has, young black men on college campuses dressing in thug attire and acting like non-conforming gangstas.

In dress and manner, many students strive mightily to shake off rappers' musical portrayal of them as wimpy nerds. The males try to give the impression that they're really gangsta killas hiding out in college to duck the Man. (McCall 1997, 53)

I recall having one of the black male students in my Introduction to American Government class come in on the first day wearing a do-rag on his head, which was draped down his neck. He wore a baseball cap on top, which was tilted to the side. His pants were sagging, and his extra-large shirt was untucked. He looked as though he had wandered off the streets of South Central Los Angeles. After the first two weeks of class, he came to my office to get some advice on his first paper assignment. I asked him where he grew up, went to high school, his major, etc. He grew up in the suburbs of Los Angeles. He went to a private high school, and his college major was electrical engineering. I said to him jokingly, "I thought you were from the 'hood." His response was "Naw Doc, I got to represent"—meaning that he had to represent the 'hood, although he had no experiences there.

If young black men posture themselves as gangstas and thugs and if they have enthusiastically embraced one model of black masculinity, how do they expect to be treated by the police and the criminal justice system? Of course, no rational person can justify the consistent acts of police brutality and the gross disparities in the criminal justice system in the United States; but should not black men accept some of the blame for embracing the gangsta-thug image? Yes.

It is unrealistic for blacks to expect a police officer, a jury, or a judge, who have already accepted certain stereotypes about young black men, to be sympathetic to them when they posture as gangsta-thugs. I agree that many professional black men have been the victims of racial profiling. So have I—although I will bet that the one time I was pulled from my car on suspicion of attempted burglary would have been multiplied had I routinely embraced the image of the gangsta-thug.

An irony reveals itself when we examine the defiant symbols of black masculinity and the enormous impact of black males on popular culture. As young black men have become more defiant, popular culture has fervently accepted and embraced this defiance to the point where it has become mainstream. In essence, each new symbol of defiance is ironically sterilized, because it is immediately popularized and widely accepted. The shock value and deviant symbolism are undermined.

Although popular culture has embraced the defiant symbols of black masculinity, so has the criminal justice system. Whereas these symbols may be tolerated and condoned by the entertainment and sports industries, this imagery is having a tragic effect on young black men entangled in the criminal justice system.

Patriarchy

Historically, black men have gone through various stages that have led to current pathologies. In his classic book *The Negro Family in the United States*, E. Franklin Frazier states that the Negro woman was schooled during slavery to be self-sufficient and self-reliant.

> As a rule, the Negro woman as wife or mother was the mistress of her cabin, save for the interference of master or overseer...her wishes in regard to mating and family matters were paramount. Neither economic necessity nor tradition had instilled in her the spirit of subordination to masculine authority. Emancipation only tended to confirm in many cases the spirit of self-sufficiency which slavery taught. (Frazier 1966, 102)

Although some slave masters had humanitarian concerns for the family structure of their slaves, many lacked this sensitivity. Hence, they traded individuals like goods. In this scenario, it was difficult for bonding to take place between the slave male and female. The worth of a black man during slavery depended on his strength, durability, and virility.

Daniel P. Black states that the black man is still struggling with the effects of slavery. According to Black, enslaved fathers did not have the time or cultural resources to teach their sons the meaning and functions of manhood. Survival was the primary concern of enslaved fathers. Hence, this is the skill they passed to their sons. "Manhood became an individual pursuit to black men as opposed to a communal, familial male ideal" (Black 1997, 89).

During slavery the black man's concept of manhood was influenced by the patriarchal practices of the white masters. Black men sought to be their captors' equal. "The white man and his world, especially his perception of men and manhood, became the yardstick by which black men began to measure their own manhood" (Black 1997, 100).

At the end of slavery, the euphoria that greeted the Emancipation Proclamation and the Thirteenth Amendment quickly subsided as blacks realized they were wedded to a system of sharecropping. The period after slavery was especially hard on black men because they could not reach the status of their white counterparts. In American society, the man has traditionally been the breadwinner. He was the one designated to "bring home the bacon." Black men felt ashamed that they could not fulfill this role, so they rebelled. They took out the pain of their embarrassment on their families. In many cases, they left the home altogether. Frazier asks:

How did the Negro family fare when it left the house of the master and began its independent career in the stormy days of emancipation? What authority was there to take the place of the master's in regulating sex relations and maintaining the permanency of marital ties? Where could the Negro father look for a sanction of his authority in family relations, which had scarcely existed in the past? (Frazier 1966, 73)

According to Frazier, family desertion was the inevitable consequence of Negro urbanization. The search for work and new opportunities pulled many Negro men from their families. Many more stable Negro men left their wives and children after World War I to follow the masses migrating to the North (Frazier 1966, 249).

When Daniel Patrick Moynihan released his 1965 report on the status of the black family, it created a firestorm of controversy. Moynihan asserted that one-third of black families were headed by females and that this statistic had devastating consequences on the upward mobility of blacks. His report was seen by many as being racist and anti-black. Nevertheless, his report was accurate. For decades, economists have found a correlation between family structure and poverty.

Today females head an overwhelming majority of black families. Where are the black men? Journalist Dwight Lewis asks this question in one chapter of the book *Thinking Black*. Lewis states that 90 percent of the 250 students at his son's high school were black but in an entire year, only 6 fathers had shown up to check on their kids (Lewis 1996, 61). Teachers and principals do not have conferences with black fathers because these fathers are not around.

I once told my father that I did not know why people celebrated Father's Day. Although some of my friends' fathers were active in raising them, the overwhelming majority grew up in fatherless households. Even if the fathers were physically present, they were spiritually absent. Few of them were loving nurturers who were active and concerned with every aspect of their sons' lives. I agree with Nathan McCall when he states in *Makes Me Wanna Holler*:

> I never heard my friends say they wanted to be like their fathers when they grew up.... A two-parent home is no better off than a single-parent one if the father is fucked up in the head and beaten down. There's nothing more dangerous and destructive in a household than a frustrated, oppressed black man. (McCall 1994, 83)

Perhaps it is the black man's inferior economic status-referred to by McCall—that is the root cause of many of the black man's vices— e.g., gambling, excessive drinking, drug use, and domestic violence. The black father forfeits his right to lecture and chastise his children when he has embraced these vices himself. In other words, what can a father tell his children about not getting hooked on drugs if indeed he is a drug addict?

In the film *Love and Basketball*, Omar Epps plays a high school basketball star who is contemplating his university scholarship offers. This decision, like others, is heavily influenced by his father, who is his idol. In his eyes, his father is perfect; he cannot do wrong. However, at some point late in the film his mother tells the son that his dad is a no-good womanizer. The son refuses to believe it until his mother shows him pictures of his father romancing with different women. The son is devastated. He never looks at his father the same way. In fact, after this episode they rarely speak again. His father had forfeited his right to give his son any advice.

What does this mean? It means that being a perfect father is extremely difficult. Because of societal pressures—real or perceived—it is even more difficult to be a perfect father if you are black. When I counsel young African American men on their responsibility as fathers and companions—without knowing what type of family environment they grew up in—I tell them they have to be pioneers. In other words, they should not necessarily look at the way they were raised by their fathers as their model. Instead, they should look at ways in which they can improve on their father's mistakes.

Bell hooks writes,

> Feeling as though they are constantly on edge, their lives always in jeopardy, many black men truly cannot understand that this condition of 'powerlessness' does not negate their capacity to assert power over black females in a way that is dominating and oppressive; nor does it justify and condone sexist behavior. Coming home from a hard day of work at a low-paying job, or after a day of searching for work or feeling the burden of unemployment, an individual black man demanding, in a coercive or aggressive way, that his wife serve him may not see his actions as sexist or involving the use of power. This 'not seeing' can be, and often is, a process of denial that helps maintain patriarchal structures. (1995, 74)

Louis Farrakhan responded to the contemporary crisis of the black man by coordinating the *Million Man March*, held in the fall of 1995. The objective of this gathering was to demonstrate the black man's sense of social responsibility. While many looked at this event as a magnificent positive representation of black maleness, others looked at it as an attempt to assert black patriarchy. Itabari Njeri states in The Farrakhan Factor that the Nation of Islam and its leaders promulgated a "patriarchal world-view" of family values at the *Million Man March*. In a commentary about the *Million Man March* in *The Progressive*, political scientist Adolph Reed, Jr., boldly stated that "beneath the unctuous, pro forma tones of apology and tender concern for black women's need for relief" was a "resurgent demand for a pride of patriarchal place" in the black community and family structure (Njeri 1998, 233). According to Njeri, "black nationalist organizations have always been incubators of virulent sexism masquerading as deferential, Madonna-like elevation of women coupled with homophobia" (P. 233).

Hooks argues that a distinction must be made between the nineteenth-century "masculinist vision" of black patriarchy—rooted in the notion that black men should strive for racial uplift, education, and security for their families—and the contemporary model of black masculinity which is primarily defined by a desire to dominate women. "The shift from benevolent patriarchy to a concern with the assertion of brute domination represents a crucial difference between the radical thinking of nineteenth-century black male leaders and their twentieth-century counterparts" (hooks 1995, 65).

Hypermasculinity

Cornell West argues in *Race Matters* that patriarchy among blacks comes in the form of a cultural conservatism. Whereas white cultural conservatism comes in the form of degrading blacks, women, and homosexuals, black cultural conservatism scapegoats women and homosexuals (West 1993, 42). Black men have not only mirrored the patriarchy of their white counterparts, they have moved beyond it.

Former NFL player Danny Buggs was suspended as a motivational speaker for the Dekalb County School District outside of Atlanta because in a speech he repeated the oft-quoted, Bible-based phrase, "God made Adam and Eve, not Adam and Steve." Buggs's sentiment is emblematic of other black men. Homophobia among black men is rampant. Black men have acted out their ultra-macho behavior by verbally and physically assaulting homosexuals. One way for black men to prove their gangsta-thugness is to be extremely harsh towards homosexuals. The homosexual black man represents the anti-thug.

Some black men get overtly hostile at the mere sight of a gay man. It's as if the level of their hostility is correlated with their manliness. For instance, moments after he hugged a male friend good-bye, Trev Broudy-who is gay-was attacked in West Hollywood by two black men wielding a baseball bat. Broudy was hospitalized for more than a week with serious head injuries that left him in critical condition (Gorman 2003, 3). At Morehouse College, the all-male black institution that is the alma mater of Martin Luther King, Jr., a student beat a gay classmate to numbness with a baseball bat. According to a campus police report, the perpetrator became angry when he saw his classmate peek at him in the shower. Reporter Lyle Harris states, "Gay-bashing may be illegal, but some African Americans don't think it's the least bit immoral" (Harris 2002, D1).

In a powerful and insightful article in the *Atlanta Journal-Constitution*, Harris states that minority groups marginalized by mainstream society often view homosexuality with disdain. He continues:

> You can't learn the best qualities of black manhood by fathering and abandoning a brood of babies, or attending marches, listening to role-models-for-rent, or aping the brutish machismo in rap videos. The only way to do that, I think, is to reject the insular, intolerant attitudes about color and class and sexuality that separate us from one another. Instead of hiding behind homophobia, we have to confront these issues honestly, without fear of scorn or physical abuse. (Harris 2002, D1)

So much of black masculinity is defined by one's relationship with women. One reason homosexuals are deeply despised by black men is because heterosexual black men cannot fathom someone not being attracted to women. Moreover, many black men cannot understand the failure to pursue multiple women.

Physician, psychologist, researcher, and educator George Edmond Smith states in *More Than Sex: Reinventing the Black Male Image* that the collective history of black men has too often conspired to create in us "a fragmented, distorted, or incomplete sense of what it means to be a man" (Smith 2000, 9).

In the beginning of the John Singleton film *Baby Boy*, Jody (played by Tyrese Gibson) states that one thing he is good at is making pretty babies. The narrative involves Jody dividing time between the mothers of his two babies, and other women. Jody claims to be a man. However, what is it that makes him a man? He does not have a real job. He cannot support his family. He lives at home with his mother. Jody defines his masculinity according to his sexual prowess. Whenever there is a problem in one of his relationships, Jody attempts to solve it with his penis. Sex is his answer to everything.

The character Franklin in Terry McMillan's *Disappearing Acts* also attempts to solve the problems in his relationship through sex. He gets fired from his job and takes his frustration out on his companion. When she cannot take any more of his negative ways, he attempts to win her back through sex.

> In summary, sexuality is the main ingredient within the black man's repertoire of self. Many black men traditionally bring unhealthy attitudes and behaviors to relationships guided by physical sex. Life events and social myths force us to live up to the standards others create; the stress of meeting societal expectations can be extreme. (Smith 2000, 9)

Mark Anthony Neal states that some black men think that just because they own a penis, they are men. "Biologically that makes you a male but culturally it does not make you a man" (Neal 2001). Perhaps some black men like Jody have embraced the notion that they are a sexually superior species and that this gift will be the answer to all their problems. This so-called gift of the black man has become counterproductive. As Robert Staples states:

Denied equal access to the prosaic symbols of manhood, they manifest their masculinity in the most extreme form of sexual domination. When they have been unable to achieve the status in the workplace, they have exercised the privilege of their manliness and attempted to achieve it in the bedroom. (Staples 1985, 85)

A black professional once asked me the following hypothetical question: "What if so much attention was not focused on this so-called 'gift' of the black man?" I immediately knew where he was going with the question. He followed his question by stating that we might have countless black physicists, engineers, doctors, etc. We both laughed and then discussed the implications of black men internalizing their status as "sexually superior."

Are stereotypes of black men so powerful that black men are compelled to live down to these low expectations? Who is to blame for boastful and wanton behaviors? Is it the white power structure? From a psychosociological perspective, what has the white power structure done to cause black men to embrace such irresponsible behavior? The notion that black men would vent their anger toward each other and toward black women because of the unfairness of the oppressive system is counterintuitive.

One fundamental reason mistrust exists between black men and black women in relationships is because of their individual experiences as they grew up. The black man was taught by his older brothers, uncles, father, and in some cases grandfather that being in love was a sign of weakness. As Staples states, "Feeling a constant need to affirm their masculinity, tenderness and compassion are eschewed as signs of weakness, which leave them vulnerable to the ever-feared possibility of female domination" (Staples 1985, 85).

Moreover, the black man is inundated with talk about running "game" and being a "player." Hence, early in his life he learns to equate masculinity with being a slick-talking player with lots of game. His masculinity is not defined by the amount of respect and compassion he shows to females in particular and to other individuals in general. His masculinity is not defined by his honesty, integrity, or moral fortitude.

The challenge for black men is to redefine masculinity. The consequences of not redefining masculinity are too great. The continued embrace of more extreme symbols of defiance, homophobia, anti-intellectualism, and sexism are enormously detrimental to the black community. If Richard Majors is correct in asserting that being cool is a black man's raison d'être, black men need to find ways to make indiscriminate compassion and achievement in all forms, "cool."

References

Barnes, Ken. 2003. 50 Cent rules year in radio. USA Today, 3 July.

Black, Daniel P. 1997. Dismantling Black Manhood: An Historical and Literary Analysis of the Legacy of Slavery. New York: Garland Publishing.

Frazier, E. Franklin. 1966. The Negro Family in the United States. Revised and abridged edition with foreword by Nathan Glazer. Chicago: University of Chicago Press.

Gorman, Anna. 2003. Gay beating victim testifies at hearing. Los Angeles Times, 16 January.

Harris, Lyle. 2002. How my gay brother helped me be a better man. Atlanta Journal-Constitution, 17 November.

hooks, bell. 1995. Killing Rage: Ending Racism. New York: Henry Holt.

Jordan, Vernon. 2001. Vernon Can Read. New York: Public Affairs.

Lewis, Dwight. 1996. Where are the black fathers? In Thinking Black, edited by D. Wickham. New York: Crown Publishers.

Majors, Richard, and Janet Mancini Billson. 1992. Cool Pose: The Dilemmas of Black Manhood in America. New York: Lexington Books.

McCall, Nathan. 1994. Makes Me Wanna Holla. New York: Random House.

McCall, Nathan. 1997. What's Going On. New York: Random House.

Moynihan, Daniel P. 1965. The Negro Family: The Case for National Action. Washington, D.C.: Office of Policy Planning and Research, U.S. Department of Labor.

Neal, Mark Anthony. 2001. Interview on Black Entertainment Television (BET). 6 August.

Njeri, Itabari. 1998. The Farrakhan Factor: African-American Writers on Leadership, Nationhood, and Minister Louis Farrakhan. Edited by Amy Alexander. New York: Grove Press.

Smith, George Edmond. 2000. More Than Sex: Reinventing the Black Male Image. New York: Kensington Books.

Staples, Robert. 1985. Black Masculinity: The Black Male's Role in American Society. San Francisco: Black Scholar Press.

West, Cornel. 1993. Race Matters. Boston: Beacon Press.

Chapter 5

The Roots of the Black Rebel in Sport

Lawlessness

This chapter attempts to explain why black star athletes consistently rebel against the status quo. The lawless behavior of many black athletes has troubled blacks and nonblacks alike. Indeed, it is perplexing to see multimillionaire black athletes consistently run afoul of the law. Although many cultural critics are quick to blame the establishment for solidifying negative stereotypes of black men, few have deconstructed why many black men have embraced these negative stereotypes. The black athlete represents the multiple definitions of black masculinity; in fact, there is no greater icon. He is strong and agile, fierce and aggressive. His untamed aggression and raw energy on the athletic field are seen as positives. However, the same aggression and energy off the field have led to negative consequences.

First, there are the so-called good guys who have had encounters with the law. Jayson Williams, Steve McNair, and Kobe Bryant could be considered the "anti-thugs." Their squeaky clean images have been tainted.

The former New Jersey Nets forward Jayson Williams had it all. He was nice looking, intelligent, articulate, and humorous. His laugh and smile were contagious, and his personality was radiant. Williams was charged with manslaughter, accused of recklessly handling the shotgun that killed a limousine driver in his home in 2002 and then creating a scene to make the death appear to be a suicide.

NFL star-quarterback and golden boy Steve McNair was charged with drunk driving and handgun possession in 2003. Only months after the McNair incident, Kobe Bryant, the NBA's clean-cut superstar, was arrested and charged for felony sexual assault in Eagle County, Colorado. Bryant admitted to committing adultry with his 19-year-old accuser. Perhaps these individuals just made human mistakes. But perhaps they were subconsciously rebelling against being perfect. The burden of being a perfect role model is daunting and formidable for anyone. However, it is especially difficult for young black men because they live in a society that sends mixed messages about those with wholesome images. Ironically, their drive to be role models and their drive to be perceived as "real" black men are mutually exclusive. In other words, in order to have one identity, they must give up the other. There are those who have sidestepped this complex identity issue altogether by consistently engaging in lawless behavior.

While finishing the final draft of this book, I was compelled to revisit several chapters after reading a story in the *Atlanta Journal-Constitution* during July 2003. The sports section featured a report from the *Associated Press* about the arrests of Orlando Magic guard Darrell Armstrong and Portland Trailblazers guard Damon Stoudamire. Armstrong was arrested after scuffling with a female police officer who tried to stop him from standing in the street and blocking traffic. Stoudamire was arrested on marijuana charges after allegedly trying to go through a an airport metal detector in Tucson, Arizona, with almost one and one-half ounces of marijuana wrapped in aluminum foil. According to police, after Stoudamire set off the security alarm, he proceeded to put the marijuana and the rolling papers into a plastic security bin.

A review of court and arrest records found an average of thirty college and professional athletes arrested for marijuana possession or distribution in the three-year span between 2000 and 2002 (Red, Quinn, and O'Keefe 2003). Former Dallas Cowboys offensive lineman Nate Newton, already serving a five-year sentence in Texas for drug trafficking, was sentenced in Louisiana to an additional five years for possession of 213 pounds of marijuana. He is serving time for both crimes concurrently, according to an article in the *New Orleans Times-Picayune*.

It seems that one or another black athlete is featured weekly in the news or on ESPN for having an encounter with the law.

I admire the way Allen Iverson plays basketball. However, his embrace of the "gangsta-thug" image is troubling. Over the years, Iverson has had a number of run-ins with the law. For a brief period during his NBA career, he was partially successful in reconstructing his image. However, in 2002 Iverson had a highly publicized confrontation with his wife that seemed to set back his efforts to improve his image.

Allen Iverson is not the only professional athlete who has had image problems. NBA forward Glenn Robinson was arrested in 2002 and charged with domestic battery, assault, and illegal possession of a firearm. Derrick Coleman of the NBA was arrested after he was stopped for speeding and refused to take a Breathalyzer test. Ron Artest of the Indiana Pacers was arrested for allegedly harassing a former girlfriend. Miami Dolphins linebacker Derrick Rodgers was arrested for allegedly kicking and punching his wife and hitting her friend with a chair during a fight at a restaurant. NBA player Ruben Patterson was arrested on domestic assault charges. The day he was to be arraigned, teammates Rasheed Wallace and Damon Stoudamire were scheduled to appear in court on drug charges-unrelated to and preceding by a full year Stoudamire's arrest in Tucson for possession of marijuana.

The public has also witnessed similarly ill-advised behavior on the part of Minnesota Vikings All-Pro wide receiver Randy Moss. Moss was arrested for "nudging" a Minneapolis traffic officer with his car. He was charged with two misdemeanors, careless driving and failure to obey a traffic-control agent. Moss was also charged with one count of drug possession after police found a small amount of marijuana in his car. The star wide receiver first ran afoul of the law in 1995 during his senior year at DuPont High School in Rand, West Virginia. He pleaded guilty to two counts of battery and was sentenced to thirty days in jail for kicking another student. Sixty days were tacked on to Moss's sentence after he tested positive for marijuana during his first week in jail.

Moss's market value dropped prior to the 1998 NFL draft because of questions about his character. During his first two years at Minnesota, he seemed to prove his critics wrong. Since that time, however, he has only confirmed initial doubts about his character. Before the 2001 season, Moss signed an eight-year, $75 million contract with the Vikings. In spite of his lucrative contract, however, he continues to periodically display a negative attitude both on and off the football field.

While many people are critical of the lawless behavior of some black athletes, few provide adequate explanations for this behavior. Where gang violence, teen pregnancy, and inner-city crime are concerned, the traditional liberal argument is that the government has failed black youth. The proponents of this argument make the case that without adequate resources for first-rate schools, recreational facilities, and job-skills training, youth lose their motivation to succeed, and they give up hope. Consequently, they turn to lives of lawlessness and destructive behaviors. The reasoning behind this argument is sound and logical.

However, this argument cannot be used for young black millionaires. They have money and ample opportunities to create their own best futures. I am sure that many people— black as well as nonblack—would like to know why these wealthy individuals consistently run afoul of the law. These sports stars have embraced an illogical ritual of affirming black maleness. According to *The American Heritage Dictionary*, a ritual is "a detailed method of procedure faithfully or regularly followed."

While some black men find their formula for gaining street credibility and succeeding, others never do. For many black men, especially professionals, this exercise is a passing phase. Growing up, street credibility is important; but later, they realize that success is an important measure of manhood. For others, however, street credibility is always the measure by which they define their manhood. Black star athletes who run afoul of the law in senseless ways are going through the same ritual that black men on the streets go through—only they go through it in front of a bewildered public.

Many star athletes grow up in environments that harbor lawless and wreckless behavior. For at least the first eighteen years of their lives, they are immersed in the rituals of their immediate environment. They spend five years or less in a university setting, which gives them a respite from their home environment. Finally, they sign lucrative contracts. These contracts cannot immediately rectify the ways in which these individuals have been socialized. In other words, you can take them out of the streets, but you can't take the streets out of them. As disparaging as this sounds, it is a reality. A college student who spent his first eighteen years on a farm is bound to have countrified ways in college and beyond. You can take him out of the country—to New York, London, or Paris—but you cannot take the country out of him.

The Integration of Sport

Thomas E. Foreman wrote in 1957 that in the post-Civil War era, the segregation of organized sports in America was not a declaration of the law. Segregation during this period was more of a "gentlemen's agreement." Two of the most popular sports during this era were baseball and boxing. No Negro was allowed to participate in white-organized, professional-league baseball from 1890 to 1946. With the exception of a seven-year period between 1908 and 1915, no Negro was allowed to contest for the heavyweight boxing title (Foreman 1957, 1).

Prior to 1890, professional baseball did feature a few blacks. In 1872, John W. "Bud" Fowler was the first black to be salaried in organized baseball. He signed on with an all-white team in New Castle, Pennsylvania (Rust and Rust 1985, 3). In the early 1880s there were approximately twenty Negroes on minor league teams and two on major league teams (Foreman 1957, 8). In 1884, Moses Fleetwood "Fleet" Walker became the first black major leaguer. His brother, Welday Walker, became the second black major leaguer in July of the same year. Although these two well-educated players seemed to get along well with their teammates, they were consistently harassed by the other teams and the fans (Rust and Rust 1985, 4).

It was Fleet Walker's traumatic experiences as the first black major leaguer that inspired him to write the book, *Our Home Colony-A Treatise on the Past, Present and Future of the Negro Race in America*. In his book, Walker advocates the segregation of the races. He suggests that the only way the Negroes could deal with the insidious and pervasive racial prejudices in the U.S. was to return to Africa-echoing the views of the black separatist Marcus Garvey. Walker's adamant stance coupled with other forces prompted the segregation of organized professional baseball (Rust and Rust 1985, 5).

Adrian "Cap" Anson, manager and first baseman of the Chicago White Stockings, was the driving force behind ousting blacks from organized professional baseball. He hated blacks with a passion and vehemently opposed them playing on white teams. He was successful in his quest and Harrisburg, Pennsylvania, dropped the last Negro players from their professional rosters in 1890 (Foreman 1957, 8-9).

Booker T. Washington, the prominent black educator, intellectual, and spokesman, was the most influential voice of blacks during the 1890s. Washington's message of racial separatism was captured in his notable 1895 *Atlanta Exposition Address*. It was in this speech that Washington stated in regard to the races, "In all things that are purely social we can be as separate as the fingers, yet one as the hand in all things essential to mutual progress" (Rust and Rust 1985, 9). In this speech Washington called for blacks to end demands for social and political equality and stress what was essentially important, economic self-sufficiency (Foreman 1957, 2). The forces of Booker T. Washington, "Cap" Anson, Fleet Walker, and the ruling of Plessy v. Ferguson solidified segregation in most organized sports for a half-century (Rust and Rust 1985, 9).

Reintegrating organized sports in America took patience, persistence, and strategy. The integration of sports became the backdrop for the integration of U.S. society. For a long period of time, university athletic departments did not advocate the full and equal participation of black athletes. They started with a few "well-mannered" superstars as tokens. Increasingly, these departments had to evaluate the benefit of playing black athletes against the cost of undermining the social order. Once the barriers were down and the floodgates were open, having black athletes on the field was a matter of survival. The integration of university sports gradually came to mean good business.

While the civil rights movement played on the guilty conscience of America, the initial philosophy of university sports was to use an image-construction strategy. They sought to prove that whites were somewhat misguided in their sweeping generalizations of blacks.

Moreover, the blacks that universities handpicked to integrate their teams were "Ideal Negroes," those who were manner able, well disciplined, and non-rebellious. Of course, some of these athletes—Paul Robeson, for example—grew to become social activists later in life; but during their tenure on white athletic fields they played by the rules. Universities did not adopt the dialectical approach of the civil rights movement. Instead, they attempted to show that not all blacks were bad and that university sports would benefit from their participation.

The Ideal Negro

Paul Robeson states in his book *Here I Stand* that he knew the code of racial etiquette growing up. He says disdainfully, "Even while demonstrating that he is really equal the Negro must never appear to be challenging white superiority. Climb up if you can but don't act 'uppity.' Always show that you are grateful....above all do not give them cause to fear you" (Robeson 1971, 20).

Section one of this chapter offers a contemporary explanation of why so many black athletes have embraced rebellious behavior. In many ways, these black athletes have rebelled against the image of the Ideal Negro. To be considered the Ideal Negro is the worst label a contemporary black athlete can have. It means they have sold out to whitey and bought into the system. Few black athletes take chances on being perceived as sell-outs or Uncle Toms. Instead, they move so far in the opposite direction that it appears odd—earrings and jewelry on the athletic field, for example. Sometimes the earrings are dangling. Today the earrings, jewelry, tattoos, and expressive behaviors are used effectively to tell teammates, coaches, and the fans, "I'm not an Ideal Negro."

I remember seeing an ESPN special featuring the life of NBA point guard Baron Davis. While at UCLA, Davis was well-known for being an excellent point guard. He was also known for being articulate and clean-cut. In the ESPN special, Davis made a concerted effort not to appear so clean-cut. He stated in the special that he is himself and does not care what people think of him. The show featured him rapping freestyle. In his rap, he used profanity, derogatory terms for women, and the word "nigga." I was shocked that Davis would make such an energetic effort to be a "bad boy."

For several years Ken Griffey, Jr., was the perfect role model for the game of baseball. When I lived in Seattle, Junior was the icon of the city. For the game of baseball he symbolized youthfulness, innocence, enthusiasm, and the fun of the game. Gradually, however, his attitude toward the media, the fans, and his teammates began to sour. One reason might have been his frustration at being consistently plagued with injuries. However, I surmise that Griffey also rebelled against being the ideal role model—the poster boy for the game of baseball.

The roots of the Ideal Negro in sports can be traced to the days of Jack Johnson, not because Johnson was an Ideal Negro, but because he represented the antithesis of this concept. Joe Louis, Jesse Owens, and Jackie Robinson were all considered Ideal Negros in their time. Today's athletes-including Allen Iverson, Ray Lewis, Terrell Owens, and Barry Bonds—have rebelled against the image constructed for their predecessors. Instead, they have aligned themselves fully with the "Bad Nigger" image of Jack Johnson. Perhaps it is the controlling, manipulative, and paternalistic nature of the Ideal Negro concept-constructed by whites—that makes many black athletes vehemently reject it today. This might explain seemingly unexplainable outbursts of rage exhibited by some black players; for example, Latrell Sprewell chocking his coach, P.J. Carlesimo, in 1997.

During the 2001-2002 NFL season, Randy Moss berated a Minnesota Vikings corporate sponsor on a team bus because he felt that the sponsor had no business sitting with the players and taking up space. He was fined $15,000 by the team for his verbal attack. The corporate sponsor did not move when Moss requested the seat, so Moss lashed out at him. Perhaps Moss was outraged at the sponsor's sense of entitlement. Maybe he was perturbed that the NFL and his team exert a disagreeable amount of control over him. Indeed, the first thing a player learns when he signs a contract is not to say or do anything that will negatively reflect on the franchise. Teams socialize players not to say anything controversial about their opponents. The NFL fines players if they do or say just about anything that is untoward. Players have been fined for criticizing the refereeing of a game, for excessive celebrating, for not having their jerseys tucked in, and for not having their socks pulled up.

Fighting in the black-dominated NFL and NBA can draw hefty fines, while more vicious brawls in the white-dominated National Hockey League are considered part of the entertainment of the sport. Why is violence an acceptable part of the NHL but not of the NFL or the NBA? One of the latent goals of many institutions in American society is to control and modify the behavior of the overly aggressive black male. This is certainly the case with the NFL and the NBA. One irony, however, in the control agenda scenario is that football and baseball teams at the university and professional levels allow players to wear earrings. The NFL fines for nearly everything but wearing earrings. Perhaps black players and administrators have successfully made the case that the earring has cultural significance and to outlaw it on the field would be racist. Nevertheless, the earring, the tattoos, and the expressive behavior on and off the field are responses by contemporary black athletes to the Ideal Negro concept.

Jack Johnson's Black Male Image

Three of the most prominent black athletes of the first half of the twentieth century were Jack Johnson, Joe Louis, and Jesse Owens. These three individuals had an enormous impact on race relations in America. The comparison of the two boxers—Jack Johnson and Joe Louis-and their effect on race relations is the most striking.

Jack Johnson, the first black heavyweight champion, held the title for seven years before losing it to Jess Willard in Cuba in 1915. Johnson had a profound effect on race relations. His flamboyant personality and his incessant appetite for confrontation and white women ultimately led to his demise. Johnson married three white women and had numerous affairs with others. He was fearless and had little respect for the conventions of the day (Wiggins 1993, 27).

It was this behavior that earned him the name "Bad Nigger." *A Bad Nigger*, in black folklore, was the name given to those black men who did not play by the rules of convention. They dressed well and reputedly had unquenchable sex drives. They lived hedonistic lifestyles with a blatant disregard for death or danger. The term was used as a badge of reverence among blacks (Roberts 1983, 69).

In December of 1908, Johnson beat Tommy Burns in Sydney, Australia, for the world heavyweight title. In 1910, he beat former heavyweight champion Jim Jeffries so badly that it humiliated whites. Not only did Jackson beat Jeffries; he also taunted him and rubbed his victory in the face of white Americans. Race riots ensued all over America as a result of this event (Rust and Rust 1985, 147).

Because of Johnson's arrogance and love for white women, many whites considered him a serious threat to racial order. Many blacks were lynched as result of his actions. After Johnson married Lucille Cameron (a white woman), two white ministers in the South recommended lynching him (Gilmore 1975, 107). Some suggest that Johnson's brazen and sometimes reckless behavior did a tremendous amount of damage to race relations in America. Booker T. Washington detested Johnson's self-centered lifestyle, stating that "Johnson's actions had injured his race and his personal rebellion would result in a more general racial oppression" (Roberts 1983, 149).

Johnson was eventually convicted of violating the Mann Act, which made the interstate transportation of a woman for immoral purposes a federal offense. He was found guilty of transporting a white woman over state lines. After his planned fall to Willard in Cuba, he returned to the U.S. to serve all but a few days of his sentence in the federal prison at Leavenworth, Kansas (Wiggins 1993, 27). Roberts captures the essence of Jack Johnson's character and legacy when he states:

> The real Jack Johnson was not a stereotype. His hatred of the white world was almost as deep as his longing to be part of it. Although he was admired by thousands of blacks during his own day, he refused to accept the responsibility of leadership.... On only one point was Johnson consistent throughout his life: he accepted no limitations. He was not bound by custom, background, or race. (Roberts 1983, 229)

While many contemporary black athletes have adopted the mind-set of Jack Johnson, only a few can afford to mimic his behavior. Allen Iverson, Rasheed Wallace, Randy Moss, Terrell Owens, Ray Lewis, Warren Sapp, Dion Sanders, and Mike Tyson could all display the characteristics of Jack Johnson because they possessed extraordinary athletic talent that cannot easily be replaced. Others who want to be like Jack Johnson have to be mindful of their expendability. The player with average skills who is too expressive gets cut, released, traded, or blackballed from the league.

Joe Louis' Black Male Image

Jack Johnson had such a negative effect on race relations that many who came after used him as a reference for what not to do or how not to behave. Joe Louis was one who learned from the mistakes of Johnson. Louis directed his sexual energies only toward black women. He did not challenge the conventions of the day as Johnson had done, and he was a man of few words-dignified and respectful (Roberts 1983, 24). Louis was the antithesis of Johnson. He was a mild-mannered hero who took pride in being a role model for blacks during his era. Two of Louis's managers, John Roxborough and Julian Black, realized his potential and began to tutor him in social etiquette. Early in Louis's career, they saw he had the potential to be a champion; and they wanted his behavior to reflect that of a champion both in and out of the boxing ring. Because of his nonthreatening demeanor, Louis also became popular among whites (Rust and Rust 1985, 158, 159).

In the year following his loss to the German Max Schmeling, Louis won seven consecutive fights leading up to his championship bout against James Braddock. Louis knocked Braddock out in the eighth round to capture the heavyweight title (Jones and Washington 1972, 75). Blacks were euphoric after Louis was crowned the heavyweight champion of the world.

> With the news of the knockout, the crowds that had been waiting beneath radio loudspeakers suddenly were on the move. From all the flats poured young and old, men and

women, to shout Joe Louis's fame. Taxicabs screeched down the street with tooting horns.... Bonfires were built in the streets and around them Negroes danced. (Rust and Rust 1985, 170)

Louis defended his title three times before a rematch bout with Schmeling. The rematch was a symbolic war between America and Nazi Germany-so much so that President Franklin D. Roosevelt invited Louis to the White House and said, "Joe, we're depending on those muscles for America" (Rust and Rust 1978, 137). In June of 1938, Louis avenged his earlier loss to Schmeling with a bout that lasted only 124 seconds. Louis dominated Schmeling, hitting him forty-one times and sending him to the hospital (Jones and Washington 1972, 76). This time, it was a victory for all Americans. Joe Louis's greatness was "not just because of the hope that he offered the black man, but his public image of a clean-living, God-fearing, decent man who could conquer the incumbent forces was an inspiration to the depression-weary whites as well. Joe Louis transcended race and became a hero to all people" (Rust and Rust 1985, 171).

Joe Louis did not transcend race solely because of his great skills as a pugilist. Louis transcended race because he was an Ideal Negro. Unlike Jack Johnson, he knew his place. Knowing one's place was a prerequisite for white America to lionize a black athlete. As Carter G. Woodson stated:

> While he is a part of the body politic, he is in addition to this a member of a particular race to which he must restrict himself in all matters social. While serving his country he must serve within a special group. While being a good American, he must above all things be a good Negro; and to perform this definite function he must learn to stay in a Negro's place. (Woodson 1990, 6)

The success of black athletes such as Joe Louis and Jesse Owens in the 1930s provided the backdrop for integration in sports and in American society. As the widely popular Louis emerged as the world heavyweight champion, many whites had to question their prejudices (Tygiel 1983, 35). After all, he was an American hero and he was black. Similarly, at the 1936 Olympic Games in Berlin, Jesse Owens was not just a black runner from America—he was symbolic of the

anti- Hitler sentiment in the world and the source of American na-
tionalistic pride. When he won four gold medals, all Americans
cheered. All Americans beamed with pride. Jesse Owens, too, was an
American hero (Baker 1986).

Louis and Owens were both American heroes and the pride of all
blacks. However, if these two athletes excelled in today's environment
and possessed their same demeanors, they would not be revered by all
sectors of the black community. Indeed, young black men would be
likely to view both Louis and Owens as sell-outs. Neither superb athletic skill nor great success is enough for black athletes of today to be
seen as icons by other blacks. The most revered black athletes of today
couple outstanding athletic achievements with a rebellious attitude.

When Charles Barkeley played for the Philadelphia 76ers, he called
himself a "90s Nigga." He stated in an interview, "Just because you
give Charles Barkeley a lot of money, it doesn't mean I'm not going
to voice my opinions." When a reporter mentioned to Barkeley that
he was writing a magazine profile on the NBA legend Julius "Dr. J"
Erving, Barkeley stated, "Man, I ain't got no time to talk about no
Uncle Tom" (Platt 2002, 128).

Jackie Robinson's Black Male Image

The great baseball integration strategist Branch Rickey chose Jackie
Robinson to integrate baseball because the former UCLA All American embodied the "total package." On April 10, 1947, Robinson signed
a contract with the Brooklyn Dodgers. On April 15, he became the
first black baseball player in modern times to play in a major league
baseball game. Robinson endured "racial slurs, fans throwing water-
melons and placing shoe shine kits outside of the team's dugout; they
likened him to an animal and disparaged his family" (Rust and Rust
1985, 60).

Robinson was articulate, educated, disciplined, carefully spoken,
and a great athlete. Many black baseball players at the time were just
as good as Robinson or even better. In fact, Josh Gibson, Leroy

"Satchel" Paige, William "Judy" Jones, James Thomas "Cool Papa" Bell, and Walter "Buck" Leonard could have been the greatest major leaguers ever (Rust and Rust 1985, 18-22). However, athletic prowess was not the sole concern of integrationists. They had to be sure that the individual who would integrate major league baseball had the character to face character assaults. His behavior on and off the field had to be spotless. A great athlete would not accomplish anything for integration if his behavior confirmed stereotypes. One cannot underestimate the impact that selectivity had on the general perception of American society and the eventual integration of sports.

Many writers at the time wanted Robinson to pattern his personality and demeanor after that of Joe Louis. Louis received unprecedented popularity among whites. Whites accepted Louis as a folk hero, not only because he was the best boxer in the world, but also because he appeared to be the Ideal Negro. He was "polite, well mannered, and knew his place" (Tygiel 1983, 75). Integrationists knew that image construction was fundamental to their goals.

Tiger Woods is cut in the mold of Jackie Robinson and Arthur Ashe. Like Robinson in baseball and Ashe in tennis, Woods was responsible for breaking the color barrier in golf. Along with outstanding golfing skills, Woods is articulate, educated, disciplined, and carefully spoken. Although no person since Robinson in baseball and Ashe in tennis has been as singularly responsible for integrating a sport as has Woods, his ranking on my Realness Scale reveals many young black men do not perceive him as being an "authentic" black man. Only 40 percent of those surveyed ranked Woods as being "real." Woods's realness score is the lowest of all of the sports icons.

David Robinson vs. Allen Iverson

Joe Louis's and Jackie Robinson's images were constructed and regulated by white management teams. The black athletes of today have rebelled against this construction and regulation. Moreover, few contemporary black athletes are cut in the mold of Joe Louis or Jackie Robinson. David Robinson, recently retired from the NBA, however, is a contemporary model of Joe Louis and Jackie Robinson. Robinson graduated from the United States Naval Academy with a degree in mathematics. He was the consummate team player and a professional on and off the court. He is clean-cut, intelligent, well-mannered, and noncontroversial. He is the antithesis of nearly every stereotype of the black male. Nevertheless, on the Realness Scale, only 42 percent of those surveyed stated that he was a real black man. The pattern of the survey suggests that young black men do not look at the well-mannered and disciplined black man as being authentic. They are not revered or idolized.

Most of the young black men that I interviewed for this book stated that they really did not know why, but Robinson was not real. One person stated that "he is not real because he has not done anything controversial or had trouble with the law." I asked, "Does that make a person real?" Realizing the illogic of his statements, the young man said, "I guess not." Robinson does not wear an earring nor does he have tattoos. He did not define his image in those ways. Instead, he established his persona by such actions as making a $5 million donation in 1997 to help create the Carver Academy at San Antonio's Carver Culture Center, a multicultural and multiethnic resource facility to serve pre-kindergarten through eighth-grade students who live primarily on the east side of San Antonio.

Ironically, an objective observer could easily see Robinson as being the most real or authentic black man. Why? Because he has been true to himself. As a player, he did not give in to the trends or styles du jour. He did not waver from being a gentleman no matter what criticisms were leveled at him. He did not embrace the gangsta-thug image just to fit in. Moreover, he has made philanthropic contributions to multiethnic communities. Robinson retired from the San Antonio Spurs with two NBA championships. But more importantly, he retired as the NBA's greatest ambassador.

Allen Iverson, on the other hand, is cut in the mold of Jack Johnson. In dress, speech, and attitude, Iverson mirrors Johnson. He does not embrace the Ideal Negro image. In fact, he has rebelled against it. Some 84 percent of young black men surveyed view Iverson as being a real black man. This is twice the number that viewed Robinson as real. Just as there were consequences for black men who emulated

Jack Johnson in the early 1900s, today there are consequences for black men who want to emulate Allen Iverson.

With his baggy pants, bandannas, cornrow braids, multiple tattoos, and big diamond earrings, Iverson is telling the establishment that he is like neither Joe Louis nor Jackie Robinson. Perhaps it is a sign of the times that Iverson and others can behave outside the boundaries of the established rules and still be tolerated, accepted, and even celebrated.

The ability of some young black men to be expressive and behave outside the boundaries could be viewed as a positive development in the racial climate in the United States. This is not so. These athletes are tolerated because they are moneymaking machines. The average young black man is not being tolerated for being expressive and acting outside of the rules. Instead, he is being racially profiled, arrested, tried, and convicted for rebellious behavior.

The Commodification of the Black Rebel In Sport

Prior to World War II, blacks competed in football, basketball, baseball, and track at white universities. Black athletes such as Paul Robeson of Rutgers; Fritz Pollard of Brown; Eddie Tolan and Willis Ward of Michigan; Jerome "Brud" Holland of Cornell; William Bell, David Albritton, and Jesse Owens of Ohio State; Ralphe Metcalfe of Marquette University; and Ralph Bunche, Jackie Robinson, and Kenny Washington of UCLA were all standout athletes who were handpicked to integrate white universities (Wiggins 1993, 28; Grundman 1986, 77).

At the end of World War II, college sports started to become more appealing, more glamorous to the general population. This transformed university athletics as institutions realized that they could capitalize on this growing appeal by allowing superb black athletes to participate (Grundman 1986, 77). Universities in the north experimented with the concept of integration by having one or two black athletes on their teams. For their experiment they chose young men who were not only superb athletes but also good students who possessed unquestioned moral character. Some have seen this approach as racist, but in fact this selective approach to integration was extremely effective. Northern universities chose black athletes such as Paul Robeson and "Fritz" Pollard to be iconoclasts—image-breakers. These athletes had to counter the rigid stereotypes of blacks that had calcified over a century and a half. University officials had to prove American society wrong. They could not do this with black athletes who were prone to go down the wrong path. Indeed, a black athlete who was a poor student, sexually aggressive, or inclined to commit crimes would have elicited "I-told-you-so's" from the strict segregationists. On the other hand, a black athlete who represented the opposite gave university officials an opportunity to say, "You were wrong." This was indeed the philosophy of Branch Rickey.

Contemporary black athletes are no longer trying to fit in. They are not attempting to counter rigid stereotypes; they are embracing these stereotypes. They are rebelling against the past—a past that told them what to do and when to do it. There were harsh consequences for not following the established rules.

Today, unlike the past, there are not harsh consequences for black superstars who do not follow convention. To the contrary, there are actually incentives for being a bad boy. This is one of the most intriguing developments in this society. While Jack Johnson was despised, vilified, and imprisoned by the establishment for parting with convention, today's Jack Johnsons are being lionized, revered, celebrated, and rewarded for their rebellious behavior.

In the summer of 2002, Allen Iverson was in the spotlight for allegedly forcing his way into an apartment and threatening two men with a gun while searching for his wife, after he had thrown her out of the house following an argument. At that time, Iverson had $40.5 million and three years left on his $70.8 million, extended-year contract. One year before this incident, Reebok gave Iverson an extension of his ten-year, $50 million endorsement deal. The 2002 incident solidified Iverson's image as a gangsta-thug. Immediately after the highly publicized case, the Wall Street Journal reported that sales of the Allen Iverson Reebok shoe increased significantly.

The commodification of the rugged-thuggish image of black masculinity began in sports with former NBA All-Star Charles Barkeley.

Barkeley was the first athlete since Muhammad Ali and Bill Russell to question the role of athletes as role models. He proclaimed that he was not a role model and that kids should look to their parents and teachers instead. In the late 1980s Barkeley spit on a fan during a game. Up to that point in time, any player who showed such gross behavior would have suffered severe consequences: the cancellation of endorsement contracts, for example. After the spitting incident, however, marketing firms did the opposite. They embraced Barkeley's bad-boy image and helped make him a sports icon. After the spitting incident, Barkeley signed a number of endorsement contracts with big-name companies. His post-basketball career as an NBA commentator became highly successful because of his political incorrectness and capacity to behave outside of convention.

When Latrell Sprewell choked his coach, the public was outraged and labeled him a thug. The little known company *AND 1* immediately capitalized on Sprewell's thuggish image. They cast him in a commercial in which Sprewell states, "People say I'm America's worst nightmare. I say I'm the American Dream." Sales suddenly took off. *AND 1* went from an obscure little company to a highly visible and popular label (Platt 2002, 165).

I doubt if Allen Iverson would have been able to endorse any company in the 1980s. Today, he has a number of endorsements, including his own athletic shoe. Firms realize that Iverson is more of an icon than the clean-cut former Navy man David Robinson. This is a remarkable societal development given the historically conservative nature of the advertisement machinery in the U.S.

Nike has taken advantage of society's enormous consumption of the rugged-thuggish black male image. One of the successful attempts to commodify the black urban experience was Nike's basketball commercials featuring various NBA players dribbling basketballs that make funky rhythmic sounds. Most of these commercials have shown young black men adorned with tattoos along with their defiant street attitudes. Rasheed Wallace, the incorrigible bad boy of the NBA, even appeared in one of these commercials. Could a person of Wallace's temperment have been featured in a television commercial during the 1980s?

This example illustrates that corporate America is more concerned with promoting cultural icons rather than positive role models. The fact is that David Robinson might be a great role model for young kids, but he never sold as many shoes as Allen Iverson.

LeBron James was the most highly publicized rookie in the history of the NBA. At eighteen years old, only months after his graduation from St. Vincent-St. Mary High School in Akron, Ohio, the Cleveland Cavaliers drafted James as the number one pick in the 2003 NBA draft. His game is a mix of Magic Johnson and Michael Jordan. However, his marketing appeal is a cross between Allen Iverson and Kobe Bryant. He is articulate and intelligent, which makes him comparable to Bryant. Growing up in a single-headed household of few resources, James's upbringing mirrors that of many youth in the inner city. His multiple tattoos, flamboyant play, and swagger on the court give him the street credentials of an Iverson. James possesses the charisma that marketers love. In an era of commodifying dynamic personalities with street credibility, James has become "the" icon. How else can one explain the disparity between James's shoe contract with Nike and Bryant's shoe contract with the same company? Both athletes signed contracts during the same period. James signed a contract for approximately $90 million while Bryant, a seasoned NBA All-Star and three-time NBA champion, signed for half as much. What message is this sending to an impressionable fourteen-year-old young black male? He is encouraged to embrace the gangsta-thug image.

When Bryant was arrested for felony sexual assault in Eagle County, Colorado, many speculated that the negative publicity would tarnish his squeaky clean image and hurt his endorsements. However, there were some who ironically—and cynically—thought the charge might give Bryant the much-needed street credibility that he lacks. This is a sad reality in this new era of commodifying the gangsta-thug.

In the midst of his sexual assualt court proceedings Bryant was compelled to get two tattoos on his right arm. Why?

The black male image in sports has gone through various transformations. Each generation of young black athletes has, in part, reflected the sociopolitical sign of the times. For example, in the 1960s black athletes reflected the militancy of the civil rights and black power movements. Today, however, black athletes reflect the political apathy, materialism, and individualism of the broader society.

In many ways, the black athlete has personified the gangsta-thug. The ostentatious display of wealth, sexual misconduct, violence, and crime has increasingly defined the images of a new generation of black athletes. Today's black athlete must be taught that there was character in the humility of Joe Louis and Jesse Owens. There was strength in the discipline of Jackie Robinson. There was courage in the activism of Arthur Ashe and Muhammad Ali. There was integrity in the grace of Dr. J. These athletes were ideal citizens, not sell-outs. They were inspirational representatives of the black community. They were quintessential American heroes and role models. Today's young black athletes should first learn about, and then strive to emulate, these individuals. Perhaps unknowingly, they have rebelled against the positive images of past sports icons and embraced the legacy of Jack Johnson. Although a great heavyweight champion, Johnson did not leave a positive legacy. There is nothing honorable in following his path.

References

Baker, William J. 1986. Jesse Owens: An American Life. New York: The Free Press.

Butler, Jason, Associated Press. 2003. Blazers guard arrested. Atlanta Journal-Constitution. Sports Flash, 8 July.

Foreman, Thomas E. 1957. Discrimination against the Negro in American athletics. Master's thesis, Fresno State College and Rand Research Associates.

Gilmore, Al-Tony. 1975. Bad Nigger! The National Impact of Jack Johnson. Port Washington, New York: Kennikat Press.

Grundman, Adolf H. 1986. The image of intercollegiate sports and the civil rights movement. In Fractured Focus: Sport as A Reflection of Society, edited by Richard E. Lapchick. Lexington, Massachusetts: Lexington Books.

Jones, Wally, and Jim Washington. 1972. Black Champions Challenge American Sports. New York: David McKay.

New Orleans Times-Picayune. 2002. Sports Digest, 10 December.

Platt, Larry. 2002. New Jack Jocks: Rebels, Race, and the American Athlete. Philadelphia: Temple University Press.

Red, Christian, T.J. Quinn, and Michael O'Keefe. 2003. Reefer madness: Why more athletes are turning to marijuana. New York Daily News, 4 May.

Roberts, Randy. 1983. Papa Jack: Jack Johnson and the Era of White Hopes. New York: The Free Press.

Robeson, Paul. [1958] 1971. Here I Stand. Reprint, with introduction by Lloyd Brown. Boston: Beacon Press.

Rust, Art, Jr., and Edna Rust. 1978. Joe Louis: My Life. New York: Harcourt Brace Jovanovich.

Rust, Art, Jr., and Edna Rust. 1985. Art Rust's Illustrated History of the Black Athlete. Garden City, New York: Doubleday.

Tygiel, Jules. 1983. Baseball's Great Experiment: Jackie Robinson and His Legacy. New York: Oxford University Press USA.

Wiggins, David K. 1993. Chapter in Racism In College Athletics: The African-American Athlete's Experience. Edited by Dana Brooks and Ronald Alehouse. Morgantown, West Virginia: Fitness Informational Technology.

Woodson, Carter G. [1933] 1990. The Mis-Education of The Negro. Reprint, Trenton, New Jersey: Africa World Press.

Chapter 6

Lost Currency

Sports

A 2003 survey showed that a record 62 percent of all scholarship althletes who arrived as freshman in 1996 graduated within six years. Black athletes made the most significant strides from the previous year. Their graduation rate rose 48 percent to 52 percent. Although tough academic reforms are changing college athletics in positive ways. There is much work to be done (Wieberg 2003, 1C). Among basketball players in top programs, less than one-third have received degrees in recent years. Over the last generation, NCAA winners including the Universities of Arizona, Kentucky, Louisville, Michigan, and Nevada, Las Vegas, have had recruiting classes where not a single athlete graduated (Reddy 2003, H1). Richard Lapchick—who oversaw a 2003 study compiled by the *Institute of Diversity and Ethics in Sports* to track athletes who began college between 1992 and1995—said, "We promise all student-athletes who enter our universities that we will give them an education and help them earn a college degree. This study shows that, once again, too many universities do not fulfill their promises, especially to African American student athletes who play basketball" (Pugmire 2003, 1). Who is to blame? Of course, the institutions that have the unremitting pressure to win at all costs are blameworthy—but so are the athletes. Irrespective of the pressures to win, an athlete who really wants to get a degree will get one. I did. They will display the commitment, dedication, and discipline to succeed. Despite the assistance of tutors, academic counselors, and an extra year in school, many black athletes are not graduating from college. In the one avenue that has given young black men the greatest opportunity for vertical mobility and success in life, they have dropped the ball. They have lost their currency.

The overwhelming majority of NFL players are black. However, there are only a few black coaches in the league. In a September 2002 report entitled, "Black Coaches in the National Football League: Superior Performance, Inferior Opportunities," famed attorneys Johnnie L. Cochran, Jr., and Cyrus Mehri of the Washington law firm Mehri & Skalet contended that NFL hiring practices are discriminatory. At the time their report was released, only two of the league's thirty-two head coaches were black. According to Cochran and Mehri, black coaches are the last to be hired and the first to be fired. (Bell 2002, 11C).

Not only is there a paucity of black coaches in the NFL, there is less than a handful of black football coaches among the 117 NCAA Division I football programs. In contrast, over 60 percent of starters on the rosters in Division I football are black. The Black Coaches Association along with Professor C. Keith Harrison, are evaluating the hiring practices in Division I-A Football.

Their skill and athletic prowess give black players in college and in the NFL significant currency that they have-to this point-chosen not to use. These athletes should be leading the protest for the aggressive recruitment of more coaches who look like them. Where is the concern? Where is the activism?

When Maurice Clarett was a freshman running back for the Ohio State Buckeyes, he was denied the opportunity to go to the funeral of a close friend during the preparations for the national championship bowl game against the University of Miami. The Ohio State administration stated that Clarett could not leave to go to his friend's funeral because he did not sign all of the proper paperwork. Clarett insisted that was not the case. He went on to state that the university only cared about making money. They did not care about human life. Clarett went beyond discussing the funeral and began discussing the glaring hypocrisy of college football. Ohio State University made $13 million from the national championship game at the Fiesta Bowl, which they won. However, as Clarett stated, it is not fair to have all this money spent on this game when there is so much poverty right around the campus of Ohio State in Columbus.

Clarett's statements were poignant and refreshing. This was the first time in two decades that I have heard an active athlete harshly and publicly criticize the hypocrisy of the athletics machine in the United States. Ohio State was reluctant to chastise Clarett because they needed him to win the national championship. As an indispensable athlete on the Buckeye squad, Clarett used his currency to condemn the contradictions of college athletics. Unfortunately, Clarett lost his currency by getting entangled in a scandal, which led to his dismissal from the team in 2003. As athletes, black men are worshiped and lionized. Stripped of their jerseys, pads, and eligibility, the same black men on the streets are treated with blatant disdain.

Until the late 1960s, many black athletes had been effectively socialized to be nonpolitical. The period from 1968 to 1972 was the only time in American sports history that blacks were outwardly committed to the struggle for black liberation and equality. In 1968, protests by black athletes were widespread. Their activism reflected the sociopolitical environment of the era. According to Harry Edwards, the black athlete revolt was a culmination of extreme hatred and injustice in America, manifested in the murder of Malcolm X, the bombing of four black girls in Birmingham, Alabama, the murder of Medgar Evers, and the assassination of Martin Luther King, Jr. (Edwards 1969, xv).

Edwards, along with other activists, orchestrated a proposed boycott of the 1968 Olympic Games unless the following demands were met: 1) removal of Avery Brundage as president of the International Olympic Committee; 2) restoration of Muhammad Ali's heavyweight title; 3) exclusion of Rhodesia and South Africa from Olympic competition; 4) appointment of at least two blacks to the United States Olympic Committee; 5) complete desegregation of the New York Athletic Club (NYAC); and 6) the addition of at least two black coaches to the men's Olympic track and field team (Wiggins 1993, 37; Edwards 1969, 138).

Although the proposed boycott of the 1968 Olympic Games in Mexico City failed, black athletes challenged the system as never before or since. Tommie Smith and John Carlos symbolized the new militancy among athletes when they raised their balled fists—symbolic of black liberation and black power—as they accepted their gold and silver medals respectively and listened to the American national anthem (Edwards 1969, 138). Black athletes reacted to the unfair practice of racial stacking on the field and monitoring of those whom they dated off the field. These athletes risked their scholarships by boycotting practices, banquets, and team competitions (Harris 1993, 59).

In 1968, black athletes threatened to protest all athletic events at the University of Washington. The football players accused the head coach, Jim Owens, of blatant discrimination. In 1969 Coach Lloyd Eaton of the University of Wyoming dismissed fourteen football players from his team because they protested the treatment of blacks by the Mormon Church. At that time, the policy of the church was not to accept black priests. Coach Eaton warned the black players: "Wear armbands and you are off the team." In the same year, Wayne Vandenburg, the coach of the University of Texas at El Paso, dismissed nine track and field athletes from his team for protesting the discriminatory policies of the Mormon Church (Florio 2002, A-01). Fourteen black football players were thrown off the team at Indiana University for missing two consecutive days of practice in protest (Wiggins 1997, 125). Black athletes were involved in rebellions at Syracuse University, Oregon State University, Michigan State University, San Francisco State University, and the University of California at Berkeley, among other schools (Wiggins 1993, 36). At no other time in the history of American sports have black athletes publicly identified with the struggle and outwardly challenged the system (Wiggins 1997, 125).

If the activism of the black athlete has mirrored the sociopolitical signs of the times, where have black athletes been on the political spectrum during the past decade? Michael Jordan was never known to be active in civil rights activities. In fact, in 1990, when he had the opportunity to endorse Harvey Gantt—a legitimate African American senatorial candidate from his home state of North Carolina—he refused. Gantt, the former mayor of Charlotte, was running against long-time conservative Jesse Helms. It was puzzling to many why Jordan would not endorse Gantt over a person who had advocated anti-minority policies over the years. In a jocular statement to reporters, Jordan said, "Republicans buy Nikes too."

Notwithstanding the courageous athletes who participated in the black athlete revolts of the late 1960s and early 1970s, there have been few black athletes that could be characterized as "activist" or "race-conscious." This is troubling. Although black athletes have saturated every level of major sports such as football and basketball, their status has been limited to that of entertainer. The system has effectively socialized the black athlete to be politically unconscious and docile. What Carter G. Woodson stated in 1933 in The Mis-Education of the Negro has been accurate for most of the century:

> When you control a man's thinking you do not have to worry about his actions. You do not have to tell him not to stand here or go yonder. He will find his "proper place" and will stay in it. You do not need to send him to the back of the back door. He will go without being told. In fact, if there is no back door, he will cut one for his special benefit. His education makes it necessary. (Woodson 1990, back cover)

Music

Although critics of rap music and the hip-hop culture are appropriately vigilant about the messages of sex, violence, and harsh language, this genre offers us a paradigm of the significant potential of this art form as a platform for social justice. In the 1950s and 1960s the Beat Culture challenged the status quo in ways that unified liberals and prompted change. In the same vein, the hip-hop culture has the potential to challenge the status quo in constructive ways.

Never before have black men had the latitude to voice their opinions in public. White policymakers in the latter half of the of the nineteenth century and the first half of the twentieth century exerted their energies in trying keep the black man silent, ignorant, disenfranchised, and away from the white woman. This is another perplexing phenomenon to me. If I were an outsider from another country, I would figure that if I was deprived of the chance to voice my opinions in public for more than 300 years, I would take advantage of the opportunity when it was finally available to me. Indeed, if I were restricted from reading and then given the chance to do so, I would read all the time. If I were restricted from voting and then allowed to do so, I would vote consistently. If I were restricted from public speaking and criticizing public policies, I would become a perpetual critic when released from those restrictions. I would use this newfound platform for the uplifting of my race and other downtrodden people.

With all the talk of "The Man is holding us back" and "We can't come up because of racism," one must not forget that there are no longer voting restrictions placed on blacks. Why don't we vote? There are widely available public libraries that are free. Why don't we read? As a black person, there is no better time than today to exercise our First Amendment rights to freedom of speech. Why don't we exercise them in constructive ways?

I remember my father, who grew up in Mississippi, telling me about the impact the Emmett Till tragedy had on him. My father and Till were the same age-fourteen-in 1955, when Till came from Chicago in the summer to visit relatives in the Mississippi Delta. While standing outside a grocery store in Money, Mississippi, with his friends one Wednesday afternoon, Till is reputed to have taken a dare to go into the store and speak boldly to a white woman. The woman's husband and his half-brother found Till the following Sunday and took him for a drive. They beat him, shot him in the head, gouged out one of his eyes, and smashed in one side of his head before they dumped his body in the Tallahatchie River. His mother Mamie Till ordered an open casket at Emmett's funeral so the world could see what they did to her son.

If I were a rapper today, I would be remembering Till in my lyrics. If so much of the anger that comes from rap music is directed towards the injustice of the system, the lyrics are misguided. I do not hear calls for reforms of the system. I do not hear the call for young blacks to exercise their right to vote. I do not hear about the struggles of the freedom fighters and civil rights leaders in rap lyrics. Where are the Bob Dylans and Bob Marleys of rap music?

For instance, Dylan—who was born in the same year as Emmett Till—was so outraged by Till's brutal death that he wrote the 1963 song "The Death of Emmett Till." Told in the first person, Dylan recounts the horrible story of Till's death.

'Twas down in Mississippi not so long ago, when a young boy from Chicago town stepped through a Southern door. This boy's dreadful tragedy I can still remember well; the color of his skin was black and his name was Emmett Till.

Some men they dragged him to a barn and there they beat him up. They said they had a reason, but I can't remember what. They tortured him and did some evil things too evil to repeat.

Contrast these lyrics with the lyrics of contemporary black artists that you will read later in this chapter.

Which rappers are discussing the multiple social problems facing blacks? Who is rapping about the police brutality cases of Rodney King, Malice Green, Demetrius Dubose, Amadou Diallo, Abner Louima, Tyisha Miller, Irvin Landrum, Thomas Jones, or Donovan Jackson? Who is discussing the discriminatory policies of the criminal justice system? Who is discussing the lack of resources in urban schools? If rappers are not discussing these issues, what are they discussing? What issues could be more important to a music genre that embraces the rage of the downtrodden and victimized? Where are their lyrical bullets directed?

In the 1980s and 1990s rapper Chuck D and his group *Public Enemy* effectively used their currency to examine America's hypocritical history, institutions, and behavior. The song "Fight the Power," which debuted in 1989, became an anthem for social activism. In their 2002 album Revolverlution, the group aimed its lyrical bullets at government oppression and unfair practices in the music industry. Among other things, the album discusses President George W. Bush's domestic agenda and the number of young black men being imprisoned and executed.

If black artists are not using their talents to confront the system they supposedly despise, they are losing currency. In fact, they are engaged in a tragic charade. Granted, there are some—but too few—black artists who are using their unprecedented currency to challenge the ills of the system. The late Tupac, Mos Def, Talib

Kweli, OutKast, The Roots, Common, Blackalicious, Dilated Peoples, Black Eyed Peas, and Nas have accurately targeted their lyrical bullets internally at self-destructive behavior and externally at the system. The rapper Nas poignantly used his currency in the 2001 album *Stillmatic*. Nas's "What Goes Around" is a powerful commentary on the internal and external influences undermining black progress. In this song he does not abandon the rebellious flavor of rap, but integrates critical social commentary that is accurately directed at the main culprits of social ills in the United States. His 2003 song "I Know I Can" is equally powerful and uplifting. The chorus of the song states,"I know I can be what I wanna be. If I work hard at it, I'll be where I wanna be." The lyrics encourage black youth to read more and learn more-emphasizing how they can be doctors, architects, and television show hosts like Oprah Winfrey. This song makes a passionate plea for black youth to abandon negative behavior.

Also contrast the content of "I Know I Can" to what you will see later in this chapter. Nas has consistently produced intriguing albums with stinging and positive lyrics. His video for the song "One Mic" is filmed in Africa. In this uplifting video he is shown interacting, like family, with villagers. Nevertheless, Nas has still displayed inconsistencies in his uplifting messages. He has sustained a feud with rival rapper Jay-Z. He reciprocates and attacks Jay-Z with the viciousness of a true enemy. In essence, he undermines his powerful messages when he misdirects his lyrical bullets towards his brother. It is this type of misguided anger and machismo that has proven to be detrimental to a generation of young black men.

Men Exploiting Women

Black men are unique in that they are the only ethnic group of men in the U.S. that consistently refer to their women publicly in derogatory terms e.g., bitches, hoes, freaks, skanks, tricks. It seems that the affirmation of black masculinity consistently comes at the expense of black women. Ironically, the backbone of the black family is sub-

ject to the most vicious public ridicule. Can one imagine Japanese or
Koreans celebrating the degradation of their women? Black men have
succeeded in doing what is taboo in other cultures.

One of my friends is a music producer in Seattle. The first CD project he produced contained various streetwise songs. One of the rappers on the first song—"We've Been Caught Up?"-states, "Feels like
I'm trapped in a cage with these stankin ass hoes tryin to give a nigga
AIDS." In another song, the same rapper tells a story of a woman that
he picks up in a club. After he has sex with her he literally kicks her
out of his place and says, "Fuck them skank ass hoes they come a
dime a dozen."

The rapper Too Short made a successful career on rapping about
what he calls "Pimpology." In fact, he created ten popular albums
using this one theme. The group Dogg Pound made a song with the
chorus, "It ain't no fun, if my homies can't have none," which suggests
that it is not fun having sexual intercourse with a woman unless it is
a group experience. The artists Ludacris and Nate Dogg collaborated
to make the widely popular song "Area Codes;" with the chorus,
"Hoes. I got hoes in every area code." This song was a part of the
soundtrack for the popular movie *Rush Hour II*. It was featured and
enthusiastically received by both men and women in the audience at
the 2001 Source Hip-Hop Music Awards.

R. Kelly won the award for Best Songwriter at the 40th Annual
Grammy Awards. Kelly had fifteen Top 40 hits in the 1990s-more than
any other male solo artist—and tied for the most Top 10 hits, with
eight. He has written music for various artists including Michael Jackson, Celine Dion, Maxwell, Kirk Franklin, Mary J. Blige, Janet Jackson, Nas, and Notorius BIG. His hit song from the movie Space Jam
movie—"I Believe I Can Fly"—is a timeless classic. Kelly should be
commended for his breadth as an artist. Few people in the history of
music have been able to fuse such diverse styles of music. He cata-
pulted himself from singing on the streets of Chicago's Southside to
an international career of stardom and fame.

So what is someone of Kelly's status doing embracing the rugged-
thuggish model of black masculinity? His case is disturbingly peculiar. How can the writer/singer of "I Believe I Can Fly" also be the
writer/singer of "R&B Thug"? This song contains the following lyrics:

> I'm just an R&B thug babe
>
> Tryin' to get some ass babe
>
> Do you wanna thug babe?
>
> I'm just an R&B thug babe
>
> Lookin' for some love babe
>
> Do you wanna date babe?

What is Kelly attempting to prove with these lyrics? What is the motivation for his regression? Why is it uncomfortable for some black men to stay above the fray? R. Kelly's song "Feelin' On Yo Booty" characterizes how much respect some black men have for their women:

> Playas wanna play
>
> Ballers wanna ball
>
> Rollers wanna roll
>
> But I'm taking off after I dance, oh yeah...I'm feelin on your booty.

Kelly's video to this song was an extreme form of hypermasculinity and male chauvinism. The video shows him in a tub being bathed by multiple women. It flashes to him in the middle of a dance floor, slow dancing with a young lady in a bikini. The video shows Kelly "feelin' on her booty."

I discussed this R. Kelly video with my music producer friend. I also questioned him about the content of some of the songs on his first CD project. His response to me was that "this is what the artist had to say-it's real...and besides, this is what sells." Others use identical arguments to justify misogynistic lyrics and counterproductive behavior. This form of hypermasculinity continues to exploit and prostitute females in the name of realistic expression and profit.

There is no other platform in which the hypermasculinist behavior of black men is played out as it is in music videos. The visuals of one video are not distinguishable from the next. The setting usually includes some thugged-out guys around a car headed to the beach or to a pool party. They wantonly boast of all of the half-naked women under their trance. No matter which cable channel these videos play on—BET, MTV, or VH1—it is appalling to see black men prostitute their women and black women prostitute themselves in the name of entertainment.

Again, what other culture in the world would exploit their women in this fashion? Let's interview men and women in Egypt, Senegal, Jordan, Japan, Singapore, Malaysia, and India. Let's find out if they would be accepting of such exploitative video practices. Go to Chinatown or Koreatown in Los Angeles and ask the parents of an eighteen-year-old girl if they would allow her to be filmed half-naked in a music video with guys feeling all over her body? Tell them you will give her $2,000 for her time and see if that will change their harsh response to you.

Michael Jackson alleged in a press conference during the summer of 2002 that the recording industry is a racist conspiracy that turns profits at the expense of performers—particularly minority artists. According to Jackson, "The recording companies really, really do conspire against the artists. They steal, they cheat, they do everything they can, [especially] against the black artists." Who is holding the music industry accountable for this exploitation? Blacks cannot expect anyone else to put restrictions on this type of exploitation. Besides, non-blacks could care less whether and how blacks self-destruct. Why should they care, if blacks don't?

Women Exploiting Women

When I first saw the cover of the August 2002 issue of the excellent black magazine *Savoy* my curiosity was piqued. There was a nice picture of Will Smith on the cover and below the picture was the feature-story identifier, "Will Smith." Below Smith's name was a line attributed to his wife, Jada Pinkett Smith: "The Thug and The Intellectual." I thought the featured article would include a debate about cerebral role models like Smith versus the romanticized image of the dangerous and impulsive thug. However, as I studied Jada's quotation, I was puzzled why she used the word "and" instead of "versus." I found my answer inside.

Jada stated in a discussion with Cheo Taylor Tyehimba of *Savoy* that her husband is a combination of opposites, which includes the "the thug" and "the intellectual." She said, "I had to have both. I need a guy who can take me to the Ice Cube concert and then to the White House. It's hard to find, but I was lucky enough to come across Will. He only tends to show one side to the media, which is really smart [of him]. But I know the other side" (Tyehimba 2002, 64). What's wrong with just having an intellectual? Or, what's wrong with having someone who is athletic and intellectual? Why the need to have positive characteristics coupled with the characteristics of a thug?

After the singer Mariah Carey divorced her music executive husband she said she was looking for a "baggy pants wearing hoodlum." When the superb actress Vivica Fox began dating 50 Cent in 2003 what message was she sending to her impressionable 16-year old female fans?

Although the hypermasculinist and patriarchal behavior among black men is inexcusable, black women cannot be held completely blameless. Many black women have enthusiastically embraced the rugged-thuggish model of black masculinity. It is attractive to them. A friend of mine once courted a black female in the traditional manner. He wined and dined her. He assured her that chivalry was not dead. She eventually told him, "Chivalry might not be dead, but I want a real man." What is a "real" man? Someone who calls you a bitch instead of bringing you flowers? Someone who gives you passionate sex but never takes you out to dinner?

As this friend stated, "If black women would raise their standards, black men would be forced to raise theirs to meet them." The underlying motivation for men in our society is to appeal to the opposite sex. If black women were first and foremost attracted to the perfect gentleman, perhaps there would be an abundance of perfect gentlemen in the black community.

I remember talking to another friend about women and relationships. He said, "Believe it or not man, I'm thirty-five years old and I have never had a girlfriend." I asked him why, and he said, "for some reason women just run away from me like I have the plague or something." The irony is, this friend—who is African American—graduated from college and has a good job as a librarian. He is soft-spoken, mild-mannered, and very intelligent. He contradicts every stereotype of the black man. He did not have to explain his problem to me because I knew what it was immediately. Nevertheless, he went on to tell me how his last spark died out when the African American woman told him she needed someone with a "more dangerous edge."

Black women, like black men, have an unprecedented platform to discuss issues that are significant to the larger black female population. Although one should not trivialize the power that men have in our society, one should not view women as being powerless. For instance, black women have the power not to listen, tolerate, or dance to rap songs that refer to them in unbecoming ways. They have the power not to enthusiastically embrace the rugged-thuggish model of black masculinity.

Most of the videos that I see by women artists deal with infidelity and heartbreak, vindication, intimacy, and occasionally domestic violence. Surely there are other topics that can be discussed by black women in their songs and videos. What about health care, education, poverty, teenage pregnancy, drugs? With increasing numbers of black women being infected with HIV/AIDS, why is someone not discussing this topic-which TLC did, in the 1990s? HIV/AIDS is life-threatening to thousands of black women. It should be in the lyrical repertoire of at least some artists. Is it possible to weave these topics into one's lyrics? If not, then black women too, have lost their currency.

I beg to differ with those who argue that black men are solely responsible for sexist behavior. Many black women have enthusiastically embraced the same negative stereotypes as black men. As the rapper Ja Rule says, "Every Thug Needs A Lady," which could also be interpreted as "Every Lady Needs a Thug." The black woman has always been the backbone of our race. When she capitulates to accept counterproductive values and embrace negative stereotypes, the black community is in desperate trouble. It is happening.

For example, while in the Atlanta area visiting my folks, I went out dancing with a couple of my high-school buddies. The club was so-phisticated-looking on the outside and on the inside. The patrons were a thirtyish crowd, a mixture of professionals and nonprofessionals. About an hour after we arrived, the DJ played a song by the rap artist Ludacris entitled "Move Bitch." Ludacris sings about beating a woman up. After the chorus—"move bitch, get out the way, get out the way"—the rapper sings "Oh No! The fight's out. I'ma 'bout to punch yo lights out." The first problem was that the DJ played the song. The second problem was that several women in the place were singing it, word-for-word. The third problem was that I heard the edited version of the song on the radio when I returned to Los Angeles. The fourth and most serious problem was that BET had the video of this song in its rotation.

Instead of protesting female degradation, many black women have celebrated it. Moreover, many black women favor the gangsta-thug over the perfect gentleman. For instance, female singers such as Lil' Kim, Foxy Brown, and Da Brat do not feature men who wear suits in their videos. They do not feature men bringing them flowers and having philosophical conversations over candlelit dinners. Instead, they show shirtless, tattooed, bandana-wearing or cornrowed gangstas in bedroom or shower scenes. They show them riding on motorcycles or in tricked-out cars with hydraulics.

Foxy Brown's second album, *Chyna Doll*, contained a single entitled "Baller Bitch." The song begins, "This is for all my ballin ass bitches all over, world wide shake them thighs for them hots for all my niggas on street corners." Brown's album *Broken Silence* repeats the same themes that were popular in her first album, *Il Na Na*.

The artist Lil' Kim has made her reputation with her explicit lyrics. Why was she the most popular female rapper in the first few years of her career? The song "Spend a Little Doe" from her album *Hardcore* contains the following lyrics: "...I ain't wanna see my bird in no cage. But I'm ready to take care of you now. Now, after three years, three muthafuckin years, nigga you know what [gun cocked], hasta la vista...it's the gangstaress...." The explicit song "Magic Stick" with Lil' Kim featuring 50 Cent remained at the top of the Billboard charts for consecutive weeks in 2003.

Da Brat, like Lil' Kim, has made her reputation off of her streetwise lyrics. The song "Breeve On Em" from her album Unrestricted contains the following lyrics: "...I keep bangin', I keep slangin'...We keep watching niggas die for simple things so I keep swingin', fuckin' a nigga head up, dead up, I'm fed up feel my lead bust..." What's positive about these lyrics?

Alicia Keys, the singing sensation who has a background in classical music, coupled with the rapper Eve to make the hit song "Gangsta Love," in which they sing about a romance with a roughneck. In her video for the hit song "Fallin," Keys features a romantic relationship with a prison inmate. The video shows a number of scenes on the prison yard. What's romantic about this scenario? What is this telling the impressionable twelve-year-old African American boy who has a crush on the beautiful singer? Why are these black female artists embracing, romanticizing, and glorifying the same rugged-thuggish lifestyle that many young black men have embraced?

I was watching Ted Koppel's Up Close program the night he featured the voice and personality of the person behind Black Entertainment Television's virtual character, Cita. Producers created Cita as an animated character for the daytime rap and R&B video program called Cita's World. After just a few years on the air, this show reached a half-million viewers, one-fourth of whom were under the age of seventeen. From the beginning the Cita character was sassy, opinionated, and streetwise. The Up Close interviewer Michelle Martin asked the voice and person behind Cita, Kitty, and the program's producer, Tracey, to describe Cita. They both said that Cita was "ghetto fabulous." Martin asked what was so fabulous about the ghetto. The two both responded that you do not have to be in the ghetto to be ghetto fabulous. They said the term conveys a certain style and attitude.

In response to Martin's question about being a "baller," Kitty and Tracey stated that it was synonymous with being ghetto fabulous. The interviewees stated that one does not have to play ball to be a baller, but some athletes-like Allen Iverson—are ballers. They said that Iverson is "a ballin baller." Martin asked the two college graduates if they thought the Cita character glorified stereotypes of blacks. Kitty stated that they were not in the business of trying to make whites feel comfortable. Martin asked about the negative impact that such images had on blacks. Kitty stated that blacks, however young, have choices; they know right from wrong and they can see examples of what is right all around them. Martin challenged this statement and moved on to ask Kitty whether she would allow her young son to watch the show. Kitty said no, because the videos are too explicit and they promote too much sex. Martin then thereby exposed Kitty's glaring contradiction.

If Kitty really felt that kids, no matter what their circumstances, had choices, why would she not let her child watch Cita's World? Even a twelve-year-old, according to Kitty's logic, could exercise his discretion and make a sophisticated determination about the video world versus reality. The fact is, her attitude mirrors that of many in the entertainment industry: "I'll shield my own kids from society's negative influences, but I will let other children 'exercise their discretion.'"

References

Bell, Jarrett. 2002. Cochran-led group seeks more black NFL coaches. USA Today, 1 October.

Edwards, Harry. 1969. The Revolt of the Black Athlete. New York: The Free Press.

Florio, Gwen. 2002. Wyoming marks '69 scandal Sculpture notes university's "Black 14." Denver Post, 9 December.

Harris, Othello. 1993. Chapter in Racism In College Athletics: The African-American Athlete's Experience. Edited by Dana Brooks and Ronald Alehouse. Morgantown, West Virginia: Fitness Informational Technology.

Lusane, Clarence. 1997. Race in the Global Era: African Americans at the Millennium. Boston: South End Press.

Pugmire, Lance. 2003. Graduation rates are far from sweet. Los Angeles Times, 17 March.

Reddy, Patrick. 2003. Reforming college sports. Buffalo News, 16 March.

Tyehimba, Cheo Taylor. 2002. Will Smith. Savoy, August.

Wieberg, Steve. 2003. Grad Rates for Athletes on Rise, USA Today, 3 September.

Wiggins, David K. 1993. Chapter in Racism In College Athletics: The African-American Athlete's Experience. Edited by Dana Brooks and Ronald Alehouse. Morgantown, West Virginia: Fitness Informational Technology.

Wiggins, David K. 1997. Glory Bound: Black Athletes in a White America. Syracuse: Syracuse University Press.

Woodson, Carter G. [1933] 1990. The Mis-Education of The Negro. Reprint, Trenton, New Jersey: Africa World Press.

Chapter 7

Popular Culture

Cultural Tourism

I am convinced that were it not for popular culture, black men, especially lower-class black men, would have worn out their welcome long ago. It is this role as the ultimate pur-veyors of popular culture, always providing the excitement, angst, irony, tension, and comic relief that are needed to sus-tain any cultural movement, that has kept black men in the mix when all indicators suggest that they should have been extinct many years previous. (Boyd 1997, 14)

The impact that American popular culture has had on the global community is extraordinary. Black men have been largely responsi-ble for the contemporary influence of American popular culture on the rest of the world. In the late 1990s, Michael Jordan was consid-ered the most popular person on the planet. A documentary about the life of the mega-star stated that next to Jesus Christ, Michael Jor-dan had the most recognizable name in the world. It seemed for a while that everyone wanted to "Be like Mike." It always amazed me to see his Number 23 Chicago Bulls jersey (and later his Washington Wizards jersey) worn by teenagers around the world-in cities as di-verse as Tokyo, Tel Aviv, Budapest, Amsterdam, Cape Town, and Oslo. Now Jordan's baton has been passed to Kobe Bryant and Tiger Woods.

In his role as a trendsetter, the young African American male is unique. He looks to no other ethnic group for his ways. Others look to him for the new slang and new fashion statements. They look to him to decide what is "dope," "weak," or "played out." A few years ago, I was appalled and embarrassed to see a number of young African Americans wearing hats with the price tags still on them. I felt these kids were being outrageous and silly. However, a trend that is perceived as being outrageous and silly spreads like wildfire after young black men endorse it. I remember the first time I saw young black men with baggy pants sagging to their upper thighs. Now millions of youth emulate this style, worldwide.

I once met with a senior executive of the Bank of America to discuss fundraising opportunities for the Colorful Flags program, which I direct. A development officer from my university sat in on the meeting. I showed the executive the poignant short film, *Life Ain't No Crystal Stair*, for which I wrote the screenplay. This film integrates rap lyrics with the dialogue. After viewing the film, the development officer immediately apologized to the executive for the rap music contained in the film. The man looked at her and said, "No apologies needed. This is all my fifteen-year-old daughter and her friends listen to." The development officer was embarrassed that she was out of touch with reality and attempted to adjust her position by saying, "You know, some of that stuff is pretty good." I smiled on the inside and laughed out loud.

I should have shown the development officer the *USA Today* article entitled "Rap is Radio's Biggest Hit Source," stating that rap is now America's most popular form of music. According to Nielson BDS and Arbitron with Billboard Airplay Monitor—researched by Anthony DeBarros and Ken Barnes—some 40 percent of 2003's Top 30 hits were rap, and rap and R&B songs made up half of the Top 100 list. Pop music was second in popularity and country music was third (Barnes 2003, 1D).

In his 1957 essay "The White Negro," Norman Mailer documents how a faction of whites energetically embraces the hipness of black culture. Whether it is music, dress, language, or attitude, whites have attempted to emulate blacks for many decades. In the book *Everything But the Burden: What White People are Taking From Black Culture*, Carl Hancock Rux refers to the widely popular rapper Eminem as "The New White Negro." The book's cover shows the backside of a white guy with his pants sagging below his boxers.

The sociopolitical commentator Tony Brown once stated that whites go through three different stages in appropriating black culture: 1) They will laugh; 2) They will observe; 3) They will copy. For example, whites initially laughed at the blues and at jazz. When they perceived the richness of these musical art forms, however, they appropriated them.

The older generation of whites would let a period of time elapse before they appropriated an element of black culture. Perhaps it was a superiority complex that restricted them from appropriating black culture immediately. Perhaps it was this complex that forced them to laugh and observe before copying. Today, however, the new generation of whites lacks the smugness of their parents. There is no time delay. Brown's three stages in appropriating black culture do not apply with this new generation. Once young blacks set a trend, it is immediately mimicked and consumed by millions of whites and nonblacks worldwide. Hip-hop is now the flavor of many youth in the international community. Author Jawanza Kunjufu states the following about hip-hop:

> Hip-hop is in many respects a classic youth oppositional subculture rejecting the norms and values of the mainstream, measuring success in terms of peer approval and equating power with the ability to influence the subculture by constantly changing insider cues, taste and values. Its strengths are its energy and creativity. (Kunjufu 1997, 2)

Rich Cohen wrote in a 2001 *GQ* article, "It seemed in the 1990s most white kids wanted to be black." He quoted a black comedian who said during the mid-1990s, "I wish I were a white kid so I would know what it feels like to want to be black." Brett Rattner—the director of the *Rush Hour* films—stated, "I was one of those white kids who wanted to be black." During the1980s, Rattner spent all of his Bar Mitzvah money on Fila gear. Why? "Because it was what the coolest black kids were wearing," he says. "Today everything that is black is cool" (Cohen 2001, 126).

It is hard not to hear street vernacular in many sectors of American society. I find it amusing to hear street vernacular in the most unlikely sectors, including soap operas, nonblack movies and sitcoms, cartoons, and conservative talk shows. You can now hear in Beverly

Hills the same slang phrases that are used in Compton. The extremely popular "What's Uuuuuuuup?" Budweiser commercial was an excellent example of the commodification of street vernacular. I once heard Barbara Walters say, "You go, girl." This is a phrase that Martin Lawrence popularized on the show Martin in the mid-1990s.

Michiko Kakutani wrote in a 1997 article in *The New York Times Magazine* that young urban blacks have co-opted the dress of upper crust whites as a manifestation of their lack of power in American society. While actual material success may be unattainable, the rationale for wearing expensive polo shirts, blue jeans, and sneakers is to present an image of success. Suburban white kids scoff at the material success of their parents and their parents' friends. One way to express this disdain is to identify with the renegade image of the street. Many white kids are "cultural tourists who romanticize the very ghetto life that so many black kids want to escape. Instead of the terrible mortality rate for young black males, they see the glamour of violence. Instead of the frustration of people denied jobs and hope and respect, they see the verbal defiance of that frustration." (p.18)

Kakutani suggests that this vicarious outlet of symbolic expression is why white suburban males have become the largest audience for gangsta-rap. *The Happy Days* scene dominated popular culture in the 1950s. Black leather jackets and greased hair represented the zeitgeist. In the 1960s, the hippie and bohemian look had the greatest influence on pop culture followed by the polyester and bell-bottoms of the 1970s and the preppy influence of the 1980s. The 1990s were dominated by hip-hop fashion. In the new millennium, hip-hop continues to drive American popular culture.

This fashion consists of baggy pants worn very loosely; baseball caps worn backwards and representing NBA, NFL, or successful university athletic teams; oversized rugby or polo shirts; and expensive tennis shoes. Hip-hop fashion, unlike the fashion of other generations, has uniquely cut across almost every ethnic boundary. Tommy Hilfiger, Ralph Lauren, and other white designers once popular among black youth have been replaced by black superstars who have their own clothing labels. Indeed, Russell Simmon's *Phat Farm*, Jay Z's *Roc-A-Wear*, P. Diddy Comb's *Sean Jean*, and *Fubu* are today the most popular names in urban wear. Each of these companies brings in over $100 million annually. The popularity of hip-hop has given some young blacks an unprecedented amount of economic clout and influence.

When the rapper Snoop Doggy Dogg's song "Gin and Juice" was popular in 1994, the sale of gin increased by 10 percent. Moreover, when Nelly rapped about stomping in his Air Force One Nike tennis shoes, the sales of this old-school tennis shoe increased dramatically. Sprite's "Obey Your Thirst" campaign used old-school rappers, among others, to appeal to the hip-hop audience. This strategy was highly successful. It established Sprite as one of the leading soft-drink brands. By signing black icons such as NBA star Kobe Bryant, Sprite continues to appeal to a growing hip-hop audience. Hip-hopper Busta Rymes has been featured on commercials endorsing Mountain Dew, while Wyclef Jean has been featured on those endorsing Pepsi. Today, it is seen as good business to use the hip-hop flavor in company advertisements (Hughes 2002, 72).

According to an article in *Black Enterprise Magazine*, if one counted every dollar generated in the early 2000s from every hip-hop CD sold and included television shows, radio programs, films, and video games, hip-hop contributes $5 billion to these entertainment sectors. Indeed, a significant number of youth between the ages of twelve and twenty-two dress the same, irrespective of their ethnicity or nationality. *Black Enterprise* writer Alan Hughes captures the global impact of hip-hop when he states, "From New York to Nepal, hip-hop has become America's leading cultural export. Across the globe, it's changing how businesses are marketing their product" (Hughes 2002, 70).

I taught a young woman whose brother worked in an Ethiopian absorption camp in Israel. When he asked the young Ethiopians in this camp what they wanted to be called (for example, Black-Israelis, Ethiopian-Israelis, African-Israelis), they stated, "Niggers." They had heard the term romanticized so much in rap music from the U.S. that they actually thought it was a badge of honor.

When I think of hip-hop's influence, I am reminded of an incident that took place in Tokyo. While on a tour, one of my buddies and I spotted a young Japanese man wearing a cap with the rapper Snoop Dogg's name on the front. My friend looked at him and said, "I see you like Snoop Dogg." The guy turned around and said "Bow Wow Wooow," which is a trademark of the rapper. My buddy and I looked at each other in disbelief. I knew at that time that the hip-hop movement was about to reach unprecedented heights.

I met three young men from the Twi ethnic group in a cultural market in Accra, Ghana. Instead of giving me their tribal or Christian names, they introduced themselves as the "Doggfather" (the rapper Snoop Dogg's other nickname), Billy Ocean, and Nino Brown (the gangsta played by Wesley Snipes in the movie New Jack City). As they walked with me through the market and tried to sell me various items, they talked to me in the hip-hop vernacular. We discussed different aspects of Ghanaian culture but we also talked about Shaggy, R. Kelly, and Tupac. In fact, I saw many youngsters wearing Tupac T-shirts. I could have easily have been in New York or Los Angeles.

On a 2003 trip to Nagano, Japan, I was sitting next to a young man on the train from Narita Airport to Tokyo. He was Maori, a member of an aboriginal ethnic group from New Zealand. He was in Japan on a rugby scholarship playing for one of the Japanese universities. After about ten minutes of conversation about rugby and Japanese culture, he promptly switched to American hip-hop. He wanted to know what I thought about the widely popular rapper 50 Cent. I told him that I liked 50 but did not care for his violent lyrics. He said, "Yeah, everybody in New Zealand is crazy about him. He's bad. He got shot nine times. He's an animal. I love that guy."

In reference to the overarching question in Chapter 6, what are young black men doing with the unprecedented influence they have on popular culture? If messages of love, peace, anti-racism, anti-sexism, and human uplift are resonated among the hip-hop population, it could have an enormous impact on ethnic relations in our society. In the 1950s and 1960s the Beat Culture challenged the status quo in ways that did not compromise their rebellious spirit. In the same vein, it is possible for the hip-hop culture to keep its rebellious street flavor and speak to issues such as love and respect for all. It is possible for rap artists such as Nelly, Jay-Z, Nas, Ja Rule, and 50 Cent to empower America and the world's youth like Bob Dylan, John Lennon, Bob Marley, Marvin Gaye, and Curtis Mayfield did. Artists such as the late rapper Tupac Shakur have rapped about such compassionate issues without losing the rugged flavor of the streets. In his song, "I Wonder If Heaven's Got A Ghetto," Shakur sings:

> I see no changes, all I see is racist faces misplaced hate makes disgrace the racist...I wonder what it takes to make this one better place...take the evil out the people [then] they'll be acting right cause both black and white are smokin crack tonight and the only time we deal is when we kill each other, it takes skill to be real, time to heal each other....

Millions of hip-hoppers all over the world have heard these lyrics. If more artists concentrated on positive messages such as this, the impact could be revolutionary.

Unlike any other subculture in American history, the hip-hop culture has transcended ethnic boundaries. Because of its eclectic audience, it has the greatest opportunity to build ethnic bridges and mend ethnic relations. Hip-hop has taken hold and permeated significant regions of the world. The clothing, music, mannerisms, and lexicon are unmistakably the same in New York, Los Angeles, Paris, Zurich, Milan, and Tokyo. Indeed, this culture has the potential to make it cool not to be racist and commit hate crimes, not to commit sexual assaults and engage in domestic violence, not to kill one's brother in the struggle.

Contradicting Stereotypes

In 1922 Walter Lippman suggested that the use of stereotypes significantly influences cognitive structures. Black men have been stereotyped as being criminals, pimps, and drug dealers. They have been generally viewed as overly aggressive and lacking discipline. Negative images of black men have been discussed in various books and shown in numerous films.

Black men have enthusiastically embraced the negative stereotypes that have been constructed about them. When Richard Wright published *Black Boy* in 1937, he observed a similar phenomenon:

> I began to marvel at how smoothly the black boys acted out the roles that the white race had mapped out for them. Most

of them were not conscious of living a special, separate, stunted way of life...Had a black boy announced that he aspired to be a writer, he would have been unhesitatingly called crazy by his pals. Or had a black boy spoken of yearning to get a seat on the New York Stock Exchange, his friends-in the boy's own interest-would have reported his odd ambition to the white boss. (Wright 1945, 217)

According to Wright's narrative, the white power structure has historically limited the aspirations and dreams of black men. Hence, black men have acquiesced.

A young black man of about seventeen was on a flight with me from Los Angeles to Detroit. He wore baggy pants and a do-rag on his head with a tilted cap on top. He had on earphones and held his CD player. A silver cross dangled from his oversized, V-neck sweater. As we waited for our delayed plane to arrive, the scowling teenager got up and walked around several times. As he strutted, he was looking to see who was looking at him. As people ignored him, he started to make noises, then rap and move his hands in a rhythmic motion. It was clear that he wanted the world to notice him. He wanted to be visible. Like so many other young black men of his generation, his "tough guy" image was created to cause shock and alarm. He wore his gangsta-thug persona with pride. I wanted to tell this teenager to shut up, sit down, and wait for the plane.

So much of young black men's behavior today lacks etiquette. Playing stereos too loud, talking in movies, yelling and cussing and fighting in public, and littering-all are disrespectful. Instead of undermining various stereotypes, this behavior rigidly reinforces them.

Representing Sport, a book written by Rod Brookes in 2002, has a picture of the 4-by-100-meter team that won the gold medal in the 2000 Olympic Games in Sydney. This team was led by world-class sprinter Maurice Green. After they won the gold medal, instead of showing the class of Michael Johnson, Carl Lewis, or Edwin Moses, they embarrassed themselves, other blacks, and their country. They celebrated their win by taking off their shirts and posing with U.S. flags wrapped around them. Minutes after the race, these young men paraded around the stadium as if they were the only athletes in town. Many people in the stands booed this over-the-top display of hubris and buffoonery. The Olympic Games promote friendly and respectful international competition. These athletes were totally oblivious to the overall goals and objectives of the Games. I was thoroughly embarrassed by the behavior of these four black men. Green later apologized for his behavior and the behavior of his teammates.

While I was in graduate school, I went with a group of friends on a road trip to Vancouver, British Columbia, in Canada. While we were getting out of the car in a parking lot on our way to a restaurant, one of the fellas set two bottles down along the side of the car. I was furious. I asked him what he was doing. He had no idea what I was talking about, which was a shame. I said, "You should put those bottles back in the car until we find a trashcan; I am sure there is one close by." He picked up the bottles and said, "Man, you're trippin." I asked him what he liked most about Vancouver. He responded by saying he liked how beautiful and clean the city was. I asked, "What if everybody in this town did what you are doing now?" He finally got my point: littering is a big deal. It is showing disrespect to the environment.

While I was working on this chapter of *American Paradox*, the Los Angeles ABC news affiliate showed a home video of a gang brawl that took place at a hip-hop concert held at the Irvine Amphitheater in Irvine, California. Rival gang members, all of whom were black, threw pipes, bottles, cans, and trash at each other while they fought. The rapper LL Cool J was on stage when the fight broke out. He said that he would not continue his performance and announced he would only come back to play the venue when they could prove that they had some couth and could act in a civilized way. The private security staff at the concert could not contain the melee, so the Irvine police were brought in. They made thirty arrests. The news team interviewed a few people who stated that it was a shame the actions of a few ignorant guys spoiled the concert for everyone.

I was at home visiting my parents in Georgia when I saw on the news that a brawl had broken out at the Cincinnati Black Family Reunion festival. The three-day event was created to focus attention on the various needs of the black family. Booths offering information about colleges, jobs, health, and technology were big features of the festival. On the second day, police had to use tear gas to break up a crowd of more than 2,000 black youth who were fighting and knocking over tables and newspaper stands throughout the area. Gunfire was reported among the crowd. Ten people were hospitalized and eight people were arrested.

As I watched the news footage of the melees in Los Angeles and Cincinnati, I felt embarrassed that other people were watching the same footage. I felt intense frustration because on the one hand, I am a harsh critic of the discriminatory and racially biased criminal justice system, but on the other, I am an equally harsh critic of absurd and counterproductive behavior. Some blacks would find ways to blame the system for the brawl between the rival gangs at the Irvine concert and among the 2,000 youth in Cincinnati. Their rationale is just as irrational as the brawls.

I feel susceptible and left out on a limb when I spend my time and emotional energies discussing the unfairness of stereotyping and racial profiling, while at the same time some young black men are wallowing in stereotypes and helping to justify the practice of profiling. If young black men would spend as much time contradicting stereotypes as they do embracing them, there would be significant change in their collective progress.

A friend was waiting to pick me up at my arriving airport gate as I returned from a trip. When he spotted me, he started to yell: "That's my dog. That's my dog. What's up boy?" I immediately told him to chill. He asked, "For what?" I said, "Because there are people around." My friend—who is a professional, raised in California—said that I was afraid to be loud because I grew up in the South and was still afraid of the white man. I told him that he could not act the same way around white folks as he could around his own people-the cussing and loudness only calcified stereotypes. Whites are intimidated by the rawness of black cultural rituals. I told him he had to be respectful of their sensitivities. Perhaps growing up in the South made me more cognizant and respectful of these sensitivities; this environment also enabled me to realize the significance of contradicting stereotypes.

I always cringe and am overwhelmed with embarrassment when I see a black person reinforcing stereotypes. I once walked into my local grocery store and saw a black teenager open up a can of Mountain Dew and start drinking it. He drank about half and put the can back on the shelf. I was sick.

On a flight from New York to Los Angeles, the airline had a scratch-off contest in which passengers could win a prize. One young black man who was in the front of the plane started yelling to one of his homies who was all the way in the back: "Hey TJ, what's up nigga? What you got? You win? You win?" He later stated at the top of his lungs, "Nigga I hope this muthafuckin plane don't crash...I'm not trying to die up in this muthafucka." I was overwhelmed with embarrassment. He acted like he had just gotten out of a cage. He had no social etiquette. He was reinforcing stereotypes.

When I lived in Seattle, I was twenty-three years old and worked at a chic men's clothing store at a popular mall. During the one year I was employed at the store, I had five black managers. My first manager was at work one evening when his male partner came and put pressure on him to leave for a bite to eat. He left the store and did not return. There was no one there with the authority to close the store down. We had to contact the regional manager who drove up from Portland to close the store. My second manager was fired for stealing $1,200 worth of suits. My third manager was fired for keeping a customer's credit card and using it to charge more than $500 worth of merchandise. My first three managers were all black men. My fourth manager was a black woman. One night she left both the back door to the store and the safe open. She knocked over clothes and set the place up like there had been a burglary. Her ex-boyfriend came in and stole the money that was in the safe. It was his idea. She was still in love with him and was desperate to get him back. She was also fired. The fifth manager worked without incident.

If you are the regional manager of this store, how can you not stereotype the next black person who comes in to interview for a job as store manager? Given the store's track record, it would be tremendously difficult not to profile. Thankfully the white regional manager was liberal-minded enough to keep giving young blacks a chance until he finally found someone who contradicted society's stereotypes.

When I was growing up, Julius Erving was one of my role models. He epitomized class and professionalism. Along with being very athletic, he was articulate and intelligent. As a ten-year-old, I met Dr. J in 1977 in the Philadelphia 76ers locker room after they had competed against the Atlanta Hawks. I remember saying to him, "Let me have your autograph." He scolded me for asking for the autograph improperly. He restated my request: "May I please have your autograph?" I was embarrassed. My father, who was a sportswriter, was interviewing Henry Bibby at the other end of the locker room. He noticed something was not right, so he walked down to the Doc's locker and asked what the problem was. Erving asked him, "Is this your son?" My father replied, "Yes, what's the problem?" Erving said, "He does not know how to ask for an autograph properly?" My father nudged me to say it the proper way. I finally got Dr. J's autograph—and I balled it up and threw it away that night. Later, I realized that he was not trying to embarrass me but to teach me social etiquette.

Many young black men today lack social etiquette. This is a problem because success and upward mobility begin with respect for others and with civility. Individuals who cannot or will not conform to the informal and formal laws of society might be admired from a distance but are ultimately shunned, ostracized, and pushed to the fringes. Our prisons are filled with young black men who lacked social etiquette but "kept it real." Dr. J was on to something.

White Privilege

At least thirty institutions—including Princeton University and the University of California, Los Angeles—teach courses in Whiteness Studies. This academic discipline examines topics such as power, oppression, and hegemony and seeks to understand the implications of white privilege on the racial identity of white Americans (Fears 2003, A01).

Provocative author and filmmaker Michael Moore offers a stinging commentary on whiteness in his book *Stupid White Men*. According to Moore, every person who has ever harmed him has been white. He states that he has never been attacked by a black person, never had his security deposit ripped off by a black landlord, and never had a black person say: "We're going to eliminate ten thousand jobs here-have a nice day" (Moore, 2002, 57). Moore's description of the invisible benefits of whiteness and the systematic forgiveness of white crimes is revealing and insightful.

> You name the problem, the disease, the human suffering, or
> the abject misery visited upon millions, and I'll bet you ten
> bucks I can put a white face to it.... And yet when I turn on
> the news each night, what do I see again and again? Black
> men alleged to be killing, raping, mugging, stabbing, gang-
> banging, looting, rioting, selling drugs, pimping, ho-ing, hav-
> ing too many babies, dropping babies from tenement win-
> dows, fatherless, motherless, Godless, penniless.... (Moore
> 2002, 59)

I agree with the argument that whites often misbehave with no
consequences. I agree that there are double standards. I remember
after a football game my senior year in high school, the fellas and I
met at the local McDonald's. When we arrived, a group of rowdy
white students were popping balloons and chasing each other around
the restaurant. I remember seeing the police officer who was on duty
laugh jovially at the antics of these teenagers. As the group was leaving, my buddies and I took their seats in the back of the restaurant.
We immediately began playing the dozens—joning—and laughing.
The police officer came back to our table within fifteen minutes and
told us that we had to keep it down. We were not running around the
restaurant, nor were we popping balloons.

When I was at Vanderbilt—one of the most elite universities in the
country—I saw the worst type of behavior imaginable from my white
cohorts. When they got drunk, they were insane-throwing furniture
out of the windows, pulling fire alarms, throwing up in the hallways,
urinating in the elevators. After a weekend of random acts of wild-
ness, the custodial team came in and cleaned up and made the necessary repairs. Students were rarely reprimanded for their behavior.
It was all seen as "good college fun." Today, they call this phenomenon "white privilege." Paula Rothenberg accurately refers to this phenomenon as "invisible privilege" because it is invisible to the media
and to the broader public:

> A major East Coast bank provides some of its customers with
> a service called "privileged checking." Those who qualify are
> allowed to write checks in amounts that exceed their balance
> with the assurance that they will not bounce. In many ways,
> this service stands as metaphor for the kinds of invisible priv-

ilege some people in our society enjoy because of their class position, their race or ethnicity, their gender, or some combination of all three. The beneficiaries of a history of credit to bankroll whatever initiatives they undertake.... This provides them with advantages that most other people do not enjoy and provides their children with a head start in the race of life. (Rothenberg 2000, 1)

Rothenberg confirms George Lipsitz's observations in *The Possessive Investment in Whiteness: How White People Profit From Identity Politics*. "Whiteness is everywhere in U.S. culture, but it is very hard to see." A white rapist or murderer featured on the local news is bland. The profile does not have the same psychological impact or galvanize the same tensions as if the person were black. Richard Dyer argues, "White power secures its dominance by seeming not to be anything in particular" (Lipsitz 1998, 1).

In the eyes of the media and in the eyes of the public, there is a difference between the rowdy behavior of young blacks at a rap concert and the rowdy behavior of young whites at a big college football victory. When the Ohio State football team beat the University of Michigan in 2002 to go undefeated for the season, OSU students and fans celebrated by turning over trashcans and setting almost a dozen fires in a ten-block area of Columbus, Ohio. Although there were forty-nine arrests, the media coverage suggested that over-excited fans got a little out of control. There are double standards in the way in which the media cover black and white violence. This point is highlighted in *The Black Image in the White Mind*, written by Robert M. Entman and Andrew Rojecki and published in 2000.

Just because white youth can get away with raucous behavior does not mean that young blacks should attempt to do the same. Whites are not the ones who are trying to overcome more than 300 years of negative image construction. Blacks cannot misbehave like whites and get away with it. The fact that young black men are six times more likely than young white men to be convicted of a crime, even when they are accused of the same offense, tells you that there are double standards. Blacks should be cognizant that they have to be twice as disciplined as whites because they are under more scrutiny.

Who needs this white acceptance? Most blacks need white acceptance if they want to be successful in their respective fields. Therefore, necessary adjustments must be made to accommodate the status quo. Is that selling out? I am sure some would construe it as such. However, I would call it being pragmatic and flexible in one's identity. Anyone who wants to be successful in society has to learn to be flexible. Black men must learn to be more disciplined. They have to learn to control their rage and impulses because the margin of error for them is smaller than it is for whites.

I gave a guest lecture to a group of students in 1998 at the University of Kent at Canterbury in Great Britain. After my lecture, the students asked me a broad range of questions pertaining to race relations in the United States. After the session, one student asked me about the plight of black men in America. He wanted to know whether black men had a chance to be successful in American society. To me, this was a simple but challenging question. I gave the student a very simple answer: "Yes." Later, I attempted to uncover the complexity of this question. I came to the conclusion that the probability of a black man's success in U.S. society is correlated with his willingness either to embrace or contradict variously constructed negative stereotypes. In other words, the average black man who contradicts these stereotypes is more likely to be successful than the one who embraces them.

Commodification of the Thug

The black man was depicted as being a dangerous and undisciplined savage in D.W. Griffith's 1915 film, *Birth of a Nation*. This film, based on Thomas Dixon's book *The Clansman*, solidified white society's fear of the black man.

Today, popular culture has motivated many young black men to embrace wholeheartedly society's negative view of them. The commodification of the gangsta-thug has created a genuine dilemma for black men. In commercials, movies, and music they are idolized because they embrace the rebellious tough guy. In these arenas, black men are rewarded by how thoroughly they embrace society's stereotypes of them. This phenomenon has led to their worldwide popularity. Because this image is persistently romanticized in many popular culture venues, impressionable young black men have become susceptible to trying to emulate what they see.

After playing a number of dynamic characters who possessed integrity, Denzel Washington won his first Oscar as a leading actor by playing a gangsta-thug. Denzel's performances in *Malcolm X*, *Remember the Titans*, and *The Hurricane* were outstanding and worthy of Hollywood's top honor. However, the voters of the Motion Picture Academy decided they were more comfortable awarding him for his role as the depraved Alonzo Harris in Training Day.

> The creation of global market niches in this era is a driving force in the contemporary exploitation of black American cultural forms. The marketing of the 'other' as entertainment, an opportunity to experience the dangerously exotic, even if only abstractly, motivates both corporate producer and nonblack consumer. In the middle are 'declassed' poor black youth-that is, those who are marginalized perhaps permanently out of the labor force-whose efforts to avoid what are clearly unpleasant destinies generate innovative ways to prosper and survive. Those ways have become new modes of capital accumulation. (Lusane 1997, 96-97)

The film *Baby Boy*, is a raw representation of all the negative stereotypes regarding the black male. This film and others like it highlight a major contradiction in African American discourse. Although for decades blacks have fought the Hollywood establishment to feature more positive black characters, black directors and producers have not followed suit.

Many black films in the gangsta-thug genre are bereft of diverse representations of black men. It is troubling to see the cinematic representations of the gangsta-thug in many black films celebrated and romanticized. For instance, in the gangsta-thug classic *Menace II Society*, O-Dog—played by Larenz Tate—became an icon of black masculinity for many young black men. In this film O-Dog is claimed to be America's worst nightmare: "young, black, and doesn't give a fuck."

In the movie *Jason's Lyric*, Bokeem Woodbine plays a character just as thuggish and loco as O-Dog.

This narrowly constructed model of black masculinity has been widely embraced by whites and blacks in the film industry. Indeed, the enthusiastic embrace of this monolithic model of black masculinity has become the most detrimental element in the lives of a generation of young black men in America.

As bell hooks states in *Killing Rage*:

> Opportunistic longings for fame, wealth, and power now lead many black critical thinkers, writers, academics, and/or intellectuals to participate in the production and marketing of black culture in ways that are complicit with the existing oppressive-exploitative structure. That complicity begins with the equation of black capitalism with black self-determination. (hooks 1995, 176)

The argument used by whites and blacks in the film industry is that the young black man as gangsta-thug represents reality. Perhaps this is true. However, the gangsta-thug does not represent the only reality of young black men in America. The error in accepting this one definition of black masculinity is that it is too restrictive. Popular culture does a poor job of featuring black men who do not fit the gangsta-thug stereotype. The statistics state that one of every four black men from the ages of sixteen to twenty-six has some contact with the criminal justice system; i.e., in jail or prison, on parole or probation. That is reality. However, this means 75 percent of young black men have not had contact with the criminal justice system.

The movie *The Best Man* is a refreshing examination of an array of black male personalities. Of the four best friends, Harper Jackson—played by Taye Diggs—is the very cerebral and creative author of the bunch. Quentin, played by Terrence Howard, is a gifted guitarist, a student of human nature, and a "player." Lance is the All-Star NFL running back, played by Morris Chestnut. He graduated college magna cum laude. Finally, Murch—played by Harold Perrineau, Jr.—is a very sensitive and compassionate individual. His character is the antithesis of our society's conception of black masculinity. While Quentin and Lance reflect the representation of the hypersexed black man with a tough outer shell, Harper and Murch do not reflect any of the constructed stereotypes. In fact, none of these characters embrace a gangsta toughness.

Many black filmmakers have met the challenge of showing diverse cinematic representations of the black man with inspiring success. The screen adaptation of best-selling author Terry McMillan's *Waiting to Exhale* made box office history for a black film by grossing well over $60 million. Films such as *Soul Food, The Wood, Love and Basketball, Brothers, Two Can Play This Game, Barber Shop, Deliver Us From Eva*, and *Brown Sugar* proved that black filmmakers have the capacity to frame and construct alternative black male images without suffering at the box office. The refreshing element of these so-called middle-class black films is that they all highlight the flaws of the black man without the gangsta-thug narrative.

Many black cultural critics discuss how the white media are responsible for perpetuating the gangsta-thug image. To be sure, white media deserve a share of the blame for perpetuating negative stereotypes of black men. However, blacks deserve just as much blame, if not more, for celebrating and enthusiastically embracing the gangsta-thug model. Jawanza Kunjufu's *Countering the Conspiracy to Destroy Black Boys* (1995) provided us with an opportunity to pause and ask ourselves just who is responsible for countering stereotypes. Blacks cannot continue to rely on the white power structure to provide counter-examples of stereotypes that many blacks have embraced.

Over the years, blacks in the film industry have had ample opportunities to show counter-narratives. Instead, they have opted for highlighting the monolithic model of black masculinity in the form of films such as *Strapped, New Jack City, Colors, Boyz `N the Hood, Straight of Brooklyn, Juice, Belly, Menace II Society, South Central, Jason's Lyric, Dead Presidents*, and *Baby Boy*. The images portrayed in these films have resonated worldwide.

In the late 1990s I participated in an academic conference in Enschede, The Netherlands, hosted by the local university. On the third day of the conference I was hanging out in the lounge area of the conference center waiting for a colleague, when one of the conference-center representatives approached me. She appeared to be in her early twenties. She politely began a conversation with me. Within three minutes she asked me if I was in a gang. I was stunned by her question. I laughed and told her no, I was not in a gang. She then asked if I had ever been in a gang. I said, "No." Her questions to me were so stunning because she helped register me for the conference. She knew I was a professor; but the overwhelming image she had internalized of a young black male from the U.S. eclipsed her logic. The popular culture image of the black gangsta had undermined her rationality.

As I was working on my dissertation research in Geneva, Switzerland, in the summer of 1995, I met a young Swiss man-eighteen or nineteen—who was dressed in hip-hop attire. He walked up to me like he had just seen Tupac. He asked me where I was from and I said Los Angeles, California, in the U.S. He became so excited that he could barely control himself. He started giggling and giving me hip handshakes. He then started cussing like he was performing on a rap album. During his excitement, he asked if I had ever been in a gang. I said "No." He did not believe me so he asked me the question twice more to elicit the response he wanted to hear. I did not give it to him. He then asked if I was carrying a gun at that very moment. I said, "No." Not convinced, he asked again. He finally asked me if I had ever shot and killed anyone-had I ever been in a "drive-by." I said "No" to him once more. The young man was clearly disappointed. By the end of my brief exchange with him, he had lost his excitement and enthusiasm. He was dejected. This one time in his young Swiss life he thought he had finally met the person he had seen so many times on the movie screen and listened to countless times on his headphones: the person of his dreams. Instead, he met a fake, an imposter: someone who looked authentic but was not.

References

Barnes, Ken. 2003. Rap is radio's biggest hit Source. USA Today, 3 July.

Boyd, Todd. 1997. Am I Black Enough For You? Bloomington: Indiana University Press.

Brookes, Rod. 2002. Representing Sport. London: Arnold.

Cohen, Rich. 2001. Chris Tucker: Hollywood's new king of comedy. GQ, August.

Entman, Robert M., and Andrew Rojecki. 2000. The Black Image in the White Mind. Chicago: University of Chicago Press.

Fears, Darryl. 2003. Hue and cry on "whiteness studies" classes. Washington Post, 30 June.

hooks, bell. 1995. Killing Rage: Ending Racism. New York: Henry Holt.

Hughes, Alan. 2002. The hip-hop economy explodes! Black Enterprise Magazine, May.

Kakutani, Michiko. 1997. Common threads: Why are homeboys and suburbanites wearing each other's clothes? The New York Times Magazine, 16 February.

Kunjufu, Jawanza. 1995. Countering the Conspiracy to Destroy Black Boys. Chicago: University of Chicago Press.

Kunjufu, Jawanza. 1997. Hip-Hop vs. MAAT: A Pyscho/Social Analysis of Values. Chicago: African American Images.

Lippman, Walter. 1922. Public Opinion. New York: Harcourt Brace.

Lipsitz, George. 1998. The Possessive Investment in Whiteness: How White People Profit From Identity Politics. Philadelphia: Temple University Press.

Lusane, Clarence. 1997. Race in the Global Era: African Americans at the Millennium. Boston: South End Press.

Moore, Michael. 2002. Stupid White Men. London: Penguin Books.

Rothenberg, Paula. 2000. Invisible Privilege: A Memoir About Race, Class, & Gender. Lawrence, Kansas: University of Kansas Press.

Rux, Carl Hancock. 2003. Eminem: the new white Negro. In Everything but the Burden: What White People are Taking from Black Culture, edited by Greg Tate. New York: Broadway Books.

Tate, Greg, ed. 2003. Everything but the Burden: What White People are Taking from Black Culture, New York: Broadway Books.

Wright, Richard. [1937] 1945. Black Boy, a Record of Childhood and Youth. 10th ed. Cleveland and New York: World Publishing.

Chapter 8

The Criminal Justice System

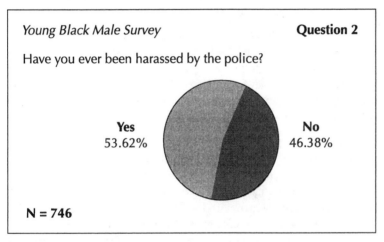

Young Black Male Survey   **Question 2**

Have you ever been harassed by the police?

Yes
53.62%

No
46.38%

N = 746

This statistic shows that at least the perception of police harassment
is significant among young black men.

Post-Rodney King

In 1997, I invited Rodney King to speak to my political science
class at California State Polytechnic University, Pomona. I also invited
his cousin and one of the jurors who sat on his civil trial to participate in a panel discussion about King's experience. Before the panel
began its discussion, I showed a documentary of the civil unrest that
included the video of King's beating. The eighty students in the lecture hall fought back tears as they watched, with King, the infamous
act of police brutality. This was King's first time speaking to a group
of students. His responses to their questions were thoughtful, candid,
and engaging. At some point in the discussion, two inevitable ques-

tions were asked: "What was the beating like?" and "Why can't you stay out of trouble?" King was candid and emotionless in the response to the first question. He had no response to the second.

Since the 1997 panel discussion, King and I have had several opportunities to discuss what the beating did to him physically and psychologically: it was devastating. For a few years, I counseled and attempted to mentor King. I met with him on a regular basis. I exercised with him and gave him books to read.

He never chose to be an icon or an agent of change. He was brutally beaten one night in 1991 and suddenly became a symbol for racial reconciliation and police reform. He was never trained to be an agent of change. He never developed the tools to lead a movement. It was unfair for us, especially African Americans, to thrust him into this role. Ultimately, he was overwhelmed by it all.

What has changed for the rest of us since the infamous beating? I am not convinced there has been much positive change in the relationship between young black men and the criminal justice system since the King beating. We still have the same race-based problems that we have been plagued with for decades. I certainly think that the King incident was an impetus for dialogue on race relations and police reform. It forced Americans to confront the multiple realities of American society. Whites who believed the system to be fair and just were forced to re-evaluate. For many blacks, however, the King case gave them an opportunity to say, "I told you so." Many blacks have family members, relatives, and friends who have been antagonized by the police. The King beating confirmed what they already knew.

Some constructive things have happened. There have been reforms in terms of police oversight. People have come to realize that policing is too important to be solely the domain of police. With each high-profile case of police brutality, there is a small, incremental step toward police reform. It took Rodney King, Malice Green, Demetrius Dubose, Amadou Diallo, Abner Louima, Irvin Landrum, Thomas Jones, and Donovan Jackson to create today's police reforms. Each of these individuals was a victim of blatant police misconduct.

Police misconduct and disparities in the U.S justice system are a cause for concern. African Americans make up 12.8 percent of the population but 49 percent of those who are incarcerated. One of every four black men from the age of sixteen to twenty-six has some connection with the penal system-i.e., in prison or jail, on parole or probation. Young black men are six times more likely to be incarcerated by adult courts as white youth for equally serious crimes. Race, in the U.S. criminal justice system, significantly affects the probability that a person will be sentenced and convicted of a crime. Race also determines the severity of the punishment. The criminal justice system has embraced noble principles and ignoble practices.

Moreover, the criminal justice system is America's big trap for young black men. Instead of devising ways to avoid this trap, young black men have been complicit. Their embrace of the rugged-thuggish model of black masculinity makes it easy for the criminal justice system to justify its discriminatory behavior towards them. This population has been nudged into this trap by the pressures to "keep it real." As long as doing time is a badge of honor in the 'hood, many young black men will fall victim to this trap. As long as achievement in school is vilified and failure is embraced, black men will fall victim to this trap. When your respected icons are those who have had frequent contacts with the criminal justice system, you are vulnerable to "America's Trap."

The peculiar thing about the relationship between young black men and the criminal justice system is that young black men know that the system is not on their side. They have seen friends, brothers, cousins, uncles, and fathers trapped by the system. Nevertheless, they participate in wanton behavior as if there will be no consequences for them.

If you have embraced a thug image, how can you blame the system for treating you in the same way you portray yourself? In other words, if you look like and behave like a thug, people will treat you like a thug. The police, judge, and jury in America's criminal justice system could care less about your "It's just an image thing" response. The system has proven that it is insensitive to your tough-guy persona.

Popular culture—including MTV, BET, VH1, and films—have romanticized the gangsta-thug. The celebration and lionization of America's "menaces to society" have caused young black men to embrace more and more radical symbols of defiance. To many fans of popular culture, these symbols of defiance are intriguing; however, they are unaware of the consequences of black men embracing deviant behavior in its rawest forms. White and Asian kids can emulate their black counterparts with no detrimental consequences. Even if they wander through the inner city looking for excitement, they can always retreat to the suburbs where they are safe from victimization. After reading the following sections, one might conclude that there is a conspiracy to rid America of its young black men. If this is so, there should be a comprehensive strategy on the part of blacks to undermine this great conspiracy.

Ignoble Practices

Critical race theory in the U.S. developed from critical legal studies. Critical legal studies were developed to analyze and deconstruct legal doctrines. The primary outcome of critical legal studies is that law cannot be relied upon to protect those who are without power. According to this school of thought, law is not designed to construct justice but instead is designed to protect those who already hold power. As a derivative of critical legal studies, critical race theory suggests that the justice system is manipulated to legitimize white supremacy and maintain a rule of law (Russell 1999).

In U.S. society, the police have acted as agents of the system. Indeed, white supremacy has been legitimized in police behavior. Those without power have come to see the police as the enemy. James Baldwin discusses the problem in his 1964 essay, "Fifth Avenue, Uptown: A Letter From Harlem":

> The only way to police the ghetto is to be oppressive. None of the police commissioner's men, even with the best will in the world, have any way of understanding the lives led by the people they swagger in twos and threes controlling. Their very presence is an insult, and it would be, even if they spent their entire day feeding gumdrops to children. They represent the force of the White world, and that force intentions are simply to keep the Black man corralled up here, in his place. The badge, the gun in the holster, and the swinging

club make vivid what will happen should his rebellion become overt. (Baldwin 1964, 60-65)

I once had an ideologically conservative white student in my "Politics of the Public Policy Process" class who had enough of me discussing the ills of American public policies. She said, "Every time I come into this class everyone is discussing how detrimental our policies are—even you. I'm tired of hearing about how bad America is. Can't you talk about some positive things? Can't you have some balance?" This was the best student in the class, and I was caught off guard by her anger. First of all, I said, in many ways this country is beautiful. I stated that I did not want to live anywhere else. Then I said to her: "when you are in K-12 you are socialized to embrace everything that is good about America. By the time you get to the university level, you should be ready for the truth." I told her that the truth is that terrorism was not invented overseas-when you lynch your own citizens, that's terrorism; when you put dogs and water hoses on your own people, that's terrorism. Finally, I said: "When police engage in terrorist behavior, let's not sugarcoat it—call it what it is."

Sensing the opportunity to show allegiance with her conservative cohort, another student joined in and asked, "So you don't think there is anything good about our criminal justice system?" I said that on paper, our criminal justice system is good. But in practice, it is foul. It seems that Americans have a strong inclination to turn away from the truth.

In U.S. society, the police have acted as agents of the system. Indeed, the white-dominated social structure has been legitimized in police behavior. Those without power have come to see the police as the enemy. Some 53.6 percent of the participants in my survey of young black males stated that the policed had harassed them. Captain Larry C. Plummer of the Mountain View, California, Police Department stated the following for the *Police Executive Research Forum*:

> Behavior motivated by bigotry and hate is endemic to the law enforcement profession. It persists not so much because we fall victim to basic "human" shortcomings, but rather because we-police professionals-have not taken the very deliberate individual and collective actions required to eliminate, or at least control, the problem.... Bigotry is fueled by many

things, but the most critical and overriding factor in our big-
otry problem is our failure-individually, organizationally, and
collectively—to expose, confront and address it. (Delattre
1996, 286)

The recurring problem of police brutality in the U.S. has taken various forms: firearms, nightsticks, chokeholds, hogtying, batons, Taser
and stun guns, pepper spray, water cannons, dogs, and high-speed
pursuits. "To Protect and Serve" is the ubiquitous motto for police departments nationwide. As agents of the government, police officers
are sworn to "protect and serve" by upholding the U.S. Constitution.
However, the behavior of many police officers, especially in urban
centers, is undermining democracy and diminishing civility and trust
among significant sectors of the American public. Racial profiling, excessive force, and police brutality reflect a blatant disregard for civil
liberties and have magnified the flaws in the liberal democracy of the
United States.

The same themes of racial profiling and police brutality have resonated throughout U.S. history. What the *Kerner Commission* found
in 1968 is true today.

Almost invariably the incident that ignites disorder arises
from police action. Harlem, Watts, Newark, and Detroit-all
the major outbursts of recent years-were precipitated by routine arrests of Negroes by white officers for minor offenses....
To many Negroes police have come to symbolize white
power, white racism and with repression. And the fact is that
many police do reflect and express these white attitudes.
(Kerner Commission 1968, 206)

In theory, the U.S. criminal justice system is based on principles of
fairness, justice, and equity. This system of justice is guided by the
principles outlined in the U.S. Constitution. In the Preamble to the
Constitution, the founders of the U.S. stated that the purpose of our
nation was to "establish justice, insure domestic tranquility, provide
for the common defense, promote the general welfare, and secure the
blessings of liberty to ourselves and our posterity."

The Bill of Rights is a fundamental component of the Constitution. Indeed, without the Bill of Rights the Constitution would be a

seriously flawed document. The founders were insightful in giving weight to the rights of the accused. From their perspective, in order for a democracy to flourish, the civil liberties of individuals had to be protected (Schmidt, Shelley, and Bardes 1999).

Ostensibly, the staunch protection of civil liberties is what separates the U.S. from totalitarian nations. In nations under a totalitarian regime, police, acting as agents of the government, have no regard for the basic civil liberties of individuals. They have no regard for human rights. In these regimes, individuals do not have equal protection under the law.

The cornerstone of the post-Civil War system of justice is the Equal Protection clause found in the Fourteenth Amendment to the U.S. Constitution. This amendment states that no state shall "deprive any person of life, liberty, or property, without due process of law; nor deny to any person within its jurisdiction the equal protection of the law."

Social Justice Theory

What is social justice? The term is socially constructed. It is based on the social, political, and economic reality of a society. In the contemporary capitalist society, social justice in the context of crime revolves around promoting and maintaining law and order (Quinney 1999). However, the definition of social justice is amorphous.

Over the years, definitions of social justice have changed. Plato and Aristotle developed versions of social justice, which lack applicability to the discussion of the U.S. criminal justice system. In the Republic, Plato states that a just state has three social classes: workers, soldiers, and rulers. Justice is said to be the performance by each class of its job and noninterference in the jobs of the other classes. In his Ethics, Aristotle starts with what all men agree is the aim of life, eudaimonia (happiness). He states that in seeking happiness all men are seeking to actualize to the best of their capabilities (Flew 1979; Arrigo 1999). Although the works of these Greek philosophers are largely inapplicable, the U.S. has developed its liberal democracy around the works of other social philosophers.

According to Immanuel Kant's ethical formalism, any behavior that cannot be categorized as "just and proper" is immoral. John Stuart Mill's theory of justice revolves around utilitarianism, the "greatest good for the greatest possible number of people." Mill's philosophy is based on "consequence of behavior" not the act itself. Thomas Hobbes sets forth his principles of justice in his *Leviathan*. According to Hobbes, justice revolves around 1) the "right of nature," which is the liberty that each man has to use his own power as he sees fit for his survival; 2) "liberty," which is the absence of external impediments; and 3) the "law of nature," by which a man is forbidden to do that which is destructive to his own life (Arrigo 1999).

John Locke theorizes in his *Two Treatises on Government* that initially people entered into a "social contract" with the government in order to protect property rights and be protected from interpersonal violence. In exchange for this protection, people gave the government their "consent to be governed." Locke states that if the government abuses its rights, it can be legitimately replaced (Locke 1967). Locke's conception of justice is applicable to the discussion of the U.S. criminal justice system because the founders relied on the writings of Locke to guide them in constructing a system of democratic governance.

Indeed, many phrases of the *Declaration of Independence* repeat parts of Locke's *Two Treatises* verbatim: people are endowed "with certain unalienable rights"; governments come about "to secure these rights" and to gain "their just powers from the consent of the governed"; and whenever government "becomes destructive of [the] ends" for which it was set up in the first place, "it is the right of the people to alter or to abolish it." Locke's argument became the basis for forming a popular government as well as a justification for revolution (Kelman 1996).

More recent social philosophers have enhanced our understanding of the concept of social justice. Howard Zinn states in *Disobedience and Democracy* that there is no moral imperative to obey an immoral law, unless the very idea of obeying a law has legitimacy and moral value. John Rawls's theory of justice relies on two principles, equal liberty and democratic equality (Crawford 1973; Rawls 1971; Zinn 1968).

While many theorists and philosophers have discussed the issue of justice in the abstract, Martin Luther King, Jr.'s conception of social justice is the most relevant to the plight of African Americans in today's society. Indeed, we should use King's definition of social justice as the context for deciding the justness of the U.S. criminal justice system. King discusses the issue of social justice in a dialectical framework that exposes the glaring contradictions between the nation's noble creed and ignoble deeds. During the most tumultuous period of the civil rights movement, King was arrested in the city of Birmingham, Alabama, for protesting the unjust laws of segregation in the South. King poignantly highlighted the contradictions in America's system of justice in his famous "Letter From Birmingham Jail" of April 16, 1963:

> Injustice anywhere is a threat to justice everywhere.... Perhaps it is easy for those who have never felt the stinging darts of segregation to say, "Wait." But when you have seen vicious mobs lynch your mothers and fathers at will and drown your sisters and brothers at whim; when you have seen hate-filled policemen curse, kick and even kill your Black brothers and sisters; when you see the vast majority of your twenty million Negro brothers smothering in an airtight cage of poverty in the midst of an affluent society...then you will understand why we find it difficult to wait. (King 1964)

What are the criteria that render a law unjust? According to King, there are many factors, and he lists four: 1) if it degrades the human personality; 2) if it binds one group and not another; 3) if it is enacted by an authority not truly representative; and 4) if, though just in itself, it is unjustly applied. The presence of one of these factors is sufficient to make a law unjust (Crawford 1973).

The U.S. has created a system of criminal justice that meets all four of King's criteria for unjust laws. In fact, the U.S. system does not consistently equate with the various theories of social justice discussed. What makes the U.S. system inconsistent with the theories of Kant, Mill, Rawls, Hobbes, Locke, and Zinn is that the laws are unjustly applied. Not only is the U.S. system incongruent with the various theories of justice, this system is unequal to other systems of criminal justice in the Western world.

America's Trap

By 2000, the total number of people in America's prisons and jails reached two million. The U.S. contains 5 percent of the world's population, but 25 percent of the world's prison population. No nation in the world incarcerates a higher percentage of its population than the U.S. (Hallinan 2001). The U.S. per capita incarceration rate is second only to Russia's and is five times higher than that of the next highest Western nation.

Since 1980 the growth of prisons in the U.S. has exploded. In the 1990s, the U.S. added nearly 700,000 prisoners to its system, almost 30 times higher than the average rate of growth from 1920 through 1970. The prison population has increased by more than 50,000 in California alone since the 1980s. The majority of these inmates are young black men. Some 60 percent are nonviolent drug offenders (Feldman, Schiraldi, and Ziedenberg 2001). I was appalled when I visited the Mississipi Department of Corrections website (at www.mdoc.state.ms.us). I saw young black men with prison sentences grossly diproportionate to their crimes e.g. marijuana possesion—5 years, cocaine possession—8 years, shoplifting—10 years, receiving stolen property—3 years, selling cocaine—60 years.

In 1994 Congress passed the *Violent Crime Control and Law Enforcement Act*, which stiffened prison sentences and proliferated the building of prisons. As a result of this legislation, the U.S. Department of Justice has implemented a mandatory minimum sentence and many states have implemented a "three strikes and you're out" law, stating that if a person is convicted of three crimes they will be sentenced to twenty-five years to life in prison (Cole(a) 2000). This law was intended for those who committed three violent crimes; however, it has been grossly misused.

The criminal justice system has proven to be unsympathetic towards the disproportionate number of black men who are victims of three-strikes laws. An example of this apathy is the case of Jerry De-Wayne Williams, known to most in California as the "pizza thief." Because of a lengthy criminal history, Williams became eligible for his third strike by stealing a slice of pizza from a group of children. His original sentence was twenty-five years to life. The Williams case is not unique. A Los Angeles man was sentenced to twenty-five years to life in prison for stealing liquor from a store on two occasions and for stealing an umbrella on a rainy night. In March 2003 the U. S. Supreme Court, in a 5-4 decision, upheld the legitimacy of three-strikes laws. What message was the highest court in the land sending to black men? The Supreme Court ruled on two California cases that the state's three-strikes law did not yield "grossly disproportionate" sentences that violate the Eighth Amendment of the U.S. Constitution. In the case of Lockyer v. Andrade, Andrade was sentenced to two consecutive terms of twenty-five years to life for several felony theft convictions, two of which involved stealing a total of $150 worth of videotapes from two K-mart stores on two separate occasions. Because of Andrade's previous theft convictions, each theft qualified as a third strike. In Ewing v. California, Ewing was sentenced to twenty-five years to life for grand theft after he stole three golf clubs worth a total of $1,200. This offense also qualified as a third strike.

In July 2002 John Walker Lindh, the white twenty-one-year-old American who fought with the Taliban in Afghanistan, pleaded guilty to charges that are likely to keep him in prison for less than twenty years. Prosecutors agreed to drop other charges, including conspiracy to murder U.S. citizens, that could have kept him in prison for life. President Bush approved the arrangement. Contrast the Lindh case with the number of cases of black men who are being sent to prison from twenty-five years to life for petty theft and minor drug offenses.

Although youth crime decreased in California during the 1980s and 1990s, the voters of California voted for Proposition 21 in 2000. Proposition 21 requires that youth as young as fourteen be automatically tried as adults for certain offenses (Dorfman and Schiraldi 2001).

Today, 49 percent of inmates are black. Typically they come from the cities. Sticking them in the boondocks where family members have a hard time visiting-and where guards have likely never encountered anyone like them—almost always leads to problems, often violent ones. Yet this is where we build our prisons. These rural communities profit most from the prison boom: from the construction jobs and the prison jobs and all the spin-off business that prisons create. Yet it is hard to ignore that those who are getting rich are usually white and those in prison are usually not (Hallinan 2001, xiii).

A study conducted in 2001 concluded that 86 percent of white homicides are committed by other whites; and overall, whites are three times as likely to be victimized by other whites as by minorities. The probability that a white will be the victim of a crime by a black youth is small. Moreover, African Americans are underrepresented in reporting as victims and overrepresented in the news as perpetrators. Articles about white homicide victims tend to be longer and more frequent than the articles that cover African American victims (Dorfman and Schiraldi 2001).

In the 1950s, when segregation was legal, African Americans made up 30 percent of the nation's prison population. Today African Americans make up 12.8 percent of the U.S. population but 49 percent of all prison inmates. The federal government predicts that one of every four black men will be imprisoned during his lifetime (Palmer 1999; Hallinan 2001). While some who study the issues blame poverty and lack of economic opportunity for these statistics, others blame the police for targeting and concentrating their efforts in urban, predominantly black communities.

According to self-reported data compiled by the U.S. Public Health Service in 1999, African Americans constitute about 14 percent of the nation's illegal drug users. Yet they make up 35 percent of those arrested for drug possession, 55 percent of those convicted for drug possession, and 74 percent of those sentenced to serve time for their crimes. According to Human Rights Watch, relative to population, black men are admitted to state and federal prison on drug charges at 13.4 times the rate of white men. Black men are incarcerated for all offenses at 8.2 times the rate of whites. In seven states, blacks make up between 80 and 90 percent of all drug offenders sent to prison. One in every 20 black men is either in state or federal prison, compared to one in 180 white men (Cole(a) 2000; Human Rights Watch(a) 2002).

Congress passed a bill in the 1980s during the crack epidemic that punished a first-time offender using crack cocaine with five years in prison for possession of five grams of crack. A powder cocaine first-time offender would have to be caught with 500 grams of powder cocaine to receive an equivalent sentence. Civil rights leaders explain that the reason for this enormous disparity is that crack cocaine is used by poor blacks and powder cocaine is used by rich whites. These leaders also point to scientific studies showing that crack cocaine is no more addictive than powder cocaine (Holmes 2001).

The penalties for nonviolent drug offenders in the U.S. are disproportionate and harsh. One could say in this context that there is a conspiracy against young black men. Drug sentences for those in possession or retailing drugs sometimes exceed the sentences given for offenses such as robbery, rape, or murder. There is evidence suggesting that few drug offenders who are incarcerated are major drug traffickers. The massive imprisonment of drug offenders has failed to curb the availability of drugs in the United States.

Youth of color in the state of California are more than eight times more likely to be incarcerated by adult courts as white youth for equally serious crimes. Youth of color are also treated more severely than white youth at each stage of the justice system, even when charged with the same offenses. In the most recent reporting to the Office of Juvenile Justice and Delinquency Prevention of the U.S. Department of Justice, all reporting states but one found disproportionate confinement of minority youth (Dorfman and Schiraldi 2001).

The injustices embraced by the criminal justice system represent this country's most glaring human rights violation. Policymakers who desire to make prison a punishment-only endeavor have responded to the age-old question of whether prisons should be just for punishment, or for punishment and rehabilitation. For example, the Federal Prison Industries Competition in Contracting Act proposes to restrict inmate training and employment in federal and state prisons. Other proposals that have gained support restrict the educational opportunities and recreational activities of inmates. What are the consequences of restricting inmate access to these positive rehabilitative activities?

Those who support an ideologically conservative stance on prison policy cannot have it both ways. It is unrealistic to advocate for less crime and simultaneously support a punishment-only prison policy.

Race and Incarceration in the United States
(Rates of incarceration in adult correctional and confinedment
facilities per 100,000 state residents, by race)

	White	Black	Hispanic	Ratio, Black/White	Ratio, Hispanic/White
Alabama	373	1,797	914	4.8	2.4
Alaska	306	1,606	549	5.2	1.8
Arizona	607	3,818	1,263	6.3	2.1
Arkansas	468	2,185	1,708	4.7	3.7
California	487	3,141	820	6.4	1.7
Colorado	429	4,023	1,131	9.4	2.6
Connecticut	199	2,991	1,669	15.0	8.4
Delaware	361	2,500	330	6.9	0.9
District of Columbia	46	768	260	16.5	5.6
Georgia	544	2,153	620	4.0	1.1
Hawaii	173	577	587	3.3	3.4
Idaho	502	2,236	1,103	4.5	2.2
Illinois	216	2,273	426	10.5	2.0
Indiana	373	2,575	602	6.9	1.6
Iowa	300	3,775	923	12.6	3.1
Kansas	397	3,686	753	9.3	1.9
Kentucky	466	3,375	2,059	7.2	4.4
Louisiana	421	2,475	1,736	5.9	4.1
Maine	207	1,731	759	8.4	3.7
Maryland	282	1,749	230	6.2	0.8
Massachusetts	204	1,807	1,435	8.9	7.0
Michigan	357	2,256	951	6.3	2.7
Minnesota	197	2,811	1,031	14.3	5.2
Mississippi	353	1,762	3,131	5.0	8.9
Missouri	402	2,306	730	5.7	1.8
Montana	358	3,120	1,178	8.7	3.3
Nebraska	226	2,251	824	9.9	3.6
Nevada	630	3,206	676	5.5	1.1
New Hampshire	242	2,501	1,425	10.3	5.9
New Jersey	175	2,509	843	14.3	4.8
New Mexico	311	3,151	818	10.1	2.6

Race and Incarceration in the United States
(continued)

	White	Black	Hispanic	Ratio, Black/White	Ratio, Hispanic/White
New York	182	1,951	1,002	10.7	5.5
North Carolina	266	1,640	440	6.2	1.7
North Dakota	170	1,277	976	7.5	5.8
Ohio	333	2,651	865	8.0	2.6
Oklahoma	682	4,077	1,223	6.0	1.8
Oregon	488	3,895	777	8.0	1.6
Pennsylvania	281	3,108	2,242	11.1	8.0
Rhode Island	199	2,735	817	13.8	4.1
South Carolina	391	1,979	871	5.1	2.2
South Dakota	440	6,510	1,486	14.8	3.4
Tennessee	402	2,021	790	5.0	2.0
Texas	694	3,734	1,152	5.4	1.7
Utah	342	3,356	998	9.5	2.9
Vermont	183	2,024	799	11.1	4.4
Virginia	444	2,842	508	6.4	1.1
Washington	393	2,757	717	7.0	1.8
West Virginia	375	6,400	2,834	17.1	7.6
Wisconsin	341	3,953	863	11.6	2.5
Wyoming	740	6,529	1,320	8.8	1.8
National	378	2,489	922	6.6	2.4

Figures calculated on basis of U.S. Census Bureau data
from Census 2000 on state residents and incarcerated population.
Human Rights Watch 2002(b).

Such a strategy would work ideally only if we segregated the freed-inmate population and placed them on a deserted island. Every day some 1,600 inmates are released from prison. Without job skills or education, how can these people be integrated into society? Following 272,111 state inmates released in 1994, researchers found over three years that 67.5 percent were rearrested. How can our policymakers continue to be shortsighted on prison policies? According to Knut Rostad, president of the Enterprise Prison Institute, training and work allow inmates to break the monotony of prison life. Prisoners covet jobs that pay. There is high competition for prison employment. Hence, prison employment functions as a powerful tool for behavioral control. It creates a positive environment that promotes rehabilitation.

The System

The U.S. is incarcerating an entire generation of black men. The statistics have significant social implications because this population does not have jobs, pay taxes, or care for their children at home. Because forty-five states and the District of Columbia deny the right to vote to offenders in prison, at least one of seven African American males has lost at least temporarily the right to vote. Thirty-two of these states deny the right to vote to those on parole. Fourteen states have laws prohibiting felons from voting for life. "Felony disenfranchisement" prohibits approximately four million Americans—mostly underprivileged and minority—from voting. For instance, 31 percent of black males of voting age in Alabama and Florida are barred from voting because of felony convictions. Nationally, the number of black men who are disenfranchised because of their conviction status is 13 percent, many for life, compared to less than 2 percent for whites (Cole(b) 2000, 17A).

Opportunities are restricted for many young blacks to engage in full citizenship. In order for a democracy to thrive, all citizens must have the opportunity to engage in the various aspects of public life.

Democracy recognizes the dignity and worth of each person...by authorizing the lowliest as well as the mightiest to participate in governing, our government publicly affirms the value of every human. (Kelman 1996, 7)

The unequal treatment of young black men in the United States betrays the fundamental principles of democracy. Not only are young black men subjected to unequal treatment, they are also being exploited by the system. Regions that lost manufacturing jobs and were left out of the economic boom of the 1990s are increasingly relying on prisons as a primary source of employment. Big companies involved in the prison industry are estimated to generate more than $30 billion a year. Many states have spent more on building prisons than they have on universities.

My mentally ill cousin has been in and out of jails for years. I often wondered why he could not use his phone card when he called me from the jail premises. The telephone company—AT&T—estimates that inmates place approximately $1 billion worth of long distance calls annually. Inmates are forced to use one long distance carrier-the one chosen by the prison—and they may make only collect calls. The price is sometimes inflated to $5.00 per minute—fifty times the price paid in the general market. Prisons receive "kickbacks" of up to 50 cents per call. As Joseph Hallinan states, "a single pay phone could earn its owner up to $12,000...and it has made corrections departments phone-call millionaires" (Hallinan 2001, xiv).

Prisons have to contract with businesses to provide clothes, sheets, toothpaste, soap, and a variety of other necessities. Big business has exploited the opportunity to build prisons and to contract with prisons for profit. Before 1983 there were no private prisons in the United States. Today there are more than 150 (Hallinan 2001, xvii). With the growing demand for prison construction, there is an equal demand to keep these prisons occupied. These demands have come at the expense of young black men.

How do we explain the proliferation of prisons in the U.S.? How do we explain the staggering disparities between the treatment of blacks and the treatment of whites in the justice system? Two factors generally explain these two scenarios: capitalistic exploitation and racism.

Alexis de Tocqueville stated in 1835 in *Democracy in America* that the unequal treatment of blacks in the United States would lead to a revolution. He predicted the Civil War. Unequal treatment has historically been the impetus for most of the race riots that have taken place in the U.S. Indeed, the race riots of 1919, 1965, 1992, and 2001 were caused by the unequal treatment of blacks. This pattern will likely continue unless fundamental issues are addressed.

According to Sasha Abramsky, during the 1980s approximately 600 new prisons opened, at a price of $6 billion. In 1988, during a time when the rates of AIDS and asthma and tuberculosis increased, more than eighty community hospitals that serviced the urban poor were closed.

Racial polarization, racial bias, and racial insensitivity have threatened to undermine the strong foundation of a variety of American institutions, especially the criminal justice system. The passage of the Thirteenth, Fourteenth, and Fifteenth Amendments to the U.S. Constitution ended the federal government's official endorsement of racial discrimination in the U.S. However, blatant discrimination still exists. The criminal justice system has embraced the legacy of America's unattractive past.

As the great African American leader Booker T. Washington stated in his 1895 *Atlanta Exposition Address,* "The laws of changeless justice bind oppressor with oppressed; and close as sin and suffering joined. We march to fate abreast." King eloquently stated in his 1963 Letter From Birmingham Jail, "We are caught in an inescapable network of mutuality, tied in a single garment of destiny."

Since the Rodney King beating, the situation for young black men has become drastically worse. Civil liberties law in the U.S. has evolved significantly in the past 40 years. However, in the past decade, these laws have increasingly been applied unequally. What does this say about the U.S. model of liberal democracy? Statistical disparities and unequal treatment between blacks and whites suggest the U.S. criminal justice system meets the criteria for injustice established by Martin Luther King, Jr.: the system degrades human personality, it binds one group and not another, it is enacted by an authority not truly representative, and is unjustly applied.

The United States cannot continue to ignore the disparities in the criminal justice system and the unequal treatment of a significant sector of its population. The health and well-being of America's liberal democracy is being undermined by this unjust system. In order for the U.S. to tout its system as a model of democracy for the world, it must remedy the systemic race-based problems that are at its foundation. The cornerstone of a civil society is respect for the "heterogeneous." The role of government and all its agents is to carry out duties in ways that exemplify fairness, justice, and equity. The legitimacy of the U.S. model of democracy depends on its ability to embrace these fundamental principles.

It is up to the black civil rights organizations and lobbyists to counter the inequalities of the system. Where are the civil rights organizations on this issue? How could they continue to allow America to victimize a significant portion of the African American population? Where are the black congresspersons and mayors? If this is not on their agenda, what is? If black ministers are not preaching about saving their sons from walking into America's Trap, then what are they preaching about? The disparities in the criminal justice system and the young black man's enticement into this system are the most pressing issues facing the black community. It is having a paralyzing effect on the black community.

I interviewed a friend for this book; he was once a probation officer and held the position of Senior Parole Officer for the Georgia State Board of Pardons and Parole. I asked him what he thought about young black men and the criminal justice system. He told me that "the system might be biased but brothers do not focus on trying to stay out of the system. They lack the discipline and motivation to play by the rules." He went on to say that it is very difficult for a person to get sent to prison for a first offense unless it is a violent crime. He stated that in about 80 percent of his cases, the judge will give the person a probated sentence—meaning they will give the person alternative ways to pay restitution before sending them to prison. For instance, a judge might instruct a person to take substance-abuse or anger-management classes and provide 100 hours of community service; order them to pay $100 per month as restitution for theft; and mandate that they see their probation officer once each month. My friend stated that young black men often ignore the judge's instructions and engage in the same behaviors-behaviors that ultimately land them in prison. "Instead of learning from their mistakes and correcting negative behavior, they try to perfect their crime the next time around. They try to out-slick the system. In my opinion, brothers are blindly walking into quicksand."

While I was listening to a popular hip-hop station in Los Angeles on a Sunday evening, I heard a young man interviewed at a community empowerment rally. A former gang member, he said, "We been tricked.

All of the stuff we told y'all young guys was wrong. We need to now get our heads right and focus on coming up."

Young black men cannot continue to walk into America's Trap. It seems that this trap has been specifically set for them. It has taken thought, strategy, and a comprehensive effort to construct a system that is so unjust. It will take thought, strategy, and a comprehensive effort to undermine this system. Young black men must know that there are dire consequences for embracing society's stereotypes. They cannot continue to behave without thought. Their margin of error is too small.

References

Abramsky, Sasha. 2002. Hard Time Blues. New York: St. Martin's Press.

Arrigo, Bruce A, ed. 1999. Social Justice/Criminal Justice: The Maturation of Critical Theory in Law, Crime, and Deviance. Belmont, California: West/Wadsworth.

Baldwin, James. 1964. Nobody Knows My Name: More Notes From a Native Son. London: Penguin.

Cole, David. 2000(a). Why so severe? Tough-on-crime policies burden a disempowered minority. L.P. Fulton County Daily Report, 21 January.

Cole, David. 2000(b). Denying felon vote hurts them, society. USA Today. 3 February.

Crawford, Curtis. 1973. Civil Disobedience: A Casebook. New York: Thomas Y. Crowell.

Delattre, Edwin J. 1996. Character and Cops: Ethics in Policing. Washington, D.C.: AEI Press.

de Tocqueville, Alexis. [1835] 1994. Democracy in America. New York: Knopf (distributed by Random House).

Dorfman, Lori, and Vincent Schiraldi. 2001. Off balance: youth, race, and crime in the news. Justice Policy Institute, April.

Feldman, Lisa, Vincent Schiraldi, and Jason Ziedenberg. 2001. Too little too late: President Clinton's prison legacy. Justice Policy Institute, February.

Flew, Antony. 1979. A Dictionary of Philosophy. New York: St. Martin's Press.

Hallinan, Joseph T. 2001. Going Up River: Travels in a Prison Nation. New York: Random House.

Holmes, Steven A. 2001. In his final week, Clinton issues proposals on race. New York Times, 14 January.

Human Rights Watch(a). 2002. Race and The Criminal Justice System: Summary and Recommendations. New York: Human Rights Watch. Also available at http://www.hrw.org/us/usdom.php.

Human Rights Watch(b). 2002. Race and incarceration in the United States. Press Backgrounder, 22 February.

Kelman, Steven. 1996. American Democracy and The Public Good. Fort Worth, Texas: Harcourt Brace College Publishers.

Kerner Commission. 1968. Supplemental Studies for the National Advisory Commission on Civil Disorders. New York: Praeger.

King, Martin Luther, Jr. 1964. Why We Can't Wait. New York: Harper and Row.

Locke, John. [1690] 1967. Two Treatises on Government. Introduction by Peter Laslett. Cambridge: Cambridge University Press.

Palmer, Louise D. 1999. More blacks serving time in U.S. prisons, urban patrols seen as reason. Boston Globe, 21 March.

Quinney, Richard. 1999. The prophetic meaning of social justice. In Social Justice/Criminal Justice: The Maturation of Critical Theory in Law, Crime, and Deviance, edited by Bruce A. Arrigo. Belmont, California: West/Wadsworth.

Rawls, John. 1971. A Theory of Justice. Cambridge: Harvard University Press.

Rostad, Knut A. 2002. Should companies be allowed to employ inmates at federal and state prisons? Insight on the News, 1 October.

Russell, Katheryn. 1999. Critical race theory and social justice. In Social Justice/Criminal Justice: The Maturation of Critical Theory in Law, Crime, and Deviance, edited by Bruce A. Arrigo. Belmont, California: West/Wadsworth.

Schmidt, Steffen W., Mack C. Shelley, and Barbara A Bardes. 1999. American Government and Politics Today. Stamford, Connecticut: Thomson /Wadworth.

Zinn, Howard. 1968. Disobedience and Democracy. New York: Random House.

Chapter 9

Black-on-Black Violence

I remember Johnny saying that the only thing in life a bad nigger was scared of was living too long. This just meant that if you were going to be respected in Harlem, you had to be a bad nigger; and if you were a bad nigger, you had to be ready to die. (Brown 1965, 122)

The Autobiographies of Black Men

Most of the autobiographies I have read by black male authors discuss ways in which they negotiated their black masculinity. These authors also discuss ways in which they developed their black male identity. The most common narrative is that they grew up in a household that had limited financial resources. Their fathers were either not around or were not particularly attentive or sensitive to their needs and problems. They turned to the streets to rebel against society and/or to get street credibility. They stole, fought, and did drugs. Developing respect and a tough-guy reputation among peers became the primary motivator for engaging in most illicit or rebellious activities.

This was the narrative in the autobiographies of Claude Brown, Quincy Jones, Nathan McCall, James McBride, and others that I have read over the years. The following are excerpts from their autobiographies.

Claude Brown

I still had my rep at Warwick [boy's camp]. Before I left the second time, I was running BI cottage; I had become the "main man".... Since I didn't get many visitors from home, I made other guys pay protection fees to me when they received visits or packages from home.... I didn't have to bully anybody—cats knew that I knew how to hit a guy and knock out a tooth or something like that, so I seldom had to hit a cat. My reputation for hurting cats was indisputable.... I knew that I was going to have to get a gun sooner or later and that I was going to have to make my new rep and take my place along with the bad niggers of the community. (Brown 1965, 122 and 149)

Quincy Jones

Lloyd [Quincy's brother] and I were the first kids to arrive in Sinclair Heights. For years we'd been running from and with gangs in Chicago who wouldn't think twice about punching out a stranger, tying a knotted sheet around each ankle, and dragging you face and hands down five blocks.... Finally we had graduated to our own turf. Two things you can depend on carrying through life from the 'hood are attitude and antennae. We had the run of the land, and we let everyone who arrived after us know it. We took charge of everything in Sinclair Heights like we saw the gangs do back in Chicago: all jobs, the territory, the crime—all ours. (Jones 2001, 26)

Nathan McCall

The best way to guarantee respect was simply to be able to thump. Then nobody disrespected you. If they did, they paid a price. Once a guy made somebody pay for disrespecting him, the word went out that he 'don't take no shit.' Everybody else got the message, and it stuck. One dude who hung with Scobe and his boys earned his rep by breaking another guy's nose in a fight.... I thought about that fight every time I saw him after that. Guys would say, 'Don't fuck with him. He broke a niggah's nose.' There was admiration in their tone when they said things like that. I wanted that kind of respect. Everybody I knew wanted it. So we all worked on our knuck games to earn our reps. We tried to learn various ways to hurt people, to fuck somebody up so bad it was remembered in the streets for a long, long time. (McCall 1994, 54–55)

James McBride

Me and my hanging-out boys were into the movies. Super-fly, Shaft, and reefer, which we smoked in as much quantity as possible. I snatched purses. I shoplifted. I even robbed a petty drug dealer once.... We broke into cars. We snuck onto the nearby Conrail/Long Island Rail Road tracks and broke into freight cars, robbing them of bicycles, television sets, and wine.... And then in the afternoons, coming home after a day of cutting school, smoking reefer, waving razors, and riding the subway, I would see my mother pedaling her blue bicycle. (McBride 1996, 6 and 139)

Indeed, it is intriguing to read how these successful black men balanced establishing street credentials with their desire to move beyond the code of the streets. Every male in this society has to develop a strategy for negotiating his masculinity. It is particularly difficult for black men to find the right formula in this exercise. While white men affirm their masculinity by making money, being decision makers, interacting with the outdoors—fishing, hunting, golfing—and completely achieving the American Dream, affirming masculinity for black men is based on other criteria. For instance, making money is secondary to how you make it and achieving the American Dream is secondary to how you achieve it.

The primary criteria for black maleness are toughness and rebelliousness. The toughest person is defined by fighting, stealing, killing, doing time in prison, or showing talent in sports, coupled with rebellion in work and career, dress, style, and/or speech. These characteristics define the most "authentic" black male. The most negative label one can have in the black community is that of a sell-out or an Uncle Tom. Equivalent to being the "House Negro" during slavery, these labels are so debilitating that many blacks run so far in the opposite direction that their behavior becomes radical, irrational, and counterproductive.

The pressures of achieving authenticity in the black community put the black man in a quagmire. On the streets he is revered for his toughness and rebelliousness. However, in the mainstream working-world, his merit is based on the antithesis of what is revered on the streets of his community. For instance, when interviewing a potential black male employee, the interviewer wants to know if he will be loyal, if he can follow instructions, if he can take constructive criticism, if he can be a team player. The interviewer does not give him points for doing time in the joint, smoking reefer, his gang affiliation, pistol-whipping, or—as in McCall's words—his ability to break "a niggah's nose."

Trying to achieve credibility in both worlds is indeed an exhausting exercise. There are dire consequences for not walking the tightrope. If one errs on the side of the mainstream, he is labeled a sell-out; this label is perhaps irreparable. If one errs on the side of toughness and rebelliousness, he sabotages his career and his life. He is doomed to a life on the fringes of society.

I too had to negotiate my black maleness growing up. I had to find the formula that would allow me to affirm my masculinity. I excelled in sports. The ultimate objective for me—as it was for Claude, Nathan, James, and Quincy—was to establish my street credibility without sabotaging my future.

Causes of Black-on-Black Violence

Michael Moore's 2002 film *Bowling for Columbine* is an intriguing portrayal of America's violent and contradictory past and present. In this documentary, Moore candidly examines America's fascination with guns and the ubiquitous fear of the invader. Abroad, the invader is Muslim. Domestically, he is black. America's fear of the black male is seen as a primary justification for a citizen's right to bear arms.

We live in a society that inundates us with images of blacks in handcuffs or on mug shots. Many blacks are outraged at the one-sided images that appear nightly on the news. As the media continue to demean and criminalize the black male, black men continue to give them reasons to do so.

The Los Angeles Police Department (LAPD) homicide detective Brent Josephson sums up the death and violence that he calls "The Monster." "There lies the body. There's the family behind the yellow tape. We have three minutes for them. Then they're left with all the pain and all the loss." *Los Angeles Times* crime reporter Jill Leovy examines The Monster in an intriguing story about black-on-black homicide in Los Angeles. "The homicide problem. The routine. The invisibility. The overwhelmed institutions. An entire system, which leaves little room for compassion" (Leovy 2003, A23).

According to the U.S. Department of Justice, 14.7 percent of violent crimes committed against whites in the year 2000 were caused by blacks. However, of all the violent crimes committed against blacks in 2000, 81.9 percent were caused by other blacks. Although young black men account for only 3 percent of the nation's population, they consistently account for over 40 percent of the murders annually in the U.S. This is a startling statistic. Many have sought explanations for this alarming phenomenon.

According to some, residential segregation is one of the causes of black-on-black homicide. In their article "Segregation and Crime: The Effect of Black Social Isolation on the Rates of Black Urban Violence" in Social Forces, Edward Shihadeh and Nicole Flynn examine the link between black isolation and black urban violence. Past research suggests that segregation has tended to increase rates of intra-racial victimization. Shihadeh and Flynn discovered in their research that segregation acts as a major predictor of robbery and homicide among blacks. The variables that exacerbate black-on-black violence are rates of female-headed households, youth institutional attachment, unemployment, and poverty.

In her article "White, Black, and Latino Homicide Rates: Why the Difference?" in Social Problems, Julie Phillips states, "Family dissolution reduces both formal and informal social controls at the community level, which in turn may increase propensities for violence." She suggests that if whites were subjected to the same pressures and barriers to success, they would exhibit similar behavior. No contemporary research studies have proved that particular ethnic groups are predisposed to violence. Research reveals the opposite phenomenon: living in structurally and economically impoverished environments leads to more rebellious and delinquent behavior and higher rates of violence.

Mary Eamon in her article "Poverty, Parenting, Peer and Neighborhood Influences on Young Adolescent Antisocial Behavior" in the Journal of Social Service Research states that poverty exerts a direct, independent effect on child and youth antisocial behavior. Studies suggest that parenting practices and peer influences mediate the relation between poverty and young adolescent antisocial behavior. According to Eamon, childhood peer rejection leads to antisocial behavior. Poor children, for a variety of reasons, are more susceptible to being ridiculed and rejected by their peers.

In his paper "Black-on-Black Violence," James Clarke, a professor of political science at the University of Arizona, views black-on-black violence from a historical, race-based perspective. One of his theories is that the criminal justice system has failed blacks in America. Historically, police protection has been a lower priority in the black community. As long as blacks were killing blacks, there was not a sense of urgency to step in and remedy the situation. Retired LAPD Deputy Chief Willie L. Pannell supports Clarke's argument. According to Pannell, who grew up as a sharecropper in rural Georgia, in the Jim Crow South the law was made to protect whites. He states, "A black man who killed a white man could expect to feel its full weight—and then some. But a black man who killed a black man acted with impunity. As a young black man you lived without the protection of the law" (Leovy 2003, 8). According to Clarke, the legacy of this attitude can be seen today in the inner cities.

As a board member of the Charles Drew Child Development Corporation in Watts, I have made a commitment to help reverse various negative trends in South Central Los Angeles. This organization's mission is to provide a myriad of social services to the residents there. One disconnect I see, however, is between the organization's objectives and the nature of the problem. The organization's objectives are rational—and many of the problems are based on irrationality.

Self-Loathing

The aforementioned scholarly explanations of black-on-black violence are all valid. These studies look at the external factors that have an effect on black-on-black violence. These studies do not focus on the internal and irrational aspects of black-on-black crime, however. Many ethnic groups have started their journey to success in the U.S. mired in poverty and victimized by discrimination. However, no other ethnic group has been devastated by intra-racial violence as blacks have been. I agree that no population in the U.S. has faced as much virulent and systematic demonization as the black man. Nevertheless, this traumatic past does not wholly account for the senselessness of black intra-racial violence today.

Is there a scholarly explanation for the death of Peter Drake, Jr., who was killed in Los Angeles in 2002? Drake's killers shot him from behind. As he lay wounded, his killers stood over him and shot him eleven more times. They finally put the gun in his mouth and blew out his teeth. King/Drew Medical Center trauma surgeon Bryan Hubbard says the carnage he sees inflicted by blacks on other blacks is incomprehensible (Leovy 2003, A22 and A24).

The 1990s feud between East Coast and West Coast rappers ultimately led to the deaths of two rap legends, Tupac Shakur and Notorious BIG. The deaths of these two stars highlighted the single most detrimental pathology in the black community, black-on-black violence. Many blacks continue to blame racism for the social ills facing the black community; too few are looking inward to find solutions to the problems. In other words, who is to blame for the deaths of Tupac and Notorious BIG? Can we blame the media and the music industry for blowing their feuds out of proportion? Or should we blame racist cops?

The Rolling Stones had a rivalry in the 1970s with the Who. In the 1980s Guns N' Roses had a rivalry with Mötley Crüe. The boy-band groups 'NSYNC and the Backstreet Boys had an intense rivalry in the late 1990s. However, the battles that these white bands waged against each other were limited to lyrical content. None of these groups even considered murdering their rivals. Why is there a need for black rappers to challenge rivals through violence?

When thirty-seven-year-old Jam Master Jay, the famed DJ of the pioneering group Run-DMC, was murdered in his studio in Queens, New York, in October 2002, there was no talk of race riots. Although the masked culprit was not immediately identified, everyone knew, intuitively, that the person who shot Jam Master Jay was black. Russell Simmons, co-founder of Def Jam Records and chairman of the Hip-Hop Summit, stated after the hip-hop icon's death, "The tragic death of Jam Master Jay should serve as a reminder of the condition of poverty, ignorance and lack of opportunity inherent in our urban communities across the country." Ironically, Jam Master Jay was the mentor for "the realest, the illest, the killest" rapper, 50 Cent.

During the same week as Jam Master Jay's funeral, the popular, twenty-six-year-old black television and film actor Merlin Santana of the Eddie Murphy film *Showtime* and *The Steve Harvey Show* sitcom was killed in South Central Los Angeles. Before the culprit was identified, Steve Harvey stated in an interview, "we have to stop killing ourselves." The week after Santana's killing proved to be the most violent in Los Angeles history. In an eight-day period, twenty people-most of them in a one-square-mile area of South Central Los Angeles—were gunned down. Leovy writes:

> To lose someone in this way is to endure a catastrophe the world scarcely seems to notice. It is to wait behind yellow tape as your child dies beneath the hands of paramedics. It is to pull up your son's T-shirt and count the bullet holes in his back. It is to feel angry at blacks, angry at whites, angry at police and angry at killers still on the loose. (Leovy 2003, A22)

Chief William J. Bratton of the LAPD called the killing "tit-for-tat" violence. He pointed out, "people will think nothing of shooting at someone because they looked at them wrong or were wearing the wrong color or drove by at the wrong time" (Garvey and Garrison 2002, 29). During 2002, homicides in Los Angeles increased by 10 percent. For the fifth year straight, African Americans—who make up just 11 percent of the population of Los Angeles—accounted for 40 percent of the murder victims. Leovy reports, "Santa Monica, for example, has a murder rate similar to that of the safest European nations. By contrast, South Central L.A.-just a few miles away by freeway-has the murder rate double that of Bogotá, Colombia" (Leovy 2003, 22).

In September of 2003, Venus and Serena Williams's oldest sister, Yetunde Price, was shot and killed in Compton, CA. This senseless murder appalled and saddened many people worldwide. The suspect is a young black man.

As I watched the local news during the spate of black-on-black murders, I listened to what the local residents had to say. One resident observed, "Why are you blaming police? They're not killing us. We're killing ourselves." In speaking about the gang violence, the mayor of Los Angeles, James Hahn, stated, "It's not the police's fault. The community has a degree of fault to share. There are places in the cities where values have broken down, there are fourth- and fifth-generation gang members." In Los Angeles County, young black men are killed at four times the rate of Latinos and eighteen times the rate of white men.

Young black men have acted out their ultra-macho behavior on each other in the form of black-on-black violence. This self-destruction is romanticized in movies and music. Two of the record industry's most successful black record labels have been Death Row and Murder Inc. What is glamorous about death row and murder? The ultimate way for a black man to get street credibility is by killing someone and doing time in prison for it. This is peculiar. Imagine trying to explain this cultural code of honor to a visitor from another country. Claude Brown affirms this phenomenon:

> In our childhood, we all had to make our reputations in the neighborhood. Then we'd spend the rest of our lives living up to them. A man was respected on the basis of his reputation. The people in the neighborhood whom everybody

looked up to were cats who'd killed somebody. The little boys
in the neighborhood whom the adults respected were the little boys who didn't let anybody mess with them. (Brown
1965, 256)

Sanyika Shakur-formerly known as Monster Kody Scott—devotes
many pages in his riveting book Monster to the consequences of false
bravado and self-destructive behavior. In the year *Monster* was released, Los Angeles experienced 1,077 killings, most of which were
gang-related. Shakur discusses how he "put in work" for his "set"-his
gang—to gain his reputation. "Putting in work" meant going out and
killing as many people in rival gangs as possible. Shakur came to be
revered by some and respected by many in L.A.'s black community.
When I moved to Los Angeles in 1992, I was unaware of Shakur and
his reputation. I learned of it shortly after my arrival, however.

In the following passage, Shakur describes how he saw himself after
he finally achieved the status he had long sought.

By this time, I had become very egotistical. My reputation
had finally ballooned to the third stage and, by definition, I
had moved into the security zone of O.G. [original gangsta]
status. My rep was omnipresent, totally saturating every circle of gang life. From CRASH to the courts, from Crips to
Bloods, from Juvenile Hall to death row, Monster Kody had
arrived. This, coupled with my newfound curiosity and interest in Mafia-style gangsta-ism, made me hard to approach.
(Shakur 1994, 208)

Menaces To Society

The 1993 film *Menace II Society*, written and directed by Allen and
Albert Hughes, is a raw and disturbing representation of the casual
nature of black-on-black violence. In one of the trailers that preceded
the film, actor Charles S. Dutton, on behalf of the Institute for Black
Parenting, appeals to young black men to halt their violent behavior.
Dutton says that violence is taking place "because guys who think they

are cool settle every argument with a gun." He goes on to state, "turning away from violence and rebuilding the community is your responsibility, not somebody else's." Trailers for three violent movies followed Dutton's public service advertisement.

Menace II Society is a story of poverty, drugs, alcohol, and gang warfare. It is a story about false bravado and self-destruction. The film opens with the character O-Dog (Larenz Tate)—deemed America's nightmare—walking into a Korean market with his friend Caine (Tyrin Turner). O-Dog acts in a rebellious fashion towards the male and female Korean merchants. This prompts the male merchant to express sympathy for O-Dog's mother. O-Dog responds with, "What did you say about my mama?" He then shoots the man three times in the head. He forces the woman to give him the store's monitoring video. Once he gets it, he shoots the woman three times. He then calmly proceeds to look for money in the cash register and in the slain man's pockets. Later, O-Dog brags and demonstrates to his friends how he shot the Korean gentleman. They all watch the video of the murder for entertainment. O-Dog compares himself to actor Steven Seagal.

Later in the film, O-Dog casually shoots a crack addict. The addict initially offers O-Dog a couple of cheeseburgers for money. He then offers to give O-Dog sexual favors for money. O Dog erupts with anger at this affront to his manhood. He murders the man, picks up the cheeseburgers, and casually offers them to his shocked friends who had just witnessed his maniacal act.

The son of a dope dealer and a heroin addict, Caine grew up surrounded by bad influences. When we first see him in the film, he has just graduated from high school. He is relatively innocent. However, the pressures of his immediate environment slowly transform him into a dangerous villain.

When Caine is about eight years old, a neighborhood hustler shows him how to hold a gun. Later, we see Caine as a teenager, showing an eight-year-old boy how to hold a gun. In this film, the gun is seen as a magical instrument. It has the power to transform. The film depicts how young black men idolize, revere, and worship the gun. "Being strapped"—possessing a gun at all times—is a way of life. Moreover, the gun and the respect that comes from using it are romanticized in the film. Nothing in the universe can give the poor and uneducated young black man the power and respect of the gun.

Menace II Society reflects the violence of the inner city and romanticizes it at the same time. O-Dog became an icon to a generation of young black men. His lack of respect for societal norms, his ruthlessness in taking life, and his casual attitude about death became traits that many young black men desire to emulate. For example, while working on this section of the book, I read a Los Angeles Times article about a twenty-one-year-old African American man who drove down to the local store and was confronted by some black youth flashing gang signs. When he failed to respond, the gang members fired shots, putting a bullet in his car. He was caught "slippin." Being caught slippin means that a person has been observed in a state of unawareness; they have unwittingly become relaxed in dangerous surroundings. According to O-Dog's logic, anyone who is caught slippin deserves to be killed. Imagine the hundreds of black men who have been killed in gang violence because they were caught slippin. Many young gangstas have killed other young black men because they were caught in this state.

When I first entered graduate school at the University of Southern California, I lived close to campus in what some consider South Central Los Angeles. My residence was very close to many of the notorious gang sets. Upon arrival, it was hard for me to adjust to the car alarms, the screeching cars, and the helicopters ("ghetto birds") patrolling at night. I had seen the movies and heard all of the stories about gang violence in Los Angeles. I was warned by some of my astute friends who had seen the same movies and heard similar stories, not to get caught slippin.

One night I went to a birthday party in the heart of gang territory. I could not enjoy myself because of my paranoia. I did not want to be caught slippin. Late in the night four guys came to the party, which was being held in the backyard of someone's house. They looked like they were ready to get into some trouble. One of the guys I was standing next to said, "Look's like it's about to be on." I replied with, "Man, I'm out of here." He responded, "It's too late for that now. I got you"—which meant he was packing a gun. I said to myself, "This is crazy." I had gone to a party just to celebrate someone's birthday and now I was about to be caught in the nonsensical violence of somebody's turf war. Fortunately, nothing serious happened that night; but the tension that came from the possibilities was enough to frighten others and me. During the three and a half years that I lived by USC, I was always on guard, always mindful of not being caught slippin.

False Bravado

The gang warfare between the notorious Crips and Bloods has resulted in the deaths of hundreds of young black men. What is at the heart of this feud? Throughout the history of the world, wars have been fought for various reasons. Land, religion, ethnicity, and ideology have been the most common. Some wars have been based on superficial differences. On what basis have young black men waged war against each other? Is it over land, religion, ethnicity, or ideology? If not, what is it over? They claim turf but do not own any land. They are of the same ethnic background and in some cases, they are related. If they have a religious belief, it is Christianity, although of an unpracticed form. The only issue left to justify their warfare is their ideology. Do they have different views on the government's role in our society? Do the Crips believe in a laissez-faire approach to government, while the Bloods feel strongly about a more hands-on government approach to solving our social problems? Perhaps they differ over our health care, social welfare, or fiscal policies.

When enraged, blacks have unwittingly taken out their frustrations on each other. High murder rates among black men, however, are not a recent phenomenon. Black men were twelve times more likely than white men to die by homicide as far back as the 1950s. The 1992 Los Angeles riots resulted in almost a billion dollars in property damage. Blacks and Latinos burned and looted stores in their own communities.

For all of the rhetoric that black men generate about rebellion and their dislike of the white man, black men historically have done relatively little to counter the white man's oppression and hegemony. The minor exception to this claim is the action taken by a few courageous members of the Black Panther Party during the 1960s. Franz Fanon states in *Black Skin, White Mask* that nearly every time a black population has encountered the white man on his soil, he has laid down arms and welcomed him—subsequently allowing himself to be victimized. Paul Robeson once stated that he was appalled at the extent to which African populations were dependent on their European masters for cues on how to think and how to behave. Robeson saw the source of this problem as an inferiority complex stemming from oppression (Robeson 1971, xiii).

While I was working for the Center for Multiethnic and Transnational Studies at USC, one of my colleagues—who was very active in the Black Power struggle in Los Angeles during the late 1960s—asked me a poignant question: "In the history of black people as we know it, have blacks ever killed more than a thousand whites?" I was caught off guard by the radical nature of the question. He was not advocating violence against whites; rather, he was asking a powerful question. After I gathered myself, I realized that it was the most provocative question I had ever been asked. He followed his initial question by urging me to "Add up all the slave rebellions, Nat Turner, Denmark Vesey, Gabriel Prosser, even add up those taken out by the Zulus in their encounters with the British in South Africa, the Ashanti battles with the British in Ghana—do you get 1,000 whites?" He concluded by saying that even if you can come up with 5,000 whites who have died at the hands of blacks, it is still telling because of the millions of blacks who have died at the hands of whites—the middle passage, slavery, war, lynchings, beatings, and police brutality. What does this say about the hypermasculinist behavior of black men?

A white man who wanted to sell insurance in South Central Los Angeles asked me if it was safe for him to go there. My response was, "Why not? It is safer for you to go there than it is for me." He was puzzled by my response. Statistics prove, however, that he would be multiple times safer walking the streets of South Central L.A. than I would be. This example suggests that the fictitious assault against the white man is idle rhetoric. It always has been. Blacks assault other blacks.

Gangsta rappers claim their music unifies the black masses, yet they stage those black-on-black bicoastal wars, fiercely protecting the turf that the white man owns; they claim their rhymes raise consciousness about white oppression, yet they conspire with that same white man to bring back blaxploitation in another form. (McCall 1997, 55)

Joseph Marshall, a former schoolteacher in San Francisco and the founder of the Omega Boys Club, states that many young black men are caught in a maelstrom of self-destructive behavior. Thousands of black men are in prisons because they abide by irrational rules of survival. In his poignant and insightful book *Street Soldier*, Marshall calls these rules the self-imposed "gottas."

Gotta handle my business.

Gotta do what I gotta do.

Gotta get my money on.

Gotta be down for my set [gang].

Gotta be down for my 'hood.

Gotta get my respect.

Gotta pack a gun to watch my back.

Gotta pack a gun to watch my homies' back.

Gotta be with my potna [partner], right or wrong. (Marshall 1996, 131)

The fact is that the black man's hypermasculinity is camouflaged in a false bravado that is only detrimental to his family and his community. There is nothing revolutionary about killing your own brothers. In order for young black men to be successful in society, they need to be able to distinguish the good from the bad, the negative from the positive. Currently, the values that many young black men embrace are twisted; they are dangerous and ignoble.

References

Brown, Claude. 1965. Manchild in the Promised Land. New York: Touchstone Books.

Clarke, J.W. 1996. Black-on-black violence. Online: Transaction Publishers, retrieved 9 February 2003 from http://www.sistahspace.com/nommo/bmc9.html.

Eamon, M.K. 2001. Poverty, parenting, peer and neighborhood influences on young adolescent antisocial behavior. Journal of Social Service Research 28 (1): 1–23.

Fanon, Franz. 1991. Black Skin, White Masks. New York: Grove Weidenfeld.

Garvey, Megan and Jessica Garrison. 2002. Get angry, Bratton tells L.A. Los Angeles Times, 21 November.

Jones, Quincy. 2001. Q: The Autobiography of Quincy Jones. New York: Doubleday.

Leovy, Jill. 2003. Mortal wounds: the unseen agony of black-on-black homicide. Los Angeles Times, 26 January.

Marshall, Joseph, Jr., and Lonnie Wheeler. 1996. Street Soldier. San Francisco:VisionLine Publishing.

McBride, James. 1996. The Color of Water. New York: Riverhead Books.

McCall, Nathan. 1994. Makes Me Wanna Holla. New York: Random House.

McCall, Nathan. 1997. What's Going On. New York: Random House.

Phillips, J. 2002. White, black, and Latino homicide rates: why the difference? Social Problems 49 (3): 349–373.

Robeson, Paul. [1958] 1971. Here I Stand. Reprint, with introduction by Lloyd Brown. Boston: Beacon Press.

Shakur, Sanyika. 1994. Monster: The Autobiography of an L.A. Gang Member. New York: Penguin Books.

Shihadeh, E.S., and N. Flynn. 1996. Segregation and crime: the effect of black social isolation on the rates of black urban violence. Social Forces 74 (4): 1325–1352.

Chapter 10

Black Icons

In 2002 I constructed a survey-formally titled, Survey of Young African American Men (13-19)—to gauge the perceptions, attitudes, and general knowledge of young black men aged thirteen to nineteen regarding various cultural issues. With the help of a research assistant, I distributed surveys to 756 young black men in twelve high schools in and around Los Angeles and Atlanta. I contacted various principals in the Los Angeles area and asked if they would assist me in administering the survey. I provided those principals who agreed to participate with a permission letter for them to send to the parents of the students.

I constructed the Realness Scale to gauge young black males' perceptions of which black men they view as "real" and which they view as "fake." The survey did not define what the term "real" meant. The objective was to allow the participants to decide what constituted "real" and what constituted "fake." I wanted the pattern of responses to leave room for interpretation. Instead of my attempting to decide what the participants were thinking as they responded to the Realness Scale, through various interviews with young black men I allowed them to elaborate on their rationale for ranking one person as "real" and another as "fake."

Respondents were asked to rate the following black icons according to whether they perceived them to be "real," "fake," or "in between." They were to mark 1 beside the person's name if they believed him to be real; mark 3 if they believed him to be fake; and 2 if they believed him to be in between.

Tupac Shakur   Kobe Bryant
Will Smith   Mike Tyson
Tiger Woods   David Robinson
Allen Iverson

The survey instrument, the permission letter, and other, related materials-including the tabulated results of the survey—are included in the Appendix. The charts below summarize the findings.

Some 150 surveys were completed in the Atlanta region and 606 surveys were completed in the Los Angeles region. In Atlanta, I also distributed surveys at a Christian youth conference. Initially, I distributed surveys only in the Los Angeles region; but later I wanted to see if there were significant disparities in responses between regions. There were none. Moreover, there were no significant disparities in responses between those surveys collected in the high schools and those collected at the Christian youth conference.

Tupac Shakur

Tupac Amaru Shakur was born Lesane Parish Crooks on June 16, 1971, in Brooklyn, New York. He was raised by his mother, who was a member of the Black Panther Party. When he was a small child, his mother changed his name to Tupac Amaru after an Incan revolu-

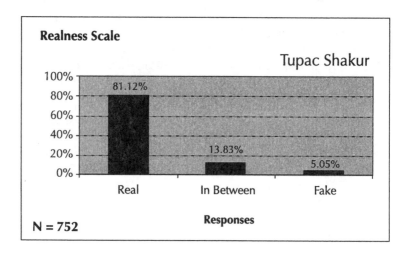

tionary, "Tupac Amaru," meaning "Shining Serpent." "Shakur" means "thankful to God" in Arabic. Tupac grew up poor and distressed; when he was very young, his mother frequently moved among various homeless shelters in New York. He once stated, "I remember crying all the time. My major thing growing up was, I couldn't fit in. Because I was from everywhere I didn't have no buddies that I grew up with" (Deggans 1996, 4A).

By the time he was twelve, Tupac had found a strong interest in acting, writing love songs, and composing poetry. As a teen, his family moved to Baltimore, and he attended the Baltimore School of the Performing Arts, where he studied acting and ballet. He left a strong impact on his teachers. His progress and development at this school was halted when he moved to Oakland, California, to join his family. At his high school in Oakland, he met and joined up with the group Digital Underground as a dancer.

After teaming with Digital Underground for a brief period, he released his own album *2Pacalypse Now* in 1992. The hit single "Brenda's Got A Baby" helped make this album a success and jumpstarted Shakur's career. Indeed, he was a rising star in music and in film. By the end of 1992, Tupac had played the role of a troubled street kid in the film *Juice*. He later starred in the films *Above the Rim* and *Poetic Justice*.

In 1994 Tupac released the album *Thug Life*. His transformation from the cerebral poet and talented actor was fast-forwarded with this album, which embraced and romanticized the rebellious behavior of thugs. He seemed to internalize his thug image when he got a machine gun tattooed on his chest and the words Thug Life on his stomach.

By the time Tupac was twenty, he had been arrested eight times. His troubles with the law began in 1992 when a six-year-old child was killed by a stray bullet—caught in the crossfire of a scuffle between Shakur and two other people. Tupac's record company agreed to settle a wrongful-death suit. A year later he was charged with shooting at two off-duty Atlanta police officers; he was cleared of this charge. One month after that incident, he and two other men were charged with sexually assaulting a woman in a New York hotel. In 1994, one day after being charged with sexual assault, he was shot five times while being mugged.

In 1995, Tupac was sentenced to four and a half years in prison. He was released on bail pending appeals after serving eleven months. In prison he found time to write lyrics. After his release from prison in 1995, Shakur released the double album *Me Against The World* and the multiplatinum *All Eyez On Me*.

On September 8, 1996, Tupac Shakur was shot as he sat in a black BMW 750 Saloon, waiting at a traffic light in Las Vegas, Nevada. The brilliant and controversial rapper died in the hospital five days later. He was twenty-five. After his passing, multiple albums of his have been released; they all have been highly successful. The films *Gridlock'd* and *Gang Related*, in which he starred, were released in 1997. A museum in his honor was built in Stone Mountain, Georgia. In death, Tupac has become a much-revered icon among hip-hoppers. His growing legend is equivalent to that of Bob Marley.

Will Smith

Willard Christopher Smith, Jr., was born on September 25, 1968, in Philadelphia. He received the nickname "Prince" from his teachers because of how he "charmed his way through." He later added the name "Fresh" to it. He grew up in a middle-class household. His mother worked for the school board, and his father was an engineer and the owner of a refrigeration company. He graduated from Over-

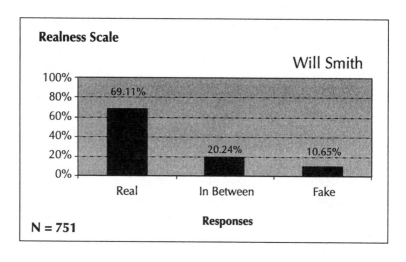

brook High School and passed up a scholarship to the Massachusetts Institute of Technology to begin a career in music. Will Smith started to rap at parties at the age of twelve. That is how he met Jeff A. Townes, better known as DJ Jazzy Jeff. Early in his career, Smith's grandmother stumbled on a rap notebook that was filled with expletive-ridden lyrics; she was angered and disappointed. Out of deference to her, Smith gave up using obscene language in his lyrics. He states, "Throughout history, the people that chose the right road have been persecuted. I feel like I'm doing the right thing when folks are hating. I use it as fuel to continue on the moral high ground" (Ogunnaike 2002, 2).

The absence of street vernacular gave Smith's music a "G" rating. While other rappers at the time were displaying the rage and anger of the urban streets, Smith's style was completely opposite. Parents favored Smith and Jazzy Jeff's version of hip-hop over the "Parental Advisory" brand. This ultimately led to a wider fan base. In 1988, the artists won a Grammy for the innocuous and playful song, "Parents Just Don't Understand." Smith made his film debut in *Where the Day Takes You* in 1992.

In 1990 Quincy Jones invited Will Smith-at the time, a rapper with no previous acting experience—to his home in Los Angeles to discuss the sitcom The Fresh Prince of Bel-Air. Smith was asked to read a few pages of dialogue for about twenty executives from NBC. After fifteen minutes of this exercise, Smith was hired. *The Fresh Prince of Bel-Air* was a hit that lasted six years. Indeed, Smith has found success in music, television, and film. He possesses as much all-around talent as anyone in entertainment history.

Smith's key albums are: as Fresh Prince with *DJ Jazzy Jeff*, *Rock the House* (1987), *He's the DJ, I'm the Rapper* (1988), *And in This Corner* (1989), *Homebase* (1991), and *Code Red* (1993); and as Will Smith, *Big Willie Style* (1997), *Willennium* (1999), and *Born to Reign* (2002). His television hit was *The Fresh Prince of Bel-Air* (NBC, 1990 to 96). His key films are *Six Degrees of Separation* (1993), *Bad Boys* (1995), *Independence Day* (1996), *Men in Black* (1997), *Enemy of the State* (1998), *Ali* (2001), *Men in Black II* (2002) and *Bad Boys* (2003).

The filming of Ali changed Smith's perspective on a number of things. Some of the filming took place in Maputo, Mozambique; while there, Smith visited South Africa. He met with leaders such as Nelson Mandela and mingled with the people in the street. He said that this was the most inspirational experience of his life. It was in Africa that Smith committed himself to having a global and more humanitarian outlook on life. Will and his wife, Jada, have contributed to various charities in Los Angeles and nationwide.

Tiger Woods

Eldrick "Tiger" Woods was born on December 30, 1975, in Cypress, California, to an African American father and a Thai mother. Tiger was nicknamed after a Vietnamese soldier who was a friend of his father. Tiger grew up in a nurturing family. His mother and father put a premium on spending time with him. Tiger's father, Earl Woods, served two tours of combat duty in Vietnam and retired as a lieutenant colonel in the U.S. Army Special Forces. He met Tiger's mother, Kultida, while he was doing service in Vietnam. She worked as a secretary in a U.S. Army office.

Woods began kindergarten in 1981. On his first day of school he was tied to a tree by older boys and taunted with racial slurs. He was still in his crib when he took an interest in the game of golf. At the age of six months, he attentively watched his father hit golf balls into a net and imitated his swing. He putted with Bob Hope on the

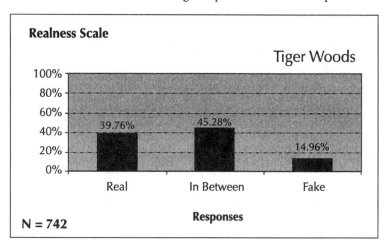

Mike Douglas Show at age two. He shot a score of 48 for nine holes at age three and was featured in Golf Digest at age five. Woods won the Optimist International Junior Tournament six times. At age fifteen, he won his first U.S. Junior Amateur Championship. By the time he was sixteen, Woods had won an overwhelming majority of his matches.

Tiger's academic performance was on a par with his golf game. At Western High School in Anaheim, California, he was nearly a straight-A student. According to his former teachers, he was an analytical and focused student. He had a natural curiosity and was determined to do well. One of his high school teachers stated, "Every career, a teacher has six or seven students he remembers for the rest of his life. Tiger was one of them, and he would be if he never won a golf tournament." Another high school teacher described him as "conscientious." This quality partially came from his mother's religion, Buddhism. According to Tiger, Buddhism has given him self-awareness. He says his religion has taught him that he is here to work on the flaws in his personality.

After graduating from high school, Woods attended Stanford University for two years. He majored in accounting. At Stanford, he won ten collegiate events and held the NCAA Individual Men's Championship, in addition to being named Pac-10 Player of the Year and NCAA First Team All-American. Woods stepped away from Stanford and made a decision to pursue a professional career in 1996. He won all of golf's four major championships consecutively and has consistently ranked as the number one golfer in the world. He is one of the most influential athletes in the world.

The mission statement for the Tiger Woods Foundation states, "We empower young people to reach their highest potential by initiating and supporting community-based programs that promote the health, education and welfare of all of America's children." Through junior golf clinics, motivational speeches, educational programs, the support of local heroes, and benevolent giving, the foundation has interacted with tens of thousands of kids across America.

Allen Iverson

Allen Iverson was born in 1975 and raised in the projects of Hampton, Virginia, by a teen mother. He lived in poverty in a house above a sewer that flooded its floors frequently. He helped care for two younger sisters. He had almost no contact with his biological father. His mother's boyfriend—who acted as father—spent time in and out of jail. Iverson's mother encouraged him to play basketball. He was a two-sport star in high school, excelling in football and basketball. He liked Georgetown University basketball coach John Thompson and chose to go there after being briefly incarcerated. He was selected as the Big East Defensive Player of the Year in consecutive seasons.

After two outstanding seasons, Iverson left Georgetown and was selected in the first round of the 1996 NBA draft. He was named the NBA Most Valuable Player in 2001, leading the league in scoring (31.1 points per game) and steals (2.51 steals per game). He has won the NBA scoring title multiple times.

Iverson founded the Crossover Foundation to save a struggling Boys & Girls Club in Greater Hampton Roads, Virginia. Since 1998, he has hosted the Annual Allen Iverson Celebrity Classic to benefit this Boys & Girls Club. He has participated in celebrity softball and

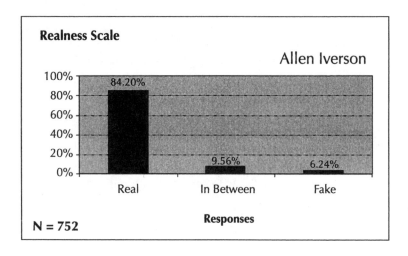

basketball games and celebrity auctions. He visits hospitals, forbidding the team's staff from attracting publicity. He refers to his teammates as family and is fiercely loyal to them.

On the other side, Iverson has exhibited less noble behavior. At 17, he got into a fight at a bowling alley and was sentenced to five years in prison for "mauling by mob." He was granted clemency and released after four months; his conviction was later overturned. In 1997, Iverson was arrested for possession of a gun and marijuana when he was a passenger in a car cited for speeding in Richmond, Virginia. Iverson pleaded no contest to a misdemeanor charge of carrying a concealed weapon in a plea agreement under which the drug charge was dropped. He performed community service and received three years' probation, after which his record was expunged.

NBA Commissioner David Stern reprimanded Iverson at the beginning of the 2000-2001 season before the debut of his rap album; the lyrics spoke negatively of women and gays. Under threat of penalty, Iverson was instructed to change the lyrics. In 2002, Philadelphia authorities charged Iverson with forcing his way into an apartment and threatening two men while searching for his wife, whom he had thrown out of the house, after an argument. He was initially charged with more than a dozen felony and misdemeanor counts that included assault, criminal trespassing, and weapons offenses. Four felony and eight misdemeanor charges were thrown out by the judge because witnesses disagreed on several points. Iverson, however, still had to face charges of allegedly bursting into his cousin's house and making terroristic threats while looking for his wife.

David Robinson

David Robinson was born in Key West, Florida, in 1965 to Ambrose and Freda Robinson. David moved around a lot because his father was in the U.S. Navy. He spent most of his childhood around the house fixing electrical things such as televisions. He grew up without basketball as a part of his life and discovered the game relatively late. He only played basketball for one year in high school at Osbourn Park in Manassas, Virginia; and even then it was only for recreation, not in preparation for his future. Robinson scored a 1320 on the College

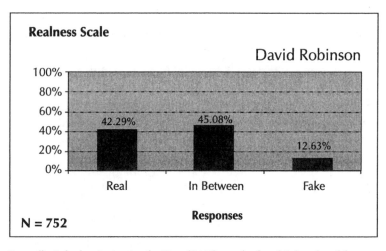

Board's Scholastic Aptitude Test (SAT), and after high school he attended the U.S. Naval Academy. While at the Naval Academy Robinson was an All-American in both his junior and senior years, and he was everyone's choice for College Player of the Year both seasons. Although excelling on the court, Robinson was also an accomplished pianist and a solid student. He graduated from the Academy with a degree in mathematics.

Known to his fans as "The Admiral," Robinson was a lean, muscular, strong, and agile athlete. He was chosen as one of the Fifty Greatest NBA Players of All Time. He is also the only U.S. male basketball player who has competed in three Olympics: in 1988, 1992, and 1996. He was the first pick in the 1987 NBA draft, chosen by the San Antonio Spurs. He sat out for two years in order to fulfill his military service obligations. He joined the Spurs for the 1989-1990 season, and that year he was named the league's Rookie of the Year. In 1992 he was named the NBA Defensive Player of the Year. Robinson scored 71 points against the Los Angeles Clippers on the last day of the 1993-1994 season to win the NBA scoring title at 29.8 points per game (Shaquille O'Neal was right behind him with 29.3). In his tenth year in the league he won his first NBA championship.

In 1992 David and his wife, Valerie, created the David Robinson Foundation, a Christian organization whose mission is to support programs that address the physical and spiritual needs of families. In

1997, the Robinsons donated $5 million to help create the Carver Academy at San Antonio's Carver Culture Center, a multicultural and multiethnic community center designed to serve pre-K through eighth-grade students who live primarily on the east side of San Antonio. Robinson retired from the NBA in 2003 after a fourteen-year career.

Kobe Bryant

Kobe Bryant was born on August 23, 1978, in Philadelphia. He is the son of former NBA star Joe "Jellybean" Bryant of 76ers, Clippers, and Rockets fame. Kobe was named after Kobe steak, which was listed on a menu at a Japanese restaurant. Growing up, Kobe's father was his main confidant. While his father was finishing his career, Kobe spent eight of his childhood years in Italy. Bryant states, "Growing up in Italy, I became more of an individual. The hardest thing in life is to know yourself and to master your own emotions. And I learned those things at a very young age" (Lieber 2000, 1C). Kobe's parents enrolled him in an Italian parochial school instead of an English-speaking school. Hence, he learned to speak fluent Italian and was immersed in the culture. His experiences living in Italy gave him a tremendous appreciation for different cultures.

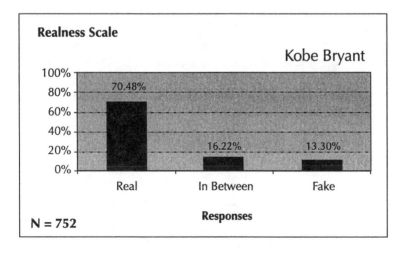

Realness Scale

Kobe Bryant

N = 752

After returning to the U.S. for high school, Kobe entered Lower Merion High School in the Philadelphia area. He was immediately a star for Lower Merion and was destined to follow in his father's footsteps. As a senior, he was voted National High School Player of the Year by both USA Today and Parade. He was also named the Naismith Player of the Year. Kobe led his team to the Class AAAA state title and broke several records on the way. He averaged 30.8 points, 12 rebounds, 6.5 assists, 4.0 steals, and 3.8 block shots per game, and accumulated a total of 2,883 points. He became the leading scorer in southeastern Pennsylvania history—beating out records set by NBA great Wilt Chamberlain.

Kobe was a good athlete, and he was intelligent. He once stated that his idea of fun was reading Dante's Inferno in Italian. He scored 1100 on his SATs but passed up college to enter the NBA draft in 1996. Bryant was initially drafted by the Charlotte Hornets as the thirteenth pick overall but was traded to the Los Angeles Lakers. He struggled in his first couple of years in the NBA; but by 1999, he found the right formula. He led the Lakers to consecutive NBA championships in 2000, 2001, and 2002. He has been named to the NBA All-Star Team and All-Defensive Team in multiple seasons. His clean-cut and wholesome image was tarnished when he was accused by a nineteen-year-old of felony sexual assault in Eagle County, Colorado, in 2003. Bryant admitted to committing adultery with his 19-year old accuser.

Kobe has established the Kobe Bryant Foundation, which strives to help at-risk youth in Los Angeles. Money raised from membership dues in his fan club goes to his foundation. With money raised from celebrity bowling tournaments, Bryant built the ERAS Center in Culver City, California; helped develop a computer room at Hollygrove Center; and sponsored a bookmobile with tutors, which traveled throughout East Los Angeles.

Mike Tyson

Michael Gerard Tyson was born on June 30, 1966, in New York City. He was raised in Brooklyn by a single mom. He fought on the streets growing up and made a name for himself as a "man." He was sent to "reform" school at thirteen, where he learned to box. A social

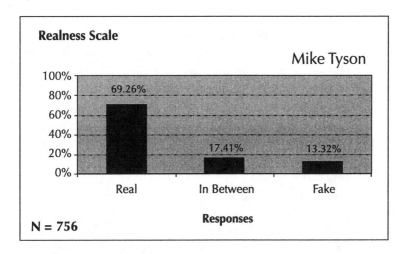

Realness Scale

Mike Tyson

100%
80%   69.26%
60%
40%
20%   17.41%   13.32%
0%
Real   In Between   Fake

N = 756   Responses

worker and boxing fan named Bobby Stewart discovered Tyson's boxing potential and led him to Constantine "Cus" D'Amato. D'Amato brought Tyson to the Catskills Mountains of New York and mentored him in and out of the ring. D'Amato eventually became Tyson's legal guardian and the most influential person in his young life. D'Amato died in 1985, leaving Tyson virtually alone.

Tyson's amateur boxing record was 24-3. Two controversial losses to Henry Tillman kept Tyson from competing as a heavyweight at the 1984 Olympics in Los Angeles. After the disappointment of not being able to compete in the Olympics, Tyson decided to turn professional. By 1987, Tyson held heavyweight titles from the three major sanctioning organizations and was the undisputed heavyweight champion of the world.

After five years as a pro with a 33-0 record, Tyson suffered one of the greatest upsets in boxing history. In 1990 in Tokyo, he lost to Buster Douglas, a 42-to-1 underdog. This fight proved that Tyson was not invincible, and it was the start of a rocky five-year period for him. The most serious of his woes was a 1992 rape conviction. He was prisoner 922335 in a jail called the Indiana Youth Center. In Tyson's two years in prison, he did not once put on boxing gloves.

In 1996, in one of the most exciting fights of the decade, Evander Holyfield scored an eleventh-round knockout of Tyson and won the match. In a highly anticipated rematch in 1997, Tyson was disqualified from the fight for biting Holyfield's ear. His boxing license was suspended temporarily. He successfully reapplied for it in 1998.

By 2002, Tyson had suffered a series of setbacks that ultimately crushed him. His second wife filed for divorce. He had to settle multiple charges of sexual antagonism. In a news conference held to promote the much-anticipated fight between Tyson and Lennox Lewis, Tyson started a brawl, bit Lewis on the leg, and hurled obscenities to the media. The Nevada boxing commission suspended his license again. The fight with Lewis was rescheduled in Memphis.

In an interview before his big fight with Lewis, Tyson told a female TV reporter that he usually has sex with women who interview him. He told other reporters that he would like to "stomp" on their children's testicles "so you could feel my pain because that's the pain I have waking up everyday." His public relations team dropped him after this interview. In the days leading up to the big fight, Lennox said, "I don't feel I need Tyson. But he's the guy in my era who's a misfit that everybody looked up to. It would be a disappointment for us not to meet" (D'Amato 2002, 1C).

The beginning of the end of Tyson's illustrious and tumultuous career was when he finally stepped in the ring with his former sparring partner Lennox Lewis on June 8, 2002. Lewis wore Tyson down and then knocked him out in the eighth round, humiliating him on his way to retaining his heavyweight championship title, effectively undermining his mystique and superstar status.

Selected Results from the Survey of Young African American Men (Ages 13-19)

- A fourteen-year-old ninth grader from McDonough, Georgia, with a C+ grade average rated the following individuals as "real" (1); "fake" (3); or "in between" (2).

Tupac Shakur	1
Will Smith	3
Tiger Woods	2
Allen Iverson	1
David Robinson	2
Kobe Bryant	3
Mike Tyson	1

The respondent offered these comments in an interview about each individual:

Tupac Shakur: I gave Tupac a "1" because he is real inside and outside. He's hard. He had heart. He lived by the sword and died by the sword.

Will Smith: I gave Will Smith a "3" because I was comparing him to Tupac. Will Smith is cool. I wish I could change that answer because I like him.

Tiger Woods: I don't know what to think about Tiger Woods. When I look at him I see him as in between. A lot of black men don't really play golf. The hardness about him is that he stands up for what he is.

Allen Iverson: I see Iverson as being real on the court. He's cocky. A lot people want to be like him. They wear his jersey.

David Robinson: I really don't know too much about David Robinson.

Kobe Bryant: I see Kobe as a pretty boy. He doesn't have any tattoos. I see tattoos as a sign of being hard.

Mike Tyson: Mike Tyson, he's hard but he's crazy—like when he talked about eating Lennox Lewis's kids. He's hard but Lewis went out and kicked his butt.

• A sixteen-year-old tenth grader from McDonough, Georgia, with an A grade average rated the following individuals as "real" (1); "fake" (3); or "in between" (2).

| Tupac Shakur | 1 |
| Will Smith | 2 |

Tiger Woods	1
Allen Iverson	2
David Robinson	2
Kobe Bryant	1
Mike Tyson	3

The respondent offered these comments in an interview about each individual:

Tupac Shakur: When I think of Tupac, I look at more than the thug image. I look at him as a poet. He basically told stories of what went on around him.

Will Smith: I think it's kind of cool that he took the whole rap thing and said that I'm not going to use cuss words and I can still win Grammys. But on the other hand, he can be looked at as being a sellout because he's not rebellious like Tupac. I think he keeps his anger low-key.

Tiger Woods: I gave Tiger a "1" because he really encouraged people to expand beyond football and basketball. He's making a name for himself. Whenever you think of golf you think of Tiger Woods. It's cool that you're seeing our race expanding and doing different things.

Allen Iverson: Allen Iverson is a very interesting character to me. He can ball—I will give him that. But it's certain things that he does that makes people think that's the way all black people act. People look at the tattoos and the braids and ask is that the way all black people are. I gave him a "2" because he can ball and that's it. Unlike Tupac, he has not proven to me that he is well read and he doesn't have anything to say about the problems of black people.

David Robinson: I haven't heard much about him. He's in the basketball scene but I've not heard about him like the Allen Iversons and the Michael Jordans. I've never heard of him attacking a police officer or a reporter or anything. He goes out and plays ball and makes his money.

Kobe Bryant: I like Kobe. He's a great baller. I saw a documentary that showed him traveling to the Great Wall of China. That was cool that he was interested in that. I like his style. I like how he rocks his casual clothes.

Mike Tyson: To be honest, he was a great boxer. In his early stages, he was real good, real popular. But like Iverson, it's a lot of things that he's doing that help stereotype blacks, like we're thugs and we make up trouble. Like when he bit Holyfield's ear, he's just been making a negative impact on black culture.

• A seventeen-year-old twelfth grader from Los Angeles, California, with an C+ grade average rated the following individuals as "real" (1); "fake" (3); or "in between" (2).

Tupac Shakur	1
Will Smith	2
Tiger Woods	1
Allen Iverson	1
David Robinson	2
Kobe Bryant	1
Mike Tyson	3

The respondent offered these comments in an interview about each individual:

Tupac Shakur: Pac's music will still go on. People look up to him. He's one of the coldest MCs. He told the truth and didn't hold nothing back—like when he came out and said he got raped in prison.

Will Smith: He is funny. He's in between because one minute he's serious and one minute he's joking. His music is cool but he basically makes his music to sell to white people not to blacks.

Tiger Woods: He's real when he tells those people at the golfing tournaments to stop taking pictures of him. But overall, he don't promote blacks enough.

Allen Iverson: He's real. He ain't caring what nobody says. He don't sugarcoat things. He grew up hard and poor like us. We ain't got nothing here in South Central and he didn't have nothing growing up.

David Robinson: He used to be all right but now his fame is fading away.

Kobe Bryant: Kobe is just real period. He is who he is. You know, he's smooth.

Mike Tyson: That man is an animal. He look for trouble from anybody.

• A sixteen-year-old tenth grader from Los Angeles, California, with an C grade average rated the following individuals as "real" (1); "fake" (3); or "in between" (2).

Tupac Shakur	1
Will Smith	2
Tiger Woods	3
Allen Iverson	1
David Robinson	2
Kobe Bryant	2
Mike Tyson	3

The respondent offered these comments in an interview about each individual:

Tupac Shakur: I put Pac at a "1" because he was down. He wasn't fakin.

Will Smith: He's trying to make everybody happy—playing both sides.

Tiger Woods: He's not even trying to be connected. He's just after money.

Allen Iverson: He's real because he ain't forgot where he came from.

David Robinson: He ain't doing nothing.

Kobe Bryant: He could be anybody. He don't represent all the time.

Mike Tyson: He's chaos—just all messed up.

• A seventeen-year-old twelfth grader from Los Angeles, California, with an C grade average rated the following individuals as "real" (1); "fake" (3); or "in between" (2).

Tupac Shakur	1
Will Smith	3
Tiger Woods	3
Allen Iverson	1

David Robinson   3

Kobe Bryant   2

Mike Tyson   2

The respondent offered these comments in an interview about each individual:

Tupac Shakur: He wasn't posin.

Will Smith: He's all light.

Tiger Woods: He too white.

Allen Iverson: All the kids can relate to AI.

David Robinson: Nobody knows him. He's not even, like, normal. He hasn't done nothing.

Kobe Bryant: (Did not have a response. Shrugged his shoulders.)

Mike Tyson: He's just drama.

• A fourteen-year-old ninth grader from Los Angeles, California, with an B grade average rated the following individuals as "real" (1); "fake" (3); or "in between" (2).

Tupac Shakur   1

Will Smith   1

Tiger Woods   2

Allen Iverson   1

David Robinson   3

Kobe Bryant   1

Mike Tyson   3

The respondent offered these comments in an interview about each individual:

Tupac Shakur: He cared.

Will Smith: He's got a cool lady.

Tiger Woods: He's not doing all he could to make stuff right.

Allen Iverson: He's just ballin'—handlin' his own.

David Robinson: Even Shaq said he thinks he's too good; clean-cut.

Kobe Bryant: He's clickin. He's just, like, on it. He's so smooth.

Mike Tyson: I don't wanna be like that.

• A fifteen-year-old ninth grader from Los Angeles, California, with an A grade average rated the following individuals as "real" (1); "fake" (3); or "in between" (2).

Tupac Shakur	1
Will Smith	1
Tiger Woods	2
Allen Iverson	2
David Robinson	2
Kobe Bryant	1
Mike Tyson	3

The respondent offered these comments in an interview about each individual:

Tupac Shakur: He was like so normal.

Will Smith: I wanna be him.

Tiger Woods: Nobody can relate to him but rich people.

Allen Iverson: He seems cool, but he's getting into trouble and that isn't good for him to be teaching kids.

David Robinson: I don't know.

Kobe Bryant: He's always on and knowing people—even the Asians wanna be him.

Mike Tyson: Mean—out for his own.

References

Tupac Shakur

Dyson, Michael Eric. 2001. Holler if You Hear Me: Searching for Tupac Shakur. New York: Basic Civitas.

Eric, Deggans. 1996. Gangsta' rapper Tupac Shakur lived, died in conflict. St. Petersburg Times, 15 September.

www.duke.edu/~de1/2pac.html

www.Hitemup.com

Will Smith

Jones, Quincy. 2001. Q: The Autobiography of Quincy Jones. New York: Doubleday.

Ogunnaike, Lola. 2002. Back in Black II. New York Daily News, 30 June.

Tyehimba, Cheo Taylor. 2002. Will Smith. Savoy, August.

Tiger Woods

Clary, Jack. 1997. Tiger Woods. Wilton, Connecticut: Belden Hill Press.

D'Amato, Gary. 2001. Woods denies letdown has hurt his game. Milwaukee Journal Sentinel, 20 August.

Diaz, Jaime. 2000. Tiger Woods, the student at the head of the class. Sports Illustrated, 21 August.

www.pgatour.com/players/bios/8793

Allen Iverson

Alexander, Rachel. 2000. Nailing the turnaround. Washington Post, 26 November.

Robbins, Liz. 2002. As Iverson moves on, his past is with him. New York Times, 14 July.

www.nba.com/playerfile/allen_iverson.html

David Robinson

www.nba.com/playerfile/david_robinson/bio.html

www.swbc-solutions.com/theadmiral/bio.htm

Kobe Bryant

Lieber, Jill. 2000. Bryant on joyous ride fueled by imagination. USA Today, 10 February.

www.nba.com/playerfile/kobe_bryant/bio.html

Mike Tyson

D'Amato, Gary. 2002. Former trainer predicted bout years ago. Milwaukee Journal Sentinel, 9 June.

D'Amato, Gary. 2002. Lewis laughs last. Milwaukee Journal Sentinel, 9 June.

Gildea, William. 2002. Dr. Jekyll and Mr. Tyson. Washington Post, 2 June.

Hamill, Pete. 2002. The Tyson I cherish. New York Daily News, 10 June.

Chapter 11

Redefining Authenticity

Embracing New Values

We strut through the world like some dusky colossus, looming larger than life itself: a nightmare, a fantasy, an American original-feared, emulated, shunned, desired.... We are as complicated, as intriguing, as American history, and in many respects, are every bit as confused. Jazz and rap, art forms that we created and in which we excel, define American music, just as basketball and boxing, two activities that we dominate, are the face of American sport. We set the standard for style and make concrete the meaning of cool. (Cose 2002, 5-6)

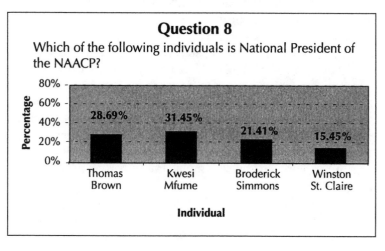

Question 8

Which of the following individuals is National President of the NAACP?

Percentage (y-axis): 0%, 20%, 40%, 60%, 80%

Thomas Brown	Kwesi Mfume	Broderick Simmons	Winston St. Claire
28.69%	31.45%	21.41%	15.45%

Individual

An impressive percentage of those surveyed responded correctly to the question, "Who is the co-founder of Death Row Records?" Suge Knight co-founded the record company. However, the percentage of those responding correctly to the question regarding the national directorship of the NAACP is disturbing.

Every young black man should know Kwesi Mfume. Mfume became president and chief executive officer of the National Association for the Advancement of Colored People (NAACP) on February 20, 1996. NAACP's Board of Directors unanimously elected him to the position. Mr. Mfume gave up his seat in the U.S. Congress, where he represented Maryland's Seventh District, to become the president of the NAACP. As a congressman, Mfume was the president of the Congressional Black Caucus. For decades, he has fought tirelessly for civil rights and social justice. Blacks should not wait on the school system to expose black students to this information.

Mfume should be acknowledged, recognized, and discussed in every black household and church. Many of those surveyed come from middle-class backgrounds. These statistics suggest that even middle-class families are not giving their children the proper exposure to important black figures and institutions.

On the other hand, this means that the NAACP is not doing a good enough job marketing itself to young black men. The fourteen- and fifteen-year-olds in South Central Los Angeles do not know Jim Brown because of his days running the football in the NFL, nor do they know him as an actor. They know him as the founder of Ameri-I-Can, an organization dedicated to ending gang violence and nurturing the positive development of young black men. These gangsters know Jim Brown because he was in the community. He had these youth over to his house. He listened to their stories and felt their pain. Can the NAACP honestly say that it has done the same? The organization at this point is a couple of million dollars in debt. Why? Maybe it is because of the various galas and Image Awards ceremonies. I am sure they serve some purpose; however, the organization's mission should extend beyond such bourgeois events.

The NAACP has lost credibility and membership because over the past two decades, the organization has not been in the trenches. If the representatives of the NAACP were in the various inner-city neighborhoods trying vigorously to stop gang violence, school dropouts, teen pregnancy, drug use and distribution, and the spread of HIV, young black men would know the organization and its leader. Just like the incessant chastisement of the strict teacher or the stern cop, young black men would say, "Here they come again. Why don't they leave us alone?" Irrespective of this sentiment, they know the teacher and cop exist because they are always in their face—they are always monitoring their behavior. The kids on the streets know the names of the teacher and the cop and are familiar with their agenda. Young black men do not know Kwesi Mfume and are not familiar with the NAACP's agenda.

The black community cannot rely on our educational system to teach its kids about the achievements of people such as Ben Carson. It is up to the black community to lionize individuals such as Carson in their speeches, lectures, and sermons. It is up to parents and teachers to encourage students to read his autobiography. In the Survey of Young African American Men, 43 percent of the respondents knew that Ben Carson was a medical doctor. This is a surprisingly good response. However, the numbers are skewed because 95 percent of the participants at a private school in Watts answered this question correctly. Someone in the school had made a point to celebrate the achievements of Carson, which is good.

Some 42.67 percent of those surveyed want to be either professional athletes or entertainers. This is disturbing. Young black men need to know that there are other career options besides sports and entertainment. By the time many young black men realize they have a much better chance pursuing a career in law, medicine, engineering, journalism, or business, it is too late. By the time they figure out they will not be the next big rap star or the next star NBA player, they have lost a significant portion of time that others are using for career development. Black families need to groom their children to pursue the myriad of career opportunities in society. Young black kids need exposure to things other than rap music and videos, video games, and athletic competitions.

Lines of people waited to see the exhibit about Albert Einstein when it opened in 2002 at the American Museum of Natural History in New York. One man who brought his ten-year-old grandson to see the exhibit stated, "With a ten-year-old, you just want to plant seeds;

then you have to see where they grow." A reporter asked the little boy what he thought of Einstein's famous equation, E=mc2, and the boy responded, "a kilogram of mass could make a light bulb burn for 30 million years" (Hotz 2002, A19). This youth was getting valuable exposure and his interests were being nurtured and cultivated.

Take someone whose career goal is to be a medical doctor. From the time the person is twelve years old, he or she participates in summer programs that are geared towards preparing them to go into the field of medicine. They read magazines about medical issues and internalize the terminology. By the time they are twelve, they have started the quest to go to medical school and become a successful doctor. The twelve-year-old black male invests the same energy, time, and enthusiasm thinking that he will be the next great rapper or professional athlete. His dedication and commitment to his future career is no less than the future doctor. The major difference deals with odds. The odds are greater that commitment and preparation will enable the future doctor to achieve his or her goals. Although commitment and preparation will increase the probability of the aspiring rapper or professional athlete's success, there is still an overwhelming long shot that their dreams will come true.

If I am sitting in a high school classroom and I am pretty certain that I am going to be signed to a major record label or if I am quite certain that I will make it to the NBA, what incentive is there for me to study? When I played football at Vanderbilt, I rarely saw guys graduate to the NFL; but I did see them go on to medical school, law school, and business school and pursue successful careers. I remember an All-American football player from Auburn University who came to visit a female friend at Vanderbilt. He walked around the dorms and met several of our football players. He commented that he could not believe that we all studied. That was no exaggeration. He knew he was going to the NFL so he was going through the motions in the classroom—taking classes from identified professors who would help keep him eligible for the season.

For those in high school and college, there are dire consequences for having unrealistic expectations. It is hard to make a cocky, standout senior in basketball think that he has a better chance of being struck by lightening than ever making it to the NBA.

The American Paradox

Ellis Cose, in his book *The Envy of the World*, points out that white men in boardrooms envy the style and confidence of black men. White kids in the suburbs try desperately to emulate the walk, talk, and dress of the black man (Cose 2002, 6). A few years ago at the NAACP Image Awards, Lawrence Fishburne recited a poignantly eloquent poem about the impact that black men have had on our society. To paraphrase Fishburne, he stated that people all over the world talk your talk, walk your walk, and dance to your rhythms. Indeed, the black man in America is one of the most enigmatic phenomena in our society. He is at once degraded, victimized, oppressed, lauded, celebrated, and revered. He represents the American Paradox.

> For as special and gifted as we are, we occupy a tenuous place on this earth. And admired as we may be in the abstract or performing on the court or floodlit stage, when we walk the streets at night, we are more likely to inspire anxiety than affection. Cradled in America's ambivalence, we embody her contradictions. (Cose 2002, 6)

During the 1996 Olympics held in Atlanta, I sat in my parents' living room on the outskirts of the Atlanta to watch the Games. Later I visited Centennial Park, the epicenter of the Olympic festivities. While I meandered around the park, I mulled over how confused the various visitors must have been about the status of black men in America. For instance, imagine visitors coming to the Olympic Games from Stavanger, Norway; Kampala, Uganda; or Nanking, China. Imagine if the only perception these visitors have of black men in the U.S. is that they are systematically degraded, victimized, and oppressed. Moreover, what if they had internalized all the negative stereotypes associated with black men in America?

As these visitors settled in to enjoy the Games, they must have been struck by the Olympic torch being passed from the former mayor of Atlanta—and former U.S. ambassador to the United Nations—Andrew Young, a black man, to Bill Cambell, the black mayor at the time. As these visitors enjoyed the opening ceremonies, they were held in suspense along with the rest of the world, waiting to see who would light the sacred torch for the 100th anniversary of the Olympics. They watched Muhammad Ali light the torch. If these visitors went back to their hotels and watched the Olympics on television, they were likely to be exposed to the African American commentators Ahmad Rashad and Greg Gumble. Back at the stadium, they were likely to watch the most publicized and celebrated athletes in those Games, Michael Johnson and Carl Lewis.

In American society, black men have been systematically degraded, victimized, and oppressed. However, no other minority population in the world is so revered. If one had to name the top ten most famous people in the world, five individuals on this list would be African American men: e.g., Michael Jackson, Michael Jordan, Muhammad Ali, Eddie Murphy, and Tiger Woods. (Oprah Winfrey would certainly make the top ten, as well.) This is a remarkable feat given that black men only make up a little more than 6 percent of the entire U.S. population. One-fifth of the world's population is Chinese. One in every six people in the world lives in India. How many famous people from these countries does the average person know? These questions are asked not to belittle the talented people of China or India, but to highlight the African American man's visibility and popularity on the world stage.

Because of his high profile and his systemic vilification, the black man remains the great American Paradox. Indeed, the paradox is confusing. One might ask, which is the true plight of the black man in America? Which scenario represents reality?

There have been signs that the U.S. has made incremental progress in its tolerance and acceptance of black men. In 1966 Robert Weaver was appointed as the first black cabinet member, Secretary of the Department of Housing and Urban Development. In the same year, Edward W. Brooke became the first black senator since Reconstruction. In 1967, Thurgood Marshall became the first black Supreme Court justice. In 1976, Andrew Young became the first black U.S. ambassador to the United Nations. The year 1989 saw a number of breakthroughs for black men. Ron Brown became the first black chairperson of the Democratic National Committee. David Dinkens became the first black mayor of New York, and Douglas Wilder of Virginia became the first black governor since Reconstruction. General Colin Powell became the first black chairman of the Joint Chiefs of Staff in 1989 and the first black Secretary of State in 2001.

Embracing the Positive

Efforts must be made to reconstruct and passionately embrace new concepts of black male authenticity. Perhaps new representations will redefine what it means to "keep it real." Perhaps keeping it real will come to mean working hard at a craft and becoming highly successful in a respective field, as have Tiger Woods, David Robinson, Derek Jeter, Bernie Williams, Stewart Scott, Will Smith, Mike Terrico, Ben Carson, Jesse Jackson, Jr., Harold Ford, Jr., Montel Williams, and Tavis Smiley.

Black men who turn their backs on their community and neglect to acknowledge the urgent social problems confronting blacks should be criticized. However, black men who have shunned society's stereotypes should not be condemned for being "fake." "Realness" should be measured in terms of setting positive examples for the thirteen-year-old who looks up to you. Realness should be defined as taking advantage of every opportunity that your parents and grandparents created for you, that they were not afforded themselves. This concept should be based on being respectful and sensitive to the needs of your women and your family.

Young black men should be socialized from birth that there is nothing heroic about destroying the dreams of people in your community by selling drugs. There is nothing supermanly about having babies by multiple women. There is nothing revolutionary about black-on-black violence. There is nothing cool about indirectly referring to your grandmothers, mothers, sisters, and daughters in derogatory ways. The black community should not continue to blame the system for this type of vicious, irresponsible, and counterproductive hypermasculinist behavior-besides, that particular blame game is old, tired, redundant, and played out.

The more I think about the power and influence that some groups have in the U.S., the more disappointed I become in the lack of power and influence that blacks have. Some groups do not tolerate any kind of injustice perpetrated on their population. Their response to injustice is cohesive and swift. How have black leaders and organizations responded to contemporary injustices?

What was the impact of the Million Man March? The idea and concept were beautiful in spirit, but what have been the results? Are music videos less misogynistic? Is rap music more uplifting? Has black-on-black crime decreased? Have black politicians helped reverse any of the draconian policies passed in the 1990s that adversely affect the black community?

Black leaders and organizations have failed to counter systematically the array of negative images of blacks in popular culture. As I asked earlier, what other ethnic group in world would allow their own women to be exploited like blacks do in their music videos? Who is holding the music industry accountable? Who is holding the film industry accountable for their consistent negative portrayals of black men?

In 1998, Hype Williams's debut film *Belly* starred the rap stars DMX, Nas, and Method Man. The story was about the black man's violence, rage, irresponsibility, and irrationality. The theater chain owned by Magic Johnson refused to show this film because of its overwhelming negative and violent depiction of African Americans. I commend Magic and his chain of theaters for being socially responsible.

Founder of Def Jam Records, Russell Simmons, threatened to boycott Pepsi in 2003 because they canceled the advertisements of the rapper Ludacris because of concerns about his vulgar lyrics. However, months later, Pepsi signed fouled-mouth Ozzy Osbourne and the rebellious rock band Papa Roach. Pepsi, which has made a considerable investment in marketing to the hip-hop community, capitulated and donated millions of dollars to Ludacris's foundation. Simmons did not give the soft drink a free pass on its contradictory stances. He effectively used his currency.

In November 2003, Sean "P. Diddy" Combs completed the 26-mile New York City Marathon, raising two million dollars for various children's charities. Combs used his currency in a remarkable and beautiful way.

I commend people like Tavis Smiley and Tom Joyner for holding people accountable for their actions. I remember when the singer Brian McKnight was on the Tom Joyner Show. He was being interviewed by Smiley. Smiley asked why he performed at the 2000 Republican National Convention. His answer was that he had gotten paid well. I could tell Smiley was livid. He did not automatically condemn McKnight for singing at the Republican Convention, but he wanted to investigate his motives.

McKnight had no justifiable motives except for money. He revealed later in the show that he did not vote because both parties were virtually the same. The fact that he said he did not vote was a cause for serious concern. He should be called out and held accountable for his negligence and lack of consciousness.

What young black male is running around saying he wants to be the next Tavis Smiley? Smiley is gifted, clean-cut, articulate, and intelligent. He is socially responsible and politically conscious. He is the best at what he does.

There is a problem when 92 percent of the participants in my survey knew that Suge Knight was the co-founder of *Death Row Records* while only 31 percent of the participants responded that Kwesi Mfume was the director of the NAACP. There is also a problem when David Robinson is not looked upon as being a real black man like Allen Iverson. What is this saying about the values of this generation of young black men?

Randall Robinson asks in his book *Defending the Spirit*, "How can we elevate Seyi Fayanju, the twelve-year-old from Verona, New Jersey, who won the National Geographic Geography Bee in competition with thousands, into a more compelling role model than gangsta rap artists and NBA players?"

It is up to the families, churches, and community organizations to teach black youth about their history and about positive black icons in every field of human endeavor. It is up to community organizations to replace billboard ads for malt liquor, pagers, and cell phones with those offering public service ads that tout the achievement of people in the community.

In a recent cover story in *Newsweek* magazine, Ellis Cose examined the gaps of achievement between black women and black men. While touting the many breakthrough achievements made by black women in the past decade, Cose highlighted the lack of progress made by black men during the same period. At least 35 percent of black women attend college, while only 25 percent of black men do.

More than 17 percent of young black males are high school dropouts while 13.5 percent of young black women are (Cose 2003, 49).

In 2000, five of my high school buddies and I founded the non-profit community outreach group, Key Elements, which is based in my hometown of McDonough, Georgia. The founding members of this group consist of two probation officers, one former professional baseball player turned teacher, one social worker, one businessman, and a university professor. The objective of this group is to provide various forums to discuss the pressing challenges facing the black community.

Each city with a black population should have leadership institutes for young black men. The purpose of these institutes would be to bring several young black men together for training each year. These young men would participate in different modules. For example, honesty, trust, responsibility, choices, commitment, and discipline are themes that participants would be exposed to throughout the training. Participants would take field trips to venues such as business and science expositions, to plays, and to museums. Not only would participants be taken to positive venues, they would also be taken to the local jail or prison. A field trip such as this would force the participants to examine the consequences of making bad choices.

The overall philosophy of the leadership institute for young black men is to cultivate a new cadre of leaders. By exposing participants to successful black men who act as mentors and by immersing these young men in an array of activities, their perception of their opportunitites and life choices will be broadened. After participating in the program, mentors would pledge their continued support to the young men by monitoring their academic progress and attending their extracurricular activities. The ultimate goal would be to counter the negative trends in the behavior of young black men, one group at a time. Imagine the impact that these leadership institutes could have if they flourished in cities and towns throughout the U.S.

In order for black men to escape the pathology related to black masculinity, a concerted effort must be made to contradict stereotypes rather than embrace them. Young black men must be shown that David Robinson is indeed a "real" black man. In order to change the self-destructive culture of black men, the black community must radically change its value system. Things will fundamentally change:

- when young black men embrace the concept that school is cool
- when "keeping it real" means excelling in any field
- when "authenticity" means working towards community uplift
- when there are concerted efforts made to contradict stereotypes.

Coupled with this, the black community needs to adamantly adopt tenets that will:

- hold those accountable who exploit the black community
- celebrate the positive non-entertainer and non-athlete who excel
- strenuously lobby to reverse policies that have an adverse affect on the black community.

References

Cose, Ellis. 2002. The Envy of the World. New York: Washington Square Press.

Cose, Ellis. 2003. The black gender gap. Newsweek, 3 March.

Hotz, Robert Lee. 2002. Einstein museum adds a human side to the equation. Los Angeles Times, 1 December.

Robinson, Randall. 1998. Defending the Spirit: A Black Life in America. New York: Plume.

Appendix

1. The instrument used for the survey of young
African American men (13-19)

SURVEY OF YOUNG AFRICAN AMERICAN MEN (13-19)

School_____Age _____ Grade
Level____ GPA____(A,B,C,D)

Rate the following individuals on whether you believe they are real Black men
or not. Mark 1 beside the person if you think he is real and 3 if you think he
is fake. Mark 2 if he is in between.

REALNESS SCALE

Real	In Between	Fake
1	2	3

Tupac Shakur _____
Will Smith _____
Tiger Woods _____
Allen Iverson _____
David Robinson ____
Kobe Bryant _____
Mike Tyson_____

Please circle your responses to the following questions.
  1. Have you read a book (outside of class work) in the past year?
     Yes   No

If "Yes" list the title of one of the last books you
    read:_____.
2. Have you ever been harassed by the police?   Yes   No
3. Do you wear an earring?   Yes   No
4. Do you have a tattoo?   Yes   No
5. Who is the co-founder and president of Death Row Records?
    A) Adam Taylor
    B) Suge Knight
    C) Wilson Davis
    D) Gene Garrison
6. Jackie Robinson integrated what professional sport?
    A) Basketball
    B) Baseball
    C) Football
    D) Boxing
7. Arthur Ashe played what professional sport?
    A) Baseball
    B) Tennis
    C) Basketball
    D) Football
8. Which of the following individuals is the National President
    of the NAACP?
    A) Thomas Brown
    B) Kwesi Mfume
    C) Broderick Simmons
    D) Winston St. Claire
9. Ben Carson is a famous:
    A) News Reporter
    B) Football Player
    C) Medical Doctor
    D) Businessman
10. You would like to pursue a future career as a:
    A) Businessman
    B) Professional Athlete
    C) Entertainer
    D) Doctor
    E) Lawyer
    Other _____

11. Do you feel like an American Citizen or an Outsider?

2. Permission letter provided to assisting principals

Dear Principal/Teacher/Parent,

My name is Renford Reese. I am an assistant professor of political science and the director of the Colorful Flags program at Cal Poly Pomona University. I am in the process of conducting research for my first scholarly book, American Paradox: Young Black Men. One chapter of this book will look at how young African American males have unwittingly accepted one model of black masculinity. The acceptance of this "tough guy" model is having detrimental consequences on a generation of young African American men.

The following survey attempts to gauge the attitudes, perceptions, and basic knowledge of African American males from ages 13-19. This survey should not take more than 10-15 minutes to complete.

Thank you for your time.

Kindest Regards,
Renford Reese, Ph.D.
Assistant Professor, Political Science
Director, Colorful Flags Program

3. Tabulated survey results

Tupac Shakur

	Frequency	Percentage
Real	610	81.12%
In Between	104	13.83%
Fake	38	5.05%
Total	752	100%

Will Smith

	Frequency	Percentage
Real	519	69.11%
In Between	152	20.24%
Fake	80	10.65%
Total	751	100%

Tiger Woods

	Frequency	Percentage
Real	295	39.76%
In Between	336	45.28%
Fake	111	14.96%
Total	742	100%

Allen Iverson

	Frequency	Percentage
Real	634	84.20%
In Between	72	9.56%
Fake	47	6.24%
Total	753	100%

David Robinson

	Frequency	Percentage
Real	318	42.29%
In Between	339	45.08%
Fake	95	12.63%
Total	752	100%

Kobe Bryant

	Frequency	Percentage
Real	530	70.48%
In Between	122	16.22%
Fake	100	13.30%
Total	752	100%

Mike Tyson

	Frequency	Percentage
Real	525	69.26%
In Between	132	17.41%
Fake	101	13.32%
Total	756	100%

4. Other Results from the Survey

Question 1

Have you read a book (outside of class work) in the past year?

	Frequency	Percentage
Yes	457	61.51%
No	286	38.49%
Total	743	100%

Question 2

Have you ever been harassed by the police?

	Frequency	Percentage
Yes	400	53.62%
No	346	46.38%
Total	746	100%

Question 3

Do you wear an earring?

	Frequency	Percentage
Yes	337	45.30%
No	407	54.70%
Total	744	100%

Question 4

Do you have a tattoo?

	Frequency	Percentage
Yes	84	11.23%
No	664	88.77%
Total	748	100%

Question 5

Who is the co-founder and president of Death Row Records?

	Frequency	Percentage
Adam Taylor	26	3.58%
Suge Knight	669	92.15%
Wilson Davis	22	3.03%
Gene Garrison	9	1.24%
Total	726	100%

Question 6

Jackie Robinson integrated what professional sport?

	Frequency	Percentage
Basketball	115	16.04%
Baseball	579	80.75%
Football	8	1.12%
Boxing	15	2.09%
Total	717	100

Question 7

Arthur Ashe played with what professional sport?

	Frequency	Percentage
Baseball	35	4.85%
Tennis	492	68.24%
Basketball	125	17.34%
Football	69	9.57%
Total	721	100%

Question 8

Which of the following individuals is the National President of the NAACP?

	Frequency	Percentage
Thomas Brown	208	28.69%
Kwesi Mfume	228	31.45%
Broderick Simmons	177	24.41%
Winston St. Claire	112	15.45%
Total	725	100%

Question 9

Ben Carson is a famous:

	Frequency	Percentage
News Reporter	219	30.93%
Football Player	115	16.24%
Medical Doctor	305	43.08%
Businessman	69	9.75%
Total	708	100%

Question 10

You would like to pursue a future career as a:

	Frequency	Percentage
Businessman	189	25.20%
Professional Athlete	195	26.00%
Entertainer	125	16.67%
Doctor	58	7.73%
Lawyer	53	7.07%
Other	130	17.33%
Total	750	100%

Question 11

11. Do you feel like an American Citizen or an Outsider?

	Frequency	Percentage
American Citizen	456	65.05%
Outsider	245	34.95%
Total	701	100%

Index